World Politics, Human Rights, and International Law

World Politics, Human Rights, and International Law

Francis A. Boyle

LEXINGTON BOOKS
Lanham • Boulder • New York • London

Published by Lexington Books
An imprint of The Rowman & Littlefield Publishing Group, Inc.
4501 Forbes Boulevard, Suite 200, Lanham, Maryland 20706
www.rowman.com

6 Tinworth Street, London SE11 5AL, United Kingdom

Cover: Francis A. Boyle (far left) on the floor of the International Court of Justice on 1 April 1993, squaring off against his adversary Shabtai Rosenne from Israel (far right) representing Yugoslavia, just before he argued and then won the first of his two World Court Orders overwhelmingly in favor of the Republic of Bosnia and Herzegovina against Yugoslavia to cease and desist from committing all acts of genocide in violation of the 1948 Genocide Convention on April 8, 1993 and then again on September 13, 1993. This was the first time ever that any Government or Lawyer had won two such Orders in one case since the World Court was founded in 1921. On August 5, 1993, he also won an Article 74(4) Order from the World Court to the same effect. Under Article 74(4) of the Statute of the International Court of Justice, when the Full Court is not in Session, the President of the Court exercises the Full Powers of the Court and can issue an Order that is binding upon the states parties in a case.

British Library Cataloguing in Publication Information Available

Library of Congress Cataloging-in-Publication Data

Names: Boyle, Francis Anthony, 1950- author.
Title: World politics, human rights, and international law / Francis A. Boyle.
Description: Lanham, Maryland : published by Lexington Books, an imprint of The Rowman & Littlefield Publishing Group, Inc., [2021] | Includes bibliographical references and index.
Identifiers: LCCN 2020050656 (print) | LCCN 2020050657 (ebook) | ISBN 9781793633392 (cloth) | ISBN 9781793633408 (epub)
Subjects: LCSH: Human rights—United States | International law and human rights—United States. | United States—Politics and government—21st century. | United States—Foreign relations—21st century.
Classification: LCC KF4749 .B695 2021 (print) | LCC KF4749 (ebook) | DDC 341.4/8—dc23
LC record available at https://lccn.loc.gov/2020050656
LC ebook record available at https://lccn.loc.gov/2020050657

∞™ The paper used in this publication meets the minimum requirements of American National Standard for Information Sciences—Permanence of Paper for Printed Library Materials, ANSI/NISO Z39.48-1992.

Contents

Introduction

International law and human rights are simply facts of world politics as well as of U.S. constitutional law and American political life and domestic public opinions around the world. Hence, they are incontestable realities that U.S. government decision-makers must routinely take into account in their formulation of American foreign affairs, counter-terrorism, and defense policies, whether in a positive or a negative sense, and whether they like it or not. Either they must view the principles of international law and human rights as something they should attempt to comply with as best as possible under the unique circumstances of an historical situation (e.g., the Cuban missile crisis),[1] or else they must view the principles of international law and human rights as something that they have to overcome in order to accomplish their illicit objectives (e.g., President Bush Junior's war of aggression against Iraq).[2] For either reason, and for both reasons, the principles of international law and human rights are therefore "relevant" to the formulation and conduct of American foreign affairs, counter-terrorism, and defense policies in what I have called and explained elsewhere in these "functionalist" terms.[3]

Let us assume, however, for the purpose of argument, that the U.S. government really pays absolutely no meaningful attention whatsoever to the principles of international law and human rights when it formulates and conducts its foreign affairs, counter-terrorism, and defense policies, but instead only invokes and manipulates those principles on an ex post facto basis in order to justify whatever decisions it has taken for Machiavellian reasons. Does this then mean that the principles of international law and human rights are indeed irrelevant? Once again, I submit that the answer to this question for all of us as teachers, students, and analysts of world politics is definitely in the negative. International law and human rights still remain critically relevant for any concerned citizen living in a democracy with a constitutional commitment to the rule of law and human rights for the purpose of formulating his or her own opinion on how to evaluate and determine the legitimacy of specific foreign affairs, counter-terrorism, and defense policies and on that basis to decide whether to support or to oppose them.

Invariably it is the case that U.S. government officials will publicly attempt to justify its foreign affairs, counter-terrorism, and defense policies in terms of international law and human rights, or, more broadly put, in terms of what is legally-morally right or wrong for the management and manipulation of domestic, allied, and world public opinion. It may be the case that the actual motivation for a particular policy had been considerations of Machiavellian power politics. But it would be extremely difficult, if not impossible, to sell pure, unadulterated Machiavellianism to the American people and Congress as the proper basis for the conduct of U.S. foreign affairs, counter-terrorism, and defense policies, let alone to the various governments and peoples of the world community of states.

Hence, U.S. government decision-makers oftentimes resort to legalistic subterfuges by pleading and manipulating and sometimes perverting principles of international law and human rights in order to disguise their Machiavellian foreign affairs, counter-terrorism, and defense policy decisions. This was certainly the case for the most part of both the neoconservative Reagan administration and the neoconservative Bush Junior administration, for a good part of the neoliberal Clinton administration and the neoliberal Obama administration, and now for almost all of the nihilistic Trump administration. Of course, this phenomenon simply confirms the worst suspicions held by political scientists that international law and human rights are therefore really irrelevant to the conduct of American foreign affairs, counter-terrorism, and defense policies as well as for world politics in general. But once again, the definition of "relevance" depends upon whether the analyst's perspective and criteria are Machiavellian or functionalist.

For even if American government decision-makers pay absolutely no meaningful attention at all to the principles of international law and human rights, nevertheless they will and indeed must attempt to justify their foreign affairs, counter-terrorism and defense policies to U.S. domestic and world public opinion by invoking and arguing these norms. This permits a foreign policy analyst or a concerned citizen who possesses a rudimentary working knowledge of international law and human rights to apply these criteria to the government's stated rationalizations in order to determine whether or not the policy can be justified as the government officials have maintained in public. If it cannot, then obviously the analyst and citizen must realize that he or she is not being told the truth and therefore something else must be going on behind the scenes that is quite different from what U.S. government officials are saying in public. By thus using the principles of international law and human rights as an analytical tool, the scholar, student, and concerned citizen can first identify such legalistic deceptions, and then proceed to pierce through the veil of legal-moral obfuscations put forth by U.S. government officials in order to grasp the real heart of what the foreign affairs, counter-terrorism, and defense policy is really all about. Such analysts and citizens might not like what they find when they get there—Machiavellian power politics. But at least a working knowledge of international law and human rights will have enabled them to pierce through the fog of perception management, propaganda, disinformation, and outright lies spewed forth by U.S. government officials. These same techniques of functionalist analysis also hold true for all other governments in the world today. All governments lie! Some more than others.

Furthermore then, most foreign governments also try to justify their policies to the U.S. government as well as to the American Congress and people and to the world at large by invoking the principles of international law and human rights. Therefore, American foreign policy decision-makers, academic foreign policy analysts, and concerned citizens need to be able to evaluate those foreign claims in accordance with the standard recognized criteria of international law and human rights. If the claims of the foreign government fall within what I have called elsewhere to be the "ballpark"[4] of international legality and humanity, then the U.S. government officials, private-sector foreign policy analysts, and the American people should be willing to give these foreign claims the benefit of the doubt and do their best to accommodate them within the overall conduct of American foreign affairs, counter-terrorism, and defense policies to whatever extent is feasible.

On the other hand, when the foreign policy of the foreign government does not even fall within the "ballpark" of international legality and humanity then it really is entitled to no recognition or support whatsoever on America's part, and U.S. foreign policy decision-makers should be wary of associating their government with it in any way, shape, or form. To the extent that American foreign policy decision-makers do so associate the U.S. government with the illegal policies of a foreign government, then a basic working knowledge of international law and human rights will put congressional, academic, and private-sector foreign policy analysts as well as concerned American citizens into a better position to intelligently criticize and oppose that policy as well as to provide for and work toward an alternative. Conversely, the same analytical methodology and analogous conclusions would also hold true when the U.S. government adopts an adversarial stance against a foreign government whose policies basically comport with the principles of international law and human rights.

Furthermore, once foreign policy analysts (congressional, scholars, students, citizens) have figured out the true nature of U.S. foreign policy by evaluating it in accordance with the standard recognized criteria of international law and human rights, if it is Machiavellian, then they can proceed to construct an alternative policy that is based upon normative considerations of international law and human rights and then organize and work in order to achieve it. Unfortunately, however, most international political scientists of the political realist school and most international lawyers of the legal positivist school really have no constructive alternatives to offer anyone. The political realists simply state that all is a matter of power and interest, which means reliance upon political and economic coercion, and ultimately upon the threat and use of U.S. military force. Whereas the legal positivists lament the fact that international law and human rights cannot be enforced and thus there is little that can be done except let the devil take the hindmost. In the final analysis, both schools of thought lead to the same Machiavellian prescriptions. Of course, the same principles of analysis hold true *ex proprio vigore* for the neoconservatives and the neoliberals and now the Trumpian nihilists.

It is never satisfactory for American foreign policy analysts just to criticize the U.S. government's decisions. Rather, we owe it to our students, to the American people and Congress, to U.S. government decision-makers themselves, as well as to foreign governments and peoples, to develop a constructive alternative approach toward resolving the major problems of world politics and human rights today. How many times have we heard the refrain, especially during the tenures of the neoconservative Reagan administration and the neoconservative Bush Junior administration and now the nihilistic Trump administration, that there are really only two alternative courses of conduct: either the threat and use of U.S. military force in a particular situation, or else the "adversaries" of the United States will prevail—whether they are terrorists, or Islamic fundamentalists, or drug smugglers, or Russians, or Chinese and so on ad nauseam in constant search of enemies abroad forever in order to scaremonger the American people and Congress. In other words, "Either you are with us or you are against us!" There is, however, a third alternative to Machiavellianism and doing nothing. It consists of deploying the principles of international law and human rights for the peaceful settlement of international disputes and the promotion of international humanitarianism. This is true internationalism as opposed to isolationism, do-nothingism, and Trumpian America-firstism.

The principles of international law and human rights provide useful criteria by which U.S. government decision-makers can, do, and should formulate their foreign affairs, counter-terrorism, and defense policies. This does not mean, however, that the principles of international law and human rights are so clear-cut that all the U.S. government has to do is to apply them. Rather, in my opinion, the principles of international law and human rights typically tell U.S. government decision-makers what they should *not* do in order to avoid foreign affairs, counter-terrorism, and defense policy blunders, disasters, and atrocities. Similarly, in a more positive and progressive sense, the principles of international law and human rights usually provide a guiding way out of some of the most urgent and pressing, if not existential, dilemmas that confront American foreign policy decision-makers and concerned citizens in today's interdependent world of international relations.

International law and human rights also comprise a most powerful analytical tool for foreign policy analysts (whether congressional, lawyers, political scientists, historians, economists, or concerned citizens) to use for the purpose of first understanding and then evaluating the conduct of American foreign policy as well as the behavior of other nation states—whether allied, friendly, neutral, nonaligned, or overtly hostile. The principles of international law and human rights can provide objective criteria for making both predictions about and value judgments upon the feasibility, the propriety, and the ultimate success or failure of interactive foreign policy, counter-terrorism, and defense behaviors among the nation states in world politics today, and then acting upon them. Finally, the principles of international law and human rights can likewise be used by concerned citizens living in a popularly elected democracy with a constitutional commitment to the rule of law and humanity in order to serve as a check-and-balance against the natural abuses of power endemic to any type of foreign and American domestic government when it comes to the conduct of foreign affairs, counter-terrorism, and defense policies.

To be sure, international law and human rights are no panacea for the numerous problems of contemporary world politics. But they do provide one promising medium for extricating the American foreign policy decision-making establishment from the oppressive Machiavellian morass that has enmired it and enmeshed for at least the past six decades of my active political and legal lifetime since the U.S. presidential campaign of 1960. By conceptualizing international law and human rights in these functionalist terms, we can objectively demonstrate their relevance to the study and analysis and practice of world politics, as well as to the future conduct of American foreign affairs, counter-terrorism, and defense policies. In the process, we can hopefully point out the way for new directions in the study and practice of world politics, international law, human rights, and the peaceful settlement of international disputes at the start of the third millennium of humankind's parlous existence.

The present danger is Machiavellian power politics. The only known antidote is international law, human rights, and the peaceful settlement of international disputes. Otherwise the future of humankind will be left to the brutal and bloody hands of geopolitical Machiavellians such as the American realists, the neo-realists, the neoliberals, the neoconservatives, and now the Trumpian nihilists.

In this thermonuclear age, humankind's existential choice is that stark, ominous, clear, and compelling. As global citizens we must not hesitate to apply this imperative anti-Machiavellian regimen of international law and human rights immediately before it becomes too late for humanity and the entire world. There will be no International War Crimes Tribunal like Nuremberg after World War III. Only humankind's deafening silence for the rest of eternity—our last will and testament to our cosmic folly of embracing Machiavellianism.

At best, history has allotted humankind only a brief interlude of time in order to avoid nuclear extinction. If we destroy ourselves at the end of that historical eyeblink, no one in the universe will hear our cries of anguish. No one in the universe will shed a tear for humankind. No one in the universe will know the glories of our civilizations. Probably, no one in the universe will ever know that we even existed. We will be no different from those numerous other races of "intelligent" beings around the universe who have committed nuclear omnicide.

Will the imperial American Republic suffer the same fate as the imperial Athenian democracy? Will World War III be far behind? Will humanity suffer the same fate as the dinosaurs? Will the planet earth become a radioactive wasteland? Our future is in the hands of you the reader. Toward that end this book has been written.

NOTES

1. See, e.g., Abram Chayes, *The Cuban Missile Crisis* (New York, NY: Oxford University Press, 1974).
2. See Francis A. Boyle, *Destroying World Order* (Atlanta, GA: Clarity Press, Inc., 2004), and *Breaking All the Rules* (Atlanta, GA: Clarity Press, Inc., 2008).
3. See Francis A. Boyle, *World Politics and International Law* (Durham, NC: Duke University Press Books, 1985).
4. See ibid.

Chapter 1

Denouncing Obama at the University of Illinois

In my book *Tackling America's Toughest Questions* (2009), I tried to analyze almost every hideous atrocity the neoconservative Bush Junior administration inflicted upon international law, human rights, the U.S. Constitution, and world politics from when they stole the American presidential election in 2000 up to 2009. I deliberately postponed writing the *Conclusion* to that book until the incoming neoliberal Obama administration had come to power and was settling into office. Then I prognosticated as follows[1]:

CONCLUSION

> Despite their presidential campaign rhetoric promoting "change," three weeks into the Obama/Clinton administration the continuity of policies across the board with the Bush administration is striking notwithstanding their change in atmospherics. It very well could be that despite our best efforts, hopes, and expectations for instituting real political "change" by means of the 2008 U.S. national elections, the American people are going to see in operation a Third Bush Term or at least a hybrid Obama/Bush/Clinton administration.

Third and fourth terms of the Bush Junior administration were more like it under Obama and his neoliberals for the next eight years.[2]

Both Barack Obama and I purposefully chose to study Jurisprudence at Harvard Law School with Professor Roberto Unger, the founder of the Critical Legal Studies Movement.[3] Speaking on the BBC news show *Hard Talk* on November 20, 2013, Professor Unger had this to say about his student President Obama: "Obama is a disaster!" I agree with the profound wisdom of our mutual teacher of the Philosophy of Law. Obama was the Black velvet glove placed upon the White racist Judeo-Christian iron fist of U.S. capitalism and imperialism. Bush Junior and Trump are just the iron fists!

On September 7, 2018, the University of Illinois awarded former president Obama the Paul H. Douglas Award for "Ethics in Government," which occasion he exploited in order to commence his campaign for winning the congressional elections of 2018 for the Democratic Party. In appalled reaction thereto, I called for and helped organize an anti-Obama protest rally right in front of the Foellinger Auditorium when Obama was in the midst of getting the award and giving his speech. What follows is my keynote address against Obama that I delivered there with a bullhorn in hand so that everyone inside and outside could hear me:

> I am Francis Boyle, Professor of Law here at the College of Law. I'm the Senior Professor at the College of Law. I've taught here 41 years in a row without a break. I know Obama. He was behind me at Harvard Law School. Obama abandoned and betrayed every principle about the rule of law that I learned at Harvard Law School including the U.S. Constitution.

I was fairly disposed toward Obama. When the Black Law Students brought him over here to the Law School from Springfield to speak, I went over there. I sat next to Obama. I introduced myself to Obama. I told Obama I couldn't stay. I had to go home for dinner with my family. He said he understood. I wished him well and I shook his hand. I was the only Law Professor there that day. I am here to condemn Obama as a war criminal and worse!

The University of Illinois is giving him an "ethics in government" award. This is a sick joke and a demented fraud! The University of Illinois, for its own typical bootlicking reasons, wants to whitewash all of Obama's international crimes. Obama should be sitting in a jail cell in The Hague with the International Criminal Court and not here getting some bogus "ethics in government" award from the bootlickers of the University of Illinois campus bigwigs.

I'm not the only one to say that. Obama and I had the same Jurisprudence teacher—Philosophy of Law—at Harvard Law School, Professor Roberto Unger, the founder of the Critical Legal Studies Movement. What did our teacher say about Obama on BBC *Hard Talk* and elsewhere? "Obama is a disaster!" Again, Professor Unger, our teacher, said: "Obama is a disaster!" I agree with Professor Unger, one of the great philosophers of law in the post–World War II era. And I have been teaching Jurisprudence since I came here in 1978.

Now don't just take Professor Unger's words for it. What does Professor Noam Chomsky have to say about Obama's drone murder extermination campaign against Muslims and Arabs and Asians of Color all over the world?

He calls it "the most extreme terrorist campaign of modern times."[4] That is Noam Chomsky, one of the great intellectuals in the world and a personal hero of mine when he was leading the forces of opposition to the Vietnam War that I was opposing as a young man. That's how Chomsky referred to Obama's drone murder campaign: "the most extreme terrorist campaign of modern times." That's amazing to think of! That's the person here that the University of Illinois is whitewashing. That figure today on his drone murder extermination campaign is up to at least ten thousand. Trump is just continuing it.

Indeed, Trump is just continuing across-the-board policies that Obama put into place. The difference between Trump and Obama and Obama and Bush Junior is that Obama knows better. He's a magna-cum-laude graduate of Harvard Law School just like I am. Obama has abandoned and betrayed every known principle of the rule of law that I ever learned at Harvard Law School including the U.S. Constitution, which he doesn't give diddly-squat about. Indeed, referring to his drone murder extermination campaign Obama bragged: "I'm really good at killing people!" Those are Obama's own words! That's the man the University of Illinois is whitewashing today with their "ethics in government" award. Indeed, Obama murdered four U.S. citizens at least that we know of, including Mr. Awlaki and his sixteen-year-old son who was completely innocent of anything. Obama is a monster! He's a criminal! As I said he should be in jail, not getting some bogus "ethics" award from the bootlickers at the University of Illinois administration.

Let's review his record. The first thing Obama does when he comes into office, Bush Junior had about 30,000 troops in Afghanistan, and Obama escalated that immediately to 100,000 troops. 100,000 troops murdering, killing, exterminating Afghans all up and down. We don't even have a body count because the Pentagon won't give us the numbers. My estimate is maybe a million people. Obama is like Genghis Khan and His Mongol Horde, raping, robbing, pillaging, and murdering all over the world innocent men, women, and children. That's the guy they're giving their "ethics in government" award to.

After he had done his genocidal work in Afghanistan, Obama moved on to Libya in order to steal their oil. Obama launched his war against Libya and exterminated about 50,000 Libyans—needlessly for no reason except Obama wanted to steal Libya's oil. Indeed, it was outright genocide for Black Africans living in Libya that Obama perpetrated upon them. Obama destroyed Libya as a state completely. It no longer exists. And we the have the massive refugee crisis coming out of Libya with thousands of Africans—Blacks and Arabs—drowning in the Mediterranean all thanks to Obama this war criminal.[5]

After he was done with Libya, then Obama moved on to Syria and destroyed Syria. He worked with his jihadi terrorists to overthrow the government of Syria and create a total catastrophe. Maybe 500,000 Syrians have been murdered because of Obama, and that country is a catastrophe today. The battles still go on. We have no idea what's going to happen over there. Just like he did in Libya, Obama used jihadi extremists to wage his wars for him. And America in Libya became the air force for Obama's jihadi extremists. Then he turned them on Syria and there the death and destruction by Obama goes on today. A second state that Obama has pretty much destroyed all by himself with his jihadi extremists—Genghis Khan and His Horde of Mongols![6]

Now, we come to Yemen started by Obama. Massive death and destruction in Yemen right now as we speak today. Obama supported Saudi Arabia and the UAE against Yemen and has killed close to 10,000 Houthis. Outright genocide! All to steal their oil and set off a humanitarian catastrophe in Yemen. Maybe 2 million Yemenis over there are suffering from cholera. It's the largest outbreak of cholera in the world today. And they are starving. Obama starved them to death. There's an embargo on them right now. They can't even eat. Obama started this policy.[7]

I could go on here forever but I'm not going to because I teach Obama's atrocities to my law students. I think we could have no better indication of where Obama really stands than the eulogy he gave last weekend in honor of the war criminal and warmonger John McCain. John McCain was a war criminal. He bombed Hanoi killing innocent civilians when he was shot down. Outright war criminal! And when he got home McCain mongered for almost every war the United States ever waged since then including in Syria and supporting Obama's Nazis in Ukraine. Let us recall John McCain's theme song: "Bomb! Bomb! Bomb! Bomb! Bomb! Iran!" Sixty million people and McCain did his best to start a war against them and kill them. Obama then appeared there to give a eulogy in support of this long-standing war criminal and warmonger.

Who else was there? Bush Junior, another Genghis Khan and His Horde of Mongols![8] They're best buddies—Bush Junior and Obama. Who else did they trot out to honor McCain? Henry Kissinger! The three of them, yes, they all spoke right after each other: Kissinger, Bush Junior, and Obama. Kissinger of the genocidal Vietnam War. Murdering 58,000 young men of my generation and exterminating 3 million Vietnamese. I call him Hank Half-An-Eichmann Kissinger. I say that from personal experience. I went through the exact same PhD program at Harvard that produced Kissinger before me. They gave me Kissinger's old office at Harvard's Center for International Affairs: "There but for the grace of God go I!" So here we have three major warmongers and war criminals honoring a fourth. You have Kissinger, Bush Junior, and Obama honoring McCain. Well as I say: Warbirds of a feather flock together! Thank you.

NOTES

1. Francis A. Boyle, *Tackling America's Toughest Questions* (Atlanta, GA: Clarity Press, 2009), 174.
2. See Charlie Savage, *Power Wars* (New York, NY: Bay Back Books, 2015). The Nazis had their lawyers too!
3. Roberto Unger, *The Critical Legal Studies Movement* (Cambridge, MA: Harvard University Press, 1983).
4. Andrea Germanos, "Noam Chomsky: Obama's Drone Program: 'The Most Extreme Terrorist Campaign of Modern Times'," *Common Dreams*, January 19, 2015.
5. Francis A. Boyle, *Destroying Libya and World Order* (Atlanta, GA: Clarity Press, 2013).
6. See Tim Anderson, *Axis of Resistance* (Atlanta, GA: Clarity Press, 2019), 62–232.
7. Vanessa Beeley, "YEMEN: Saudis, Emiratis and USA are Inflicting a War of Genocide Against the Houthis – Prof. Francis Boyle," *21st Century Wire*, Last modified March 13, 2017, https://21stcenturywire.com/2017/03/31/yemen-saudis-emiratis-and-usa-are-inflicting-a-war-of-genocide-against-the-houthis-prof-francis-boyle/.
8. Boyle, *Destroying World Order*.

Chapter 2

Civil Resistance against the Trump Administration!

In shocked reaction to the outright nihilism of the Trump administration against international law, human rights, and the U.S. Constitution for the past several months, I called for, helped to organize, and chaired a traditional half-day-long antiwar and pro-peace teach-in on the campus of the University of Illinois at Urbana-Champaign that was held on September 23, 2017, with numerous speakers. There I gave the keynote address that publicly called for civil resistance against the Trump administration as follows:

Historically this latest eruption of American militarism at the start of the twenty-first century is akin to that of America opening the twentieth century by means of the U.S.-instigated Spanish–American War in 1898. Then the Republican administration of President William McKinley stole their colonial empire from Spain in Cuba, Puerto Rico, Guam, and the Philippines; inflicted a near genocidal war against the Filipino people; while at the same time illegally annexing the Kingdom of Hawaii and subjecting the Native Hawaiian people (who call themselves the Kanaka Maoli) to genocidal conditions. Additionally, McKinley's military and colonial expansion into the Pacific was also designed to secure America's economic exploitation of China pursuant to the euphemistic rubric of the "open door" policy. But over the next four decades America's aggressive presence, policies, and practices in the so-called "Pacific" Ocean would ineluctably pave the way for Japan's attack at Pearl Harbor on December 7, 1941, and thus America's precipitation into the ongoing Second World War.[1] Today a century later the serial imperial aggressions launched, waged, and menaced by the neoconservative Republican Bush Junior administration, then the neoliberal Democratic Obama administration, and now the reactionary Trump administration threaten to set off World War III.

By shamelessly exploiting the terrible tragedy of September 11, 2001, the Bush Junior administration set forth to steal a hydrocarbon empire from the Muslim states and Peoples of Color living in Central Asia and the Middle East and Africa under the bogus pretexts of (1) fighting a war against "international terrorism" or "Islamic fundamentalism"; and/or (2) eliminating weapons of mass destruction; and/or (3) the promotion of democracy; and/or (4) self-styled humanitarian intervention and its avatar "responsibility to protect" (R2P). Only this time the geopolitical stakes are infinitely greater than they were a century ago: control and domination of the world's hydrocarbon resources and thus the very fundaments and energizers of the global economic system—oil and gas. The Bush Junior/Obama administrations targeted the remaining hydrocarbon reserves of Africa, Latin America (e.g., the Pentagon's reactivation of the U.S. Fourth Fleet in 2008), and Southeast Asia for further conquest and domination, together with the strategic chokepoints at sea and on land required for their transportation (e.g., Syria, Yemen, Somalia, Djibouti). Today the U.S. Fourth Fleet threatens oil-rich Venezuela and Ecuador for sure along with Cuba.

Toward accomplishing that first objective, in 2007 the neoconservative Bush Junior administration announced the establishment of the U.S. Pentagon's Africa Command (AFRICOM) in order to better control, dominate, steal, and exploit both the natural resources and the variegated peoples of the continent of Africa, the very cradle of our human species. In 2011 Libya and the Libyans proved to be the first victims to succumb to AFRICOM under the neoliberal Obama administration, thus demonstrating the truly bipartisan and nonpartisan nature of U.S. imperial foreign policy decision-making. Let us put aside as beyond the scope of this analysis the American conquest, extermination, and ethnic cleansing of the Native Americans from off the face of the continent of North America. Since America's instigation of the Spanish–American War in 1898, U.S. foreign policy decision-making has been alternatively conducted by reactionary imperialists, conservative imperialists, and liberal imperialists for the past 119 years and counting.

Trump is just another White racist iron fist for Judeo-Christian U.S. imperialism and capitalism smashing itself all over the world. Trump forthrightly and proudly admitted that the United States is in the Middle East in order to steal their oil. At least he was honest about it. Unlike his predecessors who lied about the matter going back to President George Bush Senior with his war for Persian Gulf oil against Iraq in 1991.[2] Just recently, President Trump publicly threatened illegal U.S. military intervention against oil-rich Venezuela. QED.

This world-girdling burst of U.S. imperialism at the start of humankind's new millennium is what my teacher, mentor, and friend the late, great Professor Hans Morgenthau denominated "unlimited imperialism" in his seminal book *Politics among Nations*:

> The outstanding historic examples of unlimited imperialism are the expansionist policies of Alexander the Great, Rome, the Arabs in the seventh and eighth centuries, Napoleon I, and Hitler. They all have in common an urge toward expansion which knows no rational limits, feeds on its own successes and, if not stopped by a superior force, will go on to the confines of the political world. This urge will not be satisfied so long as there remains anywhere a possible object of domination–a politically organized group of men which by its very independence challenges the conqueror's lust for power. It is, as we shall see, exactly the lack of moderation, the aspiration to conquer all that lends itself to conquest, characteristic of unlimited imperialism, which in the past has been the undoing of the imperialistic policies of this kind.[3]

Since September 11, 2001, it is the Unlimited Imperialists along the lines of Alexander, Rome, Napoleon, and Hitler who have been in charge of conducting American foreign policy decision-making. The factual circumstances surrounding the outbreaks of both the First World War and the Second World War currently hover like twin Swords of Damocles over the heads of all humanity.

After September 11, 2001, the people of the world witnessed successive governments in the United States that have demonstrated little respect for fundamental considerations of international law, human rights, and the U.S. Constitution. Instead, the world has watched instead a comprehensive and malicious assault upon the integrity of the international and domestic legal orders by gangs of men and women who are thoroughly Machiavellian in their perception of international relations and in their conduct of both foreign affairs and American domestic policy. Even more seriously, in many instances specific components of the U.S. government's foreign policies constitute ongoing criminal activity under well-recognized principles of both international law and U.S. domestic law, and in particular the Nuremberg Charter (1945), the Nuremberg Judgment (1946), and the Nuremberg Principles (1950), as well as the Pentagon's own U.S. Army Field Manual 27-10 on *The Law of Land Warfare* (1956), whose principles apply to the President himself as Commander-in-Chief of United States Armed Forces under Article II, Section 2 of the U.S. Constitution.

Depending on the substantive issues involved, these international and domestic crimes typically include but are not limited to the Nuremberg offenses of "crimes against peace"—for example, Libya, Afghanistan, Iraq, Somalia, Yemen, Pakistan, Syria, and their long-standing threatened war of aggression against Iran. Their criminal responsibility also concerns crimes against humanity and war crimes as well as grave breaches of the Four Geneva Conventions of 1949 and the 1907 Hague Regulations on land warfare: enforced disappearances, assassinations, murders, kidnappings, extraordinary renditions, "shock and awe," depleted uranium, white phosphorous, cluster bombs, drone strikes, and so on. Furthermore, various officials of the U.S. government have committed numerous inchoate crimes incidental to these substantive offenses that under the Nuremberg Charter, Judgment, and Principles as well as U.S. Army Field Manual 27-10 (1956) are international crimes in their own right: planning and preparation, solicitation, incitement, conspiracy, complicity, attempt, aiding and abetting, and so on. Of course the terrible irony of today's situation is that seven decades ago at Nuremberg the U.S. government participated in the prosecution, punishment, and execution of Nazi government officials for committing some of the same types of heinous international crimes that these officials of the U.S. government currently inflict upon Peoples of Color all over the world. To be sure, I personally oppose the imposition of capital punishment upon any human being for any reason no matter how monstrous their crimes, whether they be Saddam Hussein, Bush Junior, Tony Blair, Barack Obama, or Donald Trump.

According to basic principles of international criminal law set forth in paragraph 501 of U.S. Army Field Manual 27-10, all high-level civilian officials and military officers in the U.S. government who either knew or should have known that soldiers or civilians under their control (such as the CIA or mercenary contractors) committed or were about to commit international crimes and failed to take the measures necessary to stop them, or to punish them, or both, are likewise personally responsible for the commission of international crimes. This category of officialdom who actually knew or should have known of the commission of these international crimes under their jurisdiction and failed to do anything about them include at the very top of America's criminal chain-of-command the President, the Vice-President, the U.S. Secretary of Defense, Secretary of State, Director of National Intelligence, the CIA Director, National Security Advisor, and the Pentagon's Joint Chiefs of Staff along with the appropriate Regional Commanders-in-Chiefs, especially for U.S. Central Command (CENTCOM) and now U.S. Africa Command (AFRICOM).

These U.S. government officials and their immediate subordinates are responsible for the commission of crimes against peace, crimes against humanity, and war crimes as specified by the Nuremberg Charter, Judgment, and Principles as well as by U.S. Army Field Manual 27-10 of 1956. Today in international legal terms, the U.S. government itself should now be viewed as constituting an ongoing criminal conspiracy under international criminal law in violation of the Nuremberg Charter, the Nuremberg Judgment, and the Nuremberg Principles, because of its formulation and undertaking of serial wars of aggression, crimes against peace, crimes against humanity, and war crimes that are legally akin to those perpetrated by the former Nazi regime in Germany. As a consequence, American citizens possess the basic right under international law and the U.S. domestic law, including the U.S. Constitution, to engage in acts of civil resistance designed to prevent, impede, thwart, or terminate ongoing criminal activities perpetrated by U.S. government officials in their conduct of foreign affairs policies and military operations purported to relate to "defense" and "counter-terrorism." They are the real terrorists! They terrorize the entire world!

For that very reason, large numbers of American citizens have decided to act on their own cognizance by means of civil resistance in order to demand that U.S. government officials adhere to basic principles of international law, of U.S. domestic law, and of the U.S. Constitution in their conduct of foreign affairs and military operations. Mistakenly, however, such actions have been defined to constitute classic instances of "civil disobedience" as historically practiced in the United States. And the conventional status quo admonition by the U.S. power elite and its sycophantic news media for those who knowingly engage in "civil disobedience" has always been that they must meekly accept their punishment for having performed a prima facie breach of the positive laws as a demonstration of their good faith and moral commitment. Nothing could be further from the truth! Today's civil resisters are the sheriffs! The U.S. government officials are the outlaws!

Here I would like to suggest a different way of thinking about civil resistance activities that are specifically designed to thwart, prevent, or impede ongoing criminal activity by officials of the U.S. government under well-recognized principles of international and U.S. domestic law. Such civil resistance activities represent the last constitutional avenue open to the American people to preserve their democratic form of government with its historical commitment to the rule of law and human rights. Civil resistance is the last hope Americans have to prevent the U.S. government from moving even farther down the paths of lawless violence in Africa, the Middle East, Southwest Asia, military interventionism into Latin America, and nuclear confrontation with Pakistan, North Korea, Russia, and China.

Such measures of "civil resistance" must not be confused with, and indeed must be carefully distinguished from, acts of "civil disobedience" as traditionally defined. In today's civil resistance cases, what we witness are American citizens attempting to prevent the ongoing commission of international and domestic crimes under well-recognized principles of international law and U.S. domestic law. This is a phenomenon essentially different from the classic civil disobedience cases of the 1950s and 1960s where incredibly courageous African Americans and their supporters were conscientiously violating domestic laws for the express purpose of changing them. By contrast, today's civil resisters are acting for the express purpose of upholding the rule of law, the U.S. Constitution, human rights, and international law. Applying the term "civil disobedience" to such civil resistors mistakenly presumes their guilt and thus perversely exonerates the U.S. government official criminals.

Civil resistors disobeyed nothing, but to the contrary obeyed international law and the U.S. Constitution. By contrast, U.S. government officials grossly violated fundamental principles of international law as well as U.S. criminal law and thus committed international crimes and U.S. domestic crimes as well as impeachable violations of the U.S. Constitution. The civil resistors are the sheriffs enforcing international law, U.S. criminal law, and the U.S. Constitution against the criminals working for the U.S. government!

Today the American people must reaffirm their commitment to the Nuremberg Charter, Judgment, and Principles by holding their government officials fully accountable under international law and U.S. domestic law for the commission of such grievous international and domestic crimes. They must not permit any aspect of their foreign affairs and defense policies to be conducted by acknowledged "war criminals" according to the U.S. government's own official definition of that term as set forth in U.S. Army Field Manual 27-10 (1956),[4] the U.S. War Crimes Act, the Geneva Conventions, and the Hague Regulations, inter alia. The American people must insist upon the impeachment, dismissal, resignation, indictment, conviction, and long-term incarceration of all U.S. government officials guilty of such heinous international and domestic crimes. If not so restrained by civil resistance, the U.S. government could very well precipitate a Third World War. That is precisely what American civil resisters are doing today! The future of American foreign policy and the peace of the world lie in the hands of American citizens—not the bureaucrats, legislators, judges, lobbyists, think-tankers, professors, and self-styled experts who inhibit Washington, DC, New York City, Cambridge, Massachusetts, and Hyde Park/Chicago, Illinois.

After September 11, 2001, the United States has vilified and demonized Muslims and Arabs almost to the same extent that America inflicted upon the Japanese and Japanese Americans after Pearl Harbor. As the Nazis had previously demonstrated with respect to the Jews, a government must first dehumanize and scapegoat a race of people before its citizens will tolerate, if not approve, their elimination: Hiroshima and Nagasaki. In post-9/11 America we are directly confronted with the prospect of a nuclear war of extermination conducted by our White racist Judeo-Christian power elite against People of Color in the Muslim and Arab worlds in order to steal their oil and gas. The Crusades all over again! But this time nuclear Armageddon stares all of humankind right in the face!

For these reasons, the same right of civil resistance extends *pari passu* to all citizens of the world community of states and peoples. Everyone around the world has both the right and the duty under international law to resist ongoing criminal activities perpetrated by the U.S. government and its nefarious foreign accomplices in allied governments such as the NATO states, Japan, and Australia, inter alia. If not so restrained these outlaw states could readily precipitate a Nuclear Third World War.

This is our Nuremberg Moment now! We must take it! Civil resistance is the way to go![5]

NOTES

1. Boyle, *World Politics and International Law.*
2. Boyle, *Destroying World Order*, 53–64.
3. Hans Morgenthau, *Politics Among Nations*, 4th edition (New York, NY: Alfred A. Knopf, 1968), 52–53.
4. After I gave this speech, U.S. Army Field Manual 27-10 (1956) was superseded and replaced. I cannot recommend its successor. But FM 27-10 (1956) still stands as an authoritative and succinct recapitulation of the international laws of war.
5. See Francis A. Boyle, *Defending Civil Resistance Under International Law* (Ardsley, NY: Transnational Publishers, 1987), and *Protesting Power: War, Resistance, and Law* (Lanham, MD: Rowman & Littlefield, 2008).

Chapter 3

Resisting Trump's ICEstapo!

On June 23, 2018, the Immigrants' Rights Organizations in Champaign County, Illinois, held a protest rally before the Drury Inn in order to resist the agents of the U.S. Immigration and Customs Enforcement (ICE) Agency who billet and bivouac there as their in-town headquarters in order to carry out their raids apprehending some of the 16,000+ undocumented immigrants living in Champaign County. The organizers of this anti-ICE rally asked me to give a keynote speech there that I did with a bullhorn so that everyone inside and outside could hear me:

> I put the course on International Human Rights Law into the College of Law curriculum over three decades ago. One of the things I teach my law students and future lawyers is that the Undocumented have human rights because they are human beings. These rights are all set out here in the Universal Declaration of Human Rights. You can download these with no problem at all from the internet. They protect all Undocumented in this country no matter what you hear from Trump or Sessions or the Department of Injustice or the Department of Homeland Insecurity. All Undocumented have these rights.

Now the organizers told me to limit my speech to five minutes. I could lecture you all for forty-five minutes about all the human rights violations committed by Trump and Sessions and the Department of Injustice and the Department of Homeland Insecurity against the Undocumented. But I have outlined these violations in red on the Universal Declaration. Just look at it there. You can see them all for yourself, right? I don't have to lecture on them here when you can read them on your own. But in particular I wanted to call your attention to Article 16(3): "The family is the natural and fundamental group unit of society and is entitled to protection by society and the State."[1]

It's right there. Mrs. Franklin Roosevelt, Eleanor Roosevelt herself, introduced this Declaration into the United Nations General Assembly. That's how far we have regressed from Mrs. Roosevelt to Donald Trump and Melania. Think about that for a minute. Mrs. Roosevelt to Melania saying on her jacket, "I don't care." In addition, Article 25, paragraph 2 of the Universal Declaration says, "Motherhood and childhood are entitled to special care and assistance."[2] What are they doing? They are stealing and kidnapping babies and children from the arms of their mothers. Now I am a father of three sons but I could not imagine anything worse than government agents stealing my three sons from my wife. It's that simple!

I am friends with an international lawyer who prosecuted Nazis at Nuremberg, Ben Ferencz. As a twenty-seven-year-old graduate of Harvard Law School, Ben went over to Nuremberg to prosecute the Einsatzgruppen Trial. These were the Nazi death squads that went out into Eastern Europe in order to exterminate Jews, Communists, and so on—over a million of them. Ben got them convicted. He is now ninety-nine years old. Just the other day Ben put out a statement saying that what Trump is doing here constitutes a Crime against Humanity.

Let me read for you what the Nuremberg Charter of 1945 says about this matter—that was started by President Franklin Roosevelt. Again, it shows you how far we have regressed from President and Mrs. Roosevelt to President and Mrs. Trump. Here is the definition of a Crime against Humanity right out of the Nuremberg Charter of 1945 as referenced by my friend Ben Ferencz: "*Crimes against humanity*" include "inhumane acts committed against any civilian population." For all those people down there at the border right now today we are seeing inhumane acts inflicted upon them. And then second: "*Crimes against humanity*" include "persecutions on political, racial, or religious grounds."[3] Well of course this is persecution on racial grounds. These are all People of Color who are being persecuted. So of course, Ben Ferencz is right!

This is a Nuremberg Crime against Humanity that is going on here today, and the Drury Inn is aiding and abetting a Nuremberg Crime against Humanity by putting up ICE agents here to commit Crimes against Humanity. Well, at Nuremberg they also prosecuted aiders and abettors of Nuremberg crimes. So here today I am calling for a boycott of Drury Inns. I am asking this in order to stop this Crime against Humanity that is going on. We have to shut down Drury Inns. No business by anyone. No people of good faith and goodwill must do business with Drury Inns so long as they are aiding and abetting ICE to commit Crimes against Humanity. So let's do something about it! Let's boycott Drury Inns for sure and stop this Crime against Humanity! Thank you.

NOTES

1. G. A. Res. 217(III) A, *Universal Declaration of Human Rights*, at 74 (December 10, 1948).
2. G. A. Res. 217(III) A, *Universal Declaration of Human Rights*, at 76 (December 10, 1948).
3. Charter of the International Military Tribunal in Agreement for the Prosecution and Punishment of the Major War Criminals of the European Axis (London Agreement) art. 6, August 8, 1945, 58 Stat. 1544, E.A.S. No. 472, 82 U.N.T.S. 280.

Chapter 4

Resisting Trump's Lawyer at the University of Illinois College of Law

My own University of Illinois College of Law invited the U.S. deputy solicitor general Malcolm Stewart from the Trump administration's Department of "Justice" to give a public lecture on January 24, 2018. Truly appalling! In shocked reaction thereto, I called for and helped organize a protest rally to resist Trump's lawyer and Trump's Department of "Justice" held right in front of my law school building while Stewart was speaking inside. There I gave this keynote address against Trump and his lawyer and their Department of "Justice" with a bullhorn in hand so that I could be heard by everyone inside and outside:

> My name is Francis Boyle. I am the Senior Professor of Law here at the University of Illinois College of Law. That means that I have taught here longer than anyone else. I am now in my fortieth year of teaching law here.

This is one of the most despicable events I have seen organized here at the Trump College of Law. This is the first high-level official in the Trump administration to come to this campus. No doubt about it! His boss, Noel Francisco, in the Trump Department of Injustice is Number 3 and Stewart is his Deputy, to give you an idea of how high up this henchman is. The Solicitor General is the Number 3 official in the Trump Department of Injustice. He also is considered to be the so-called "10th Justice" of the U.S. Supreme Court. His office also quarterbacks and supervises all federal litigation in lower federal courts in order to get decisions against the Trump administration overturned on appeal including up to the United States Supreme Court, which this henchman has been doing for Trump and Sessions for the past year.

Sure, he worked for Obama and carried out whatever orders Obama gave him. Obama was behind me at Harvard Law School, and we can debate

Obama if you want to.[1] But Trump has said, unlike Obama, the Department of Justice is his and takes orders from him. So when Trump says "jump," this henchman says: "How high?" This is like a German lawyer working for the German Ministry of Justice when Hitler and the Nazis came to power in 1933, and instead of quitting he decides to stick around and argue their cases to the German Supreme Court. That's exactly what is going on here!

Trump has now appointed his man Gorsuch to the Supreme Court and Gorsuch is even worse than Scalia, whom he replaced. And Francisco, this henchman's boss, worked for Scalia. So you can see what we are dealing with here today. Stewart has spent the last year carrying out whatever orders Trump and Sessions and his Trump boss Francisco has given him. Hannah Arendt had an appropriate phrase for this from an essay about Eichmann on trial in Jerusalem. She called it "the banality of evil."[2] That's what's going on here. That's what we are here today to resist. We are the Trump resistance in Champaign-Urbana! We're the cutting edge of the Trump resistance!

Let's compare this henchman to Sally Yates. Sally Yates likewise spent her entire career working for the Department of Justice. But when Trump ordered her to enforce Trump's Muslim travel ban in court, she refused as a matter of principle to enforce a Muslim travel ban that was clearly unconstitutional under the First Amendment to the U.S. Constitution because it discriminated against people on grounds of religion. This henchman right now as we speak, his Office is enforcing Trump's Muslim travel ban. The U.S. Supreme Court has just ordered his Office to file documents as of February 2 and they are going to argue it in May and at the end of June we will get a decision. Regretfully it appears that the Trump Muslim travel ban will be upheld by our right-wing Supreme Court thanks in substantial part to this henchman and his Office. Thanks to his Office the Supreme Court has already temporarily upheld it. We have against us Alito, Roberts, Thomas, Gorsuch (Trump's man)—the Four Horsemen of the Apocalypse—and then of course Kennedy. It looks like they are all going to uphold the Trump Muslim travel ban that Sally Yates courageously refused to enforce and stood up against Trump.[3] Why didn't the Trump College of Law invite out Sally Yates here? She is a hero to the entire American legal profession unless you are Trump supporters like the Trump College of Law and bigots and racists against Muslims of Color. So we get a high-level Trump henchman here instead of Sally Yates. That's how bad this situation is!

The Nazis had their lawyers too and we now have a top Trump henchman here speaking for a day. We have set up this rally so that representatives of all of the victims of Trump and his Department of Injustice and this henchman can speak. We want the victims to speak for themselves!

There is no way I can possibly cover all the atrocities that the Trump Department of Injustice has inflicted in the last year. Just today it came out on the wire services that Attorney General Sessions has threatened twenty-three Sanctuary cities and states. He just threatened them now as we speak! That's the Trump Department of Injustice for you and that litigation is working its way now through to the U.S. Supreme Court. This henchman and his Office are going to try to sabotage the Sanctuary Movement!

We all know how hard we worked to get Urbana reaffirmed as a Sanctuary City. It was the only Sanctuary City between Chicago and New Orleans thanks to everyone here and the Immigrants' Rights Community. As you know we have 10,000 Undocumented here in Champaign County. We got that revised and updated Urbana Sanctuary up and running a month before Trump came to power because we knew what Trump was going to do.

President Killeen of the University of Illinois determined that all three Campuses would be de facto Sanctuaries for the Undocumented. Finally, I have to say I did not vote for Governor Rauner, but to his credit Governor Rauner signed legislation determining that the entire State of Illinois would be a Sanctuary for the Undocumented. Today the Department of Injustice, where Stewart is a high-level official, just threatened the entire State of Illinois. I kid you not! It's on the wire services. You can read it!

Let's take the DACA kids, our Dreamers. That too is in litigation right now in federal court making its way up to the United States Supreme Court. As you know Trump revoked it. The Democrats caved in over the weekend. Eight hundred thousand DACA kids are now at risk of deportation as we speak, and that case is being walked right up to the United States Supreme Court by this henchman and his Office. They are going to be arguing against our DACA kids, against our Dreamers. That's what's at stake here today![4]

Just a few weeks ago the Dean of this Law School published an article trying to sabotage the Sanctuary Movement and circulated it to lawyers and law professors and judges all over the country. Obviously trying to kiss up to Trump and Sessions to get some nice little cushy judgeship. Now we have stage two of Dean Iceman Amar kissing up to Trump/Sessions to get a nice little cushy judgeship and the rest of the Faculty is going along with it! You look here! There's not one member of this Faculty out here today supporting us! It's the Trump Law School! It's that simple!

Again, someone here has a sign on Transphobia, etc. Yeah! A federal judge just enjoined with an injunction the Trump ban prohibiting transgenders from serving in the military. Clear-cut prejudice and bigotry against transgenders that right now is working its way through federal court. It's going to be before the Supreme Court, and this henchman and his Office are going to be arguing against transgender people.[5]

In my international human rights course for years I taught LGBT human rights. They're human beings just like the rest of us. They're entitled to the same rights all the rest of us have. Certainly that's how I teach my law students to protect them. Yet what happened? We have this case in Colorado where this baker refused to serve gay people. Right now it is in the United States Supreme Court and what happened? The Department of Injustice and this henchman's Office gratuitously filed a brief against the gay plaintiffs in that case. Clear-cut bigotry. You could not do that to African Americans under federal civil rights law. That's prohibited. But against gays, Trump has no problem. And this henchman and his Office filed that brief![6]

Likewise, Labor. For three years I was greatly honored to have been elected by my Brothers and Sisters in the American Federation of Teachers Chapter here to their Executive Committee and to serve as their representative to the AFL-CIO County Board of Champaign County. Labor is having a really awful time. Right now in the Supreme Court we have the AFSCME case, as I'm sure many of you know. Hopefully we have some Labor people here who can speak. The Department of Injustice and this henchman's Office just filed a brief in the U.S. Supreme Court to break public sector unions. I kid you not! Given the current constitution of the Supreme Court, they very well might win! This will be a severe blow not just to public sector unions, but to unions across the board and organized labor.[7]

We know here on this Campus we have the Graduate Employees Union struggle so that our grad students are not treated like slave labor by university officials. I say that having been a Teaching Fellow myself for two years at Harvard. I was paid diddly-squat for sure and certainly could not have supported anyone but myself living in a dormitory and that was about it. So these are very serious issues, and this henchman and his Office are in there now to bust unions.

Finally, again I teach a course on "Constitutional Law and U.S. Foreign Affairs." I have to spend a whole course going through all the atrocities inflicted on the Constitution, civil rights, civil liberties, the poor, the oppressed, and the downtrodden by Trump and his Department of Injustice and his high-level henchman who is going to be arguing for Trump in the U.S. Supreme Court. They're going to completely gut the U.S. Voting Rights Act against African Americans. They're going to gut and destroy Affirmative Action for African Americans, that's for sure. That's coming up in the Supreme Court now too! This henchman is going to gut and destroy Affirmative Action and the Voting Rights Act in order to purge the voting rights of African Americans. Of course, at this Law School, last year only 3 percent of our entering class were African Americans—3 percent! When I publicly condemned this, they threw me off the Diversity Committee. I guess I was too "diverse" for them. Well, Black Lives Matter! But not here at the College of Law. They mean nothing. Latinos mean nothing. Muslims mean nothing. It's that simple. So I call it the Trump College of Law!

Lastly, as we know, in the negotiations over what I would call immigration "deform," Trump called all African countries "shitholes." There are fifty-four countries in Africa and he called all of them "shitholes." Why? People of Color live there, that's why. He also called Haiti a "shithole." Black People live there. He called El Salvador a "shithole." Brown People live there. Trump just revoked temporary protected status for 200,000 Salvadorans. He's going to ship them all back to El Salvador. And if there's litigation, it will make it to the Supreme Court and this henchman and his Office will act to uphold it.

I say it is the Trump Department of Injustice that is the "shithole"! I say that is the College of Law here, the Trump College of Law that brought out this high-level Trump henchman for a propaganda campaign, they are a "shithole" too! Thank you.

As mentioned above in my speech, almost immediately after Donald Trump was elected president on November 8, 2016, I recommended that the City of Urbana, Illinois, revise and update its 1986 Ordinance providing Sanctuary to undocumented immigrants in order to counteract the hostile measures that then-candidate Trump had threatened against them. Back in February of 1986, I had spent an entire evening before the Urbana City Council presenting and arguing the case for their adoption of their original Sanctuary Resolution for undocumented immigrants despite a public death threat made against me by the American Nazi Party should I do so. I detest Nazis and Klanners, both of whom had publicly opposed and campaigned against Urbana's 1986 Sanctuary Resolution. We won and they lost!

At that earlier time we had about 8,000 undocumented immigrants living in Champaign County. By 2016 there were about 16,000 undocumented immigrants living in Champaign County. Candidate Trump had threatened to summarily deport them all. I concluded that Urbana's 1986 Sanctuary Ordinance had to be updated and revised in order to take into account all of the constitutional and legal and factual and political circumstances that had taken place during the past thirty years, including and especially Trump's threats against undocumented immigrants. So I drafted and then negotiated out with the mayor of Urbana a new Sanctuary Resolution to take into account everything that had happened since 1986. My objective was to get this new Sanctuary Resolution approved by the Urbana City Council before Donald Trump was inaugurated as president on January 20, 2017, in order to counteract the campaign that he had threatened to launch against undocumented immigrants. In the late fall of 2016, I made three separate and sequential Monday evening appearances before the Urbana City Council in order to argue the case for their adoption of my new draft Sanctuary Ordinance. They did so on December 19, 2016. A nice Christmas present for the 16,000 undocumented immigrants living in Champaign County and one month ahead of my scheduled deadline for Trump's inauguration. The 2016 Urbana Sanctuary Resolution was my inauguration present for President Trump.

At the time Urbana was the only Sanctuary City between Chicago and New Orleans. I have reprinted this 2016 Urbana Sanctuary Ordinance below in the hope and expectation that other American cities, towns, villages, counties, and so on can use it as a model and a template in order to protect their own undocumented immigrants living in their midst. The Trump administration's vendetta against undocumented immigrants proved to be every bit as mean, nasty, vicious, cruel, inhumane, and illegal as I had anticipated.

RESOLUTION NO. 2016-12-070R

A RESOLUTION RE-AFFIRMING URBANA AS A SANCTUARY CITY

WHEREAS, the City of Urbana has a long history of defending human rights; and

WHEREAS, Urbana has a special relationship to immigrants because of the very large number, who come here to study, teach, do research, work and create businesses; and

WHEREAS, in 1975 the City of Urbana adopted its Human Rights Ordinance which prohibits unlawful discrimination throughout the City of Urbana; and

WHEREAS, in 1986 Urbana adopted a Resolution requiring fair and equal protection of the law for individuals without regard to their immigration status; and

WHEREAS, no federal law requires local police to routinely inquire about immigration status and any such law would likely be challenged on constitutional grounds; and

WHEREAS, in order to support the police-community relationships built up over the years with the immigrant community, ensuring they are comfortable reporting crime as witnesses or victims, local policies must not target communities based on perceived immigration status; and

WHEREAS, while recognizing the fact that undocumented immigrants who are in the United States have committed a violation of immigration law, we judge the human, moral, and practical negative costs and actual evils of deportation or other major sanctions against undocumented residents of our community and country to far outweigh the legal circumstances of their arrival and continued residence;

NOW, THEREFORE, BE IT RESOLVED THAT:

1. The City of Urbana commits to working with community advocates, policy experts, and legal advocates to defend the human rights of immigrants.

2. The Urbana Police Department will continue to respond to requests from immigrant communities to defend them against all crimes, including hate crimes, to assist people with limited language proficiency and to connect immigrants with social services.
3. The City of Urbana will reject any effort to create religious litmus tests or registries of individuals based on religion or ethnicity.
4. The Urbana City Council and the Mayor will oppose any plan that threatens to strip federal funding from cities which have adopted policies that protect undocumented immigrants and other non-citizen residents from deportation.
5. The City Council and the Mayor will join with councils and mayors from other communities around the country to stand with our immigrant residents and defend policies that welcome and protect immigrants, including New York City, Los Angeles, San Francisco, Seattle, New Orleans, Minneapolis, and others who adopt such policies.
6. No city employee or official or department or agency of the City of Urbana shall request information about or otherwise investigate or assist in the investigation of the citizenship or immigration status of any person unless such inquiry or the investigation is required by a court order. Notwithstanding this provision, the City Attorney may investigate and inquire about citizenship or immigration status when relevant to potential or actual litigation or an administrative proceeding in which the City is or may be a party.
7. No city employee or official or department or agency of the City of Urbana shall condition the provision of City benefits, opportunities or services on matters related to citizenship or immigration status unless required to do so by state or federal law or by a court order.

PASSED BY THE CITY COUNCIL this _____ day of December, 2016.
AYES:
NAYES:
ABSENT:
ABSTAINED:

Phyllis D. Clark, City Clerk

APPROVED BY THE MAYOR this _____ day of _______, _______.

Laurel Lunt Prussing, Mayor

NOTES

1. See Chapter 1 *infra.*

2. Hannah Arendt, *Eichmann in Jerusalem: A Report on the Banality of Evil* (New York, NY: Penguin Books, 1994).

3. This the U.S. Supreme Court later did in a 5 to 4 vote in *Trump v. Hawaii*, 585 U.S. ___ (2018).

4. By a 5 to 4 vote the U.S. Supreme Court gave a temporary reprieve to the DACA recipients from deportation on purely technical grounds in *Department of Homeland Security v. Regents of the University of California*, 591 U.S. ___ (2020). In immediate reaction thereto the Trump administration announced that it will set into motion another attempt to deport them.

5. Despite the contrary efforts by the Trump Department of Injustice, in *Bostock v. Clayton County*, 590 U.S. ___ (2020) the U.S. Supreme Court ruled that Title VII of the Civil Rights Act of 1964 protects employees against discrimination because of their sexual orientation or gender identity.

6. The U.S. Supreme Court upheld the right of the baker to discriminate against gays in *Masterpiece Cakeshop v. Colorado Civil Rights Commission*, 584 U.S. ___ (2018).

7. As I had predicted the U.S. Supreme Court ruled against organized labor in *Janus v. American Federation of State, County, and Municipal Employees, Council 31*, 585 U.S. ___ (2018).

Chapter 5

Resisting Trump's Consigliere Dershowitz at the University of Illinois

My own University of Illinois College of Law invited Trump's consigliere Alan Dershowitz to give a speech at the Foellinger Auditorium on the campus of the University of Illinois at Urbana-Champaign on April 26, 2018. Truly appalling! In shocked reaction thereto, I called for and helped organize a protest rally there that evening in front of the building while Dershowitz was speaking inside. Below is the keynote address I gave with a bullhorn in hand so that everyone outside and inside could hear what I had to say:

> My name is Francis Boyle. I am the Senior Professor of Law here at the University of Illinois College of Law. That means that I have taught here longer than anyone else. I am now in my fortieth year of teaching law here.

I am here to condemn not only Dershowitz but the entire College of Law for inviting him in here and sponsoring him. They know full well Dershowitz is a war criminal and they could not care less. They invited him in here, this war criminal, knowing full well that Dershowitz is a member of an Israeli Committee that approves the murder and assassination of Palestinians, which is a war crime.[1]

Indeed the consort of our former Dean Hurricane Heidi Hurd, Mikey Moore admitted that he works for the Mossad and the CIA. I kid you not! Dershowitz believes he's part of the *übermensch* and the same is true for Hurricane Heidi Hurd and her consort Mikey Moore. They have been stinking up this Campus and the Law School and this Community and the legal profession by advocating torture in and out and all the time just like Dershowitz who is speaking in there tonight. Torture in war time is also a war crime!

We have a war criminal in there under the sponsorship of the Nazi College of Law. Carl Schmitt would be proud of them all—the foremost Nazi "jurist" of his time who justified every hideous atrocity Hitler and the Nazis inflicted on everyone, including the Jews. That is exactly what Dershowitz has done to People of Color all over the world and especially Muslims of Color.

Now in addition, Dershowitz has also advocated the serial destruction of Palestinian villages. Repeatedly he has done that, including in an editorial he wrote for the *Jerusalem Post* on March 11, 2002.[2] This is a war crime in violation of the Nuremberg Charter and Judgment that convicted and condemned to death Nazi war criminals. Here let me quote from the relevant section of Article 6 of the 1945 Nuremberg Charter that the United States drafted and signed:

Article 6

. . .

The following acts, or any of them, are crimes coming within the jurisdiction of the Tribunal for which there shall be individual responsibility:

. . .

(b) WAR CRIMES: namely, violations of the laws or customs of war. Such violations shall include, but not be limited to . . . wanton destruction of cities, towns or villages, or devastation not justified by military necessity.

That is exactly what Dershowitz has advocated to be done to the Palestinians. A Nuremberg War Crime right there in the Nuremberg Charter just like the Nazis did throughout Europe during World War II. In addition, Dershowitz published it on purpose over in Israel in order to incite the Israeli government to destroy Palestinian villages. The direct incitement of Nuremberg Crimes is a war crime in its own right. And the College of Law knowing this full well nevertheless brings Dershowitz in here to advocate torture, war crimes, and crimes against humanity against Palestinians and Muslims of Color in this country and all over the world.

Also, Dershowitz deliberately went onto Fox News to encourage Trump, their biggest fan, to bomb Syria.[3] He incited Trump to bomb Syria and that is a Nuremberg Crime Against Peace, an act of aggression, a war crime as defined by international law. It also violated the United Nations Charter, the War Powers Clause of the U.S. Constitution, and the U.S. Congress's own War Powers Resolution of 1973.

Dershowitz also attacked Professor Israel Shahak, one of the leaders of the peace movement in Israel, and a Holocaust survivor himself—unfortunately, no longer with us, but a great man. I have dealt with Shahak and have great respect for him. Indeed, he was going to have a lecture tour here in the United States in the fall of 1990 and was coming to speak in Champaign. The organizers of his lecture tour asked me if I would put him up in my home as my guest in order to conserve on expenses, and I agreed. I was greatly looking forward again to meeting Professor Shahak. But with the Gulf crisis, Professor Shahak decided to cancel his lecture tour and stay at home with his own people, which was certainly understandable. Dershowitz couldn't care less! Whatever kind of outright character assassination he has to apply to anyone, even a Holocaust survivor like Professor Shahak, it doesn't bother Dershowitz. That's how shameless Dershowitz is, publicly attacking a Holocaust survivor!

He attacked and inflicted character assassination on Norman Finkelstein's mother, another Holocaust survivor. Finally, he destroyed Norman Finkelstein's academic career because Norman exposed him as a great and gross plagiarist in his book *Beyond Chutzpah*.[4]

Norman Finkelstein published a book with the University of California Press, a most distinguished press, criticizing Dershowitz and definitively proving that Dershowitz is a plagiarist. What did Dershowitz do? He set out to persecute Norman Finkelstein, a fellow Jew, and then he got Finkelstein denied tenure at DePaul University—that says it's "Catholic"—and destroyed Norman's entire academic career. Norman can no longer get into a tenure-track slot anywhere in this country or even abroad.

Now that's free speech for Alan Dershowitz! If you criticize him, he will destroy you as he did Norman Finkelstein. Don't ever forget it! So this guy even does dirty work against fellow Jews. I know that our friends from Jewish Voices for Peace are here today as a matter of principle in opposing Dershowitz's presence.

Finally, for the last year now Dershowitz has been running all over the country defending Trump. Think about that! Defending Trump all up and down in any way and in any capacity he can, defending Trump. Indeed, just read the *Champaign-Urbana News-Gazette* yesterday.[5] Dershowitz had dinner with Trump, giving legal advice to Trump. This is now the second Trump legal henchman that the College of Law has brought onto this campus. The last one was a high-level Trump legal apparatchik in the Trump/Sessions Department of Injustice that is arguing all of Trump's cases for him in the U.S. Supreme Court.

The entire College of Law Faculty know exactly where I stand on these issues. Indeed they hired me to teach criminal law, international law, and international human rights law. I know a war criminal when I see him and it's Dershowitz! Thank you.

NOTES

1. L. Ali Khan, "The Jihad of Alan Dershowitz," *Counterpunch*, September 30, 2004, https://www.counterpunch.org/2004/09/30/the-jihad-of-alan-dershowitz/.

2. Alan M. Dershowitz, "New Responses to Palestinian Terrorism," *Jerusalem Post*, March 11, 2002.

3. "Dershowitz on Trump's Response to Syria Attack, Comey's Book," *Fox News*, April 8, 2018, https://video.foxnews.com/v/5766502389001#sp=show-clips.

4. Norman G. Finkelstein, *Beyond Chutzpah: On the Misuse of Anti-Semitism and the Abuse of History*, 2nd edition (Oakland, CA: University of California Press, 2007), 17; and Ian Pindar, *Beyond Chutzpah, The Guardian: History Books*, October 3, 2008, https://www.theguardian.com/books/2008/oct/04/israel.norman.finklestein.

5. Julie Wurth, "Dershowitz: I Haven't Seen Any Evidence of Any Criminal Activity or an Impeachable Offense," *News-Gazette*, April 25, 2018, https://www.news-gazette.com/news/dershowitz-i-havent-seen-any-evidence-of-any-criminal-activity-or-an-impeachable-offense/article_d6dd6838-7cc6-5b38-b5a4-40fce7ec868f.html.

Chapter 6

Resisting Trump's CIA Director Bloody Gina Haspel

Dennis Bernstein spoke with Francis Boyle on May 10, 2018, for his Pacifica Radio Network news program *Flashpoints*. [The transcript has been updated to reflect Haspel's confirmation.]

DB: [We now have a new] CIA director who likes to get her hands dirty and participate directly in torture. She has also been actively involved in making sure nobody finds out that torture takes place.

FB: "Bloody" Gina Haspel is her nickname at the CIA. She was directly involved in the extraordinary rendition program, which is a euphemism for the enforced disappearance of human beings and their consequent torture. This was in the Complaint I filed against Bush and company in 2010 with the International Criminal Court for this crime against humanity.

Last fall the ICC Prosecutor, Fatou Bensouda, said she is going to open up an investigation into the entire CIA extraordinary rendition program for violating the Rome Statute. Although the United States is not a party to the Rome Statute, these actions took place on the territorial sovereignty of Rome Statute states, and therefore the ICC does have jurisdiction. In my opinion, Gina Haspel is a presumptive war criminal and torturer. [We now] have a torturer and war criminal as head of the CIA.

As I have argued in anti-CIA cases here in the United States, the CIA is an organized criminal conspiracy like the SS and the Gestapo. We argued that successfully back in 1987 at University of Massachusetts, Amherst. I was involved in large numbers of CIA protest cases back in the 1980s because of what was going on in Central America, with 35,000 dead in Nicaragua, 75,000 dead in El Salvador, and perhaps a quarter of a million in Guatemala. Most of those killed were Mayan Indians, which meant outright genocide.[1]

DB: Will it be difficult for our director of the CIA to travel abroad? Maybe she has to be covert forever.

FB: That is correct. Under international law today—following a terrible decision by the International Court of Justice—heads of state and foreign ministers have diplomatic immunity while they are in office. But that is not going to apply to the head of the CIA.

I have a whole dossier here against Bush Junior and the rest of them for the extraordinary rendition program. We scared him out of Switzerland over that. A Swiss parliamentarian demanded that Bush be prosecuted if he showed up in Switzerland. I know that Amnesty International and the Center for Constitutional Rights also have extensive dossiers against high-level U.S. officials involved in these torture programs, including Haspel. She would be a sitting duck for international human rights lawyers. The evidence is there.

We have a 600-page executive summary of the Senate Foreign Intelligence Committee's report on the extent of torture and extraordinary disappearances by the CIA. This is an official U.S. government document. She was not personally named in there, but she was a high-level official who was personally involved. She certainly supervised the operation in Thailand. Under international law, there is a command responsibility. She is denying that she herself physically tortured anyone, but she supervised others doing the torturing. Under international criminal law, she is accountable for the criminal behavior she oversaw.

DB: She admitted at the hearing that she had the tapes of these torture sessions, but she considered it prudent to destroy them.

FB: The Senate Committee had just announced their investigation, so her boss, Jose Rodriguez, ordered her to destroy the tapes. Arguably, this would be obstruction of justice. [We now have] a notorious international criminal heading up the CIA. In my opinion, any Senator who vote[d] to confirm her [became] an accessory after the fact to her crimes torture, war crimes, crimes against humanity, and violations of the Geneva Conventions and the Convention against Torture.

DB: This is a very difficult time. We are all worried about our friend Ray McGovern, a former CIA analyst who was brutalized while protesting the Haspel nomination. Obviously, they are very serious about shutting up anyone protesting torture.

FB: Ray arguably has the defense of prevention of crimes under international law. I am not saying it would be a winner, because it is always tough going into a federal court and defending anyone protesting and resisting criminal behavior by the United States government.

International Criminal Court Complaint Filed Against Bush, Cheney, Rumsfeld, Tenet, Rice, and Gonzales: International Arrest Warrants Requested

Professor Francis A. Boyle of the University of Illinois College of Law in Champaign, U.S.A. has filed a Complaint with the Prosecutor for the International Criminal Court (I.C.C.) in The Hague against U.S. citizens George W. Bush, Richard Cheney, Donald Rumsfeld, George Tenet, Condoleezza Rice, and Alberto Gonzales (the "Accused") for their criminal policy and practice of "extraordinary rendition" perpetrated upon about 100 human beings. This term is really their euphemism for the enforced disappearance of persons and their consequent torture. This criminal policy and practice by the Accused constitute Crimes against Humanity in violation of the Rome Statute establishing the I.C.C.

The United States is not a party to the Rome Statute. Nevertheless, the Accused have ordered and been responsible for the commission of I.C.C. statutory crimes within the respective territories of many I.C.C. member states, including several in Europe. Consequently, the I.C.C. has jurisdiction to prosecute the Accused for their I.C.C. statutory crimes under Rome Statute article 12(2)(a) that affords the I.C.C. jurisdiction to prosecute for I.C.C. statutory crimes committed in I.C.C. member states.

The Complaint requests (1) that the I.C.C. Prosecutor open an investigation of the Accused on his own accord under Rome Statute article 15(1); and (2) that the I.C.C. Prosecutor also formally "submit to the [I.C.C.] Pre-Trial Chamber a request for authorization of an investigation" of the Accused under Rome Statute article 15(3).

For similar reasons, the highest-level officials of the Obama administration risk the filing of a follow-up Complaint with the I.C.C. if they do not immediately terminate the Accused's criminal policy and practice of "extraordinary rendition," which the Obama administration has continued to implement.

The Complaint concludes with a request that the I.C.C. Prosecutor obtain International Arrest Warrants for the Accused from the I.C.C. in accordance with Rome Statute articles 58(1)(a), 58(1)(b)(i), 58(1)(b)(ii), and 58(1)(b)(iii).

January 19, 2010

Dear Sir:

Please accept my personal compliments. I have the honor hereby to file with you and the International Criminal Court this Complaint against U.S. citizens George W. Bush, Richard Cheney, Donald Rumsfeld, George Tenet, Condoleezza Rice, and Alberto Gonzales (hereinafter referred to as the "Accused") for their criminal policy and practice of "extraordinary rendition." This term is really a euphemism for the enforced disappearances of persons, their torture, severe deprivation of their liberty, their violent sexual abuse, and other inhumane acts perpetrated upon these Victims. The Accused have inflicted this criminal policy and practice of "extraordinary rendition" upon about one hundred (100) human beings, almost all of whom are Muslims/Arabs/Asians and People of Color. I doubt very seriously that the Accused would have inflicted these criminal practices upon 100 White Judeo-Christian men.

The Accused's criminal policy and practice of "extraordinary rendition" are both "widespread" and "systematic" within the meaning of Rome Statute article 7(1). Therefore the Accused have committed numerous "Crimes against Humanity" in flagrant and repeated and longstanding violation of Rome Statute articles 5(1)(b), 7(1)(a), 7(1)(e), 7(1)(f), 7(1)(g), 7(1)(h), 7(1)(i), and 7(1)(k). Furthermore, the Accused's Rome Statute Crimes Against Humanity of enforced disappearances of persons constitutes ongoing criminal activity that continues even as of today.

The United States is not a contracting party to the Rome Statute. Nevertheless, the Accused ordered and were responsible for the commission of these I.C.C. statutory crimes on, in, and over the respective territories of several I.C.C. member states, including many located in Europe. Therefore, the I.C.C. has jurisdiction over the Accused for their I.C.C. statutory crimes in accordance with Rome Statute article 12(2)(a), which provides as follows:

Article 12
Preconditions to the Exercise of Jurisdiction

. . .

2. In the case of article 13, paragraph (a) or (c), the Court may exercise its jurisdiction if one or more of the following States are Parties to this Statute or have accepted the jurisdiction of the Court in accordance with paragraph 3:

(a) The State on the territory of which the conduct in question occurred . . .

So the fact that United States is not a contracting party to the Rome Statute is no bar to the I.C.C.'s prosecution of the Accused because they have ordered and been responsible for the commission of Rome Statute Crimes against Humanity on, in, and over the respective territories of several I.C.C. member states.

Consequently, I hereby respectfully request that the Court exercise its jurisdiction over the Accused for these Crimes against Humanity in accordance with Rome Statute article 13(c), which provides as follows:

Article 13
Exercise of Jurisdiction

The Court may exercise its jurisdiction with respect to a crime referred to in article 5 in accordance with the provisions of this Statute if:

. . .

(c) The Prosecutor has initiated an investigation in respect of such a crime in accordance with article 15.

Pursuant to Rome Statute article 13(c), I hereby respectfully request that you initiate an investigation proprio motu against the Accused in accordance with Rome Statute article 15(1): "The Prosecutor may initiate investigations proprio motu on the basis of information on crimes within the jurisdiction of the Court." My detailed Complaint against the Accused constitutes the sufficient "information" required by article 15(1).

Furthermore, I respectfully submit that this Complaint by itself constitutes "a reasonable basis to proceed with an investigation" under Rome Statute article 15(3). Hence, I also respectfully request that you formally "submit to the Pre-Trial Chamber a request for authorization of an investigation" of the Accused under Rome Statute article 15(3) at this time. Please inform me at your earliest convenience about the status and disposition of my two requests set forth immediately above.

Based upon your extensive human rights work in Argentina, you know full well from direct personal experience the terrors and the horrors of enforced disappearances of persons and their consequent torture. According to reputable news media sources here in the United States, about 100 human beings have been subjected to enforced disappearances and subsequent torture by the Accused. We still have no accounting for these Victims. In other words, many of these Victims of enforced disappearances and torture by the Accused could still be alive today. Their very lives are at stake right now as we communicate. You could very well save some of their lives by publicly stating that you are opening an investigation of my Complaint.

As for those Victims of enforced disappearances by the Accused who have died, your opening an investigation of my Complaint is the only means by which we might be able to obtain some explanation and accounting for their whereabouts and the location of their remains in order to communicate this critical information to their next-of-kin and loved-ones. Based upon your extensive experience combating enforced disappearances of persons and their consequent torture in Argentina, you know full well how important that objective is. The next-of-kin, loved-ones, and friends of "disappeared" human beings can never benefit from psychological "closure" unless and until there is an accounting for the fates, if not the remains, of the Victims. In part that is precisely why the Accused's enforced disappearances of about 100 human beings constitutes ongoing criminal activity that continues as of today and will continue until the fates of all their Victims have been officially determined by you opening an investigation into my Complaint.

Let us mutually suppose that during the so-called "dirty war" in Argentina the International Criminal Court had been in existence. I submit that as an Argentinean human rights lawyer you would have moved heaven and earth and done everything in your power to get the I.C.C. and its Prosecutor to assume jurisdiction over the Argentine Junta in order to terminate and prosecute their enforced disappearances and torture of your fellow Argentinean citizens. I would have done the same. Unfortunately, the I.C.C. did not exist during those darkest of days for the Argentine Republic when we could have so acted. But today as the I.C.C. Prosecutor, you have both the opportunity and the legal power to do something to rectify this mass and total human rights annihilation, and to resolve and to terminate and to prosecute the "widespread" and "systematic" policy and practice of enforced disappearances and consequent torture of about 100 human beings by the Accused.

Unfortunately, the new Obama administration in the United States has made it perfectly clear by means of public statements by President Obama and his Attorney General Eric Holder that they are not going to open any criminal investigation of any of the Accused for these aforementioned Crimes against Humanity. Hence an I.C.C. "case" against the Accused is "admissible" under Rome Statute article 1(complementarity) and article 17. As of right now you and the I.C.C. Judges are the only people in the entire world who can bring some degree of Justice, Closure, and Healing into this dire, tragic, and deplorable situation for the lives and well-being of about one hundred "disappeared" and tortured human beings as well as for their loved-ones and next-of-kin, who are also Victims of the Accused's Crimes against Humanity. On behalf of them all, as a fellow human rights lawyer I implore you to open an investigation into my Complaint and to issue a public statement to that effect.

Also, most regretfully, the new Obama administration has publicly stated that it will continue the Accused's policy and practice of "extraordinary rendition," which is really their euphemism for enforced disappearances of human beings and consequent torture by other States. Hence the highest-level officials of the Obama administration fully intend to commit their own Crimes against Humanity under the I.C.C. Rome Statute—unless you stop them! Your opening an investigation of my Complaint will undoubtedly deter the Obama administration from engaging in any more "extraordinary renditions"—enforced disappearances of human beings and having them tortured by other States. Indeed, your opening of an investigation into my Complaint might encourage the Obama administration to terminate its criminal "extraordinary rendition" program immediately and thoroughly by means of issuing a public statement to that effect. In other words, your opening an investigation of my Complaint could very well save the lives of a large number of additional human beings who otherwise will be subjected by the Obama administration to the Rome Statute Crimes against Humanity of enforced disappearances of persons and their consequent torture by other States, inter alia.

The lives and well-being of countless human beings are now at risk, hanging in the balance, waiting for you to act promptly, effectively, and immediately to save them from becoming Victims of Rome Statute Crimes against Humanity perpetrated by the highest-level officials of the Obama administration as successors-in-law to the Accused by opening an investigation of my Complaint. Otherwise, I shall be forced to file with you and the I.C.C. a follow-up Complaint against the highest-level officials of the Obama administration. I certainly hope it will not come to that. Please make it so.

Finally, for reasons more fully explained in the Conclusion to my Complaint, I respectfully request that you obtain I.C.C. arrest warrants for the Accused in accordance with Rome Statute articles 58(1)(a), article 58(1)(b)(i), article 58(1)(b)(ii), and article 58(1)(b)(iii). The sooner, the better for all humankind.

I respectfully request that you schedule a meeting with me at our earliest mutual convenience in order to discuss this Complaint. I look forward to hearing from you at your earliest convenience.

This transmission letter is an integral part of my Complaint against the Accused and is hereby incorporated by reference into the attached Complaint dated as of today as well.

Please accept, Sir, the assurance of my highest consideration.

Francis A. Boyle
Professor of International Law

NOTE

1. Boyle, *Defending Civil Resistance Under International Law*.

Chapter 7

Trump Targets Iran!

In reaction to the dire threats against Iran by several members of the Trump administration including President Trump himself, on May 15, 2019, *Consortium News* published online the following keynote address I had delivered before the Perdana Global Peace Forum at the Putra World Trade Center, Kuala Lumpur, Malaysia, at the request of Doctor Mahathir Mohamed, then the retired prime minister of Malaysia, on June 22, 2006, when "the U.S. had deployed aircraft carriers to the Persian Gulf and tensions then, as now, were high."

Assalamu'alaikum. Dr. Mahathir, Mrs. Mahathir, distinguished Excellencies, ladies and gentlemen. Little has changed in the imperialist tendencies of American foreign policy since the founding of the United States of America in 1789. The fledgling United States opened the nineteenth century by stealing the continent of North America from the Native Americans, while in the process ethnically cleansing them and then finally deporting the pitiful few survivors by means of death marches (à la Bataan) to Bantustans, which in America we call reservations, as an instance of America's "Manifest Destiny" to rule the world.

Then, the imperial government of the United States opened the twentieth century by stealing a colonial empire from Spain—in Cuba, Puerto Rico, Guam, and the Philippines, then inflicting a near-genocidal war against the Filipino people. While at the same time purporting to annex the Kingdom of Hawaii and subjecting the Native Hawaiian people to near-genocidal conditions from which they still suffer today. All in the name of securing America's so-called "place in the sun."

And today at the dawn of the twenty-first century, the world witnesses the effort by the imperial government of the United States of America to steal a hydrocarbon empire from the Moslem states and peoples, surrounding

Central Asia and the Persian Gulf under the pretext of fighting a war against international terrorism or eliminating weapons of mass destruction or promoting democracy, which is total nonsense.

For the past 216 years, the imperialist foreign policy of the United States of America since its foundation has been predicated upon racism, aggression, ethnic cleansing, crimes against humanity, war crimes, and outright genocide. At the dawn of the third millennium of humankind's parlous existence, nothing has changed about the operational dynamics of American imperial policy. And we see this today in Afghanistan, Iraq, Palestine, and what appears to be an illegal attack upon Iran.

Now the assigned topic today is *The Middle East Agenda: Oil, Dollar Hegemony, and Islam*. So, I'm only going to limit my comments to that subject. We have to begin the story with the Arab oil embargo in 1973. As you know in 1967, Israel launched an illegal war of aggression against the surrounding Arab states, stole their land, and ethnically cleansed their people. But eventually Egypt offered a peace treaty to Israel, which Israel rejected, and the Egyptians and the Arab states decided then to use force to recover their lands.

Israel almost collapsed, the United States and Europe came to their support by providing weapons, and in reaction the Arab states imposed an oil embargo on the United States and Europe and brought their economies to their knees. Whereupon, the then U.S. Secretary of State, Henry Kissinger threatened them and said, "This will never happen again, and if you do, we will prevent it." And it was not just a threat. The United States government then at that time, planned, prepared, and conspired, to steal the oil of the Persian Gulf. They did not have the military capability to do this at that time, to carry out the Kissinger threat, which was also then repeated by the Ford administration, and the Carter administration under Harold Brown and Zbigniew Brzezinski.

So they put into planning an interventionary force, designed expressly for the purpose of stealing Arab oil fields, and that was called the Rapid Deployment Force. And it took ten years of training, planning, positioning, and supply to build that interventionary force of that capability and eventually it was called the U.S. Central Command. The purpose of the U.S. Central Command is to steal and control and dominate the oil and gas resources of the Persian Gulf and Central Asia. And that's exactly what the U.S. Central Command proceeded to do in the Bush Senior war against Iraq, their first military expedition.

And as we know, that war exterminated probably two hundred thousand Iraqis.[1] Half of them innocent civilians. Simply wiped out in a bombing campaign and a military expedition of unprecedented dimensions. But remember, it took fifteen years for the Pentagon and three different administrations both

Republicans and Democrats to get the capability to do this. And then, when that genocidal conflict was over, what happened? The United States carved Iraq up into three pieces with their air force, the so-called no-fly zones, a zone for the Kurds in the North, a zone for the Shi'a in the South, and the Sunni in the middle. Why? To destroy Iraq as an effectively viable state.

In his book *Clash of Civilizations*,[2] Huntington from Harvard who advised the Pentagon and advised the State Department pointed out that the only Arab state with the capability to lead the Arab world and challenge the United States and Israel was Iraq. And so Iraq had to be destroyed, to maintain the domination of the United States and its proxy, Israel. And remember after 1973, whatever it was before then, Israel is nothing more than a cat's-paw of the United States. They do what America tells them to do! Otherwise Israel is nothing more than a failed state.

In addition to destroying Iraq as a state, carving it up into three pieces, was the decision to debilitate and destroy the Iraqi people. And so they continued the genocidal economic sanctions on the people of Iraq, that my colleagues, Denis Halliday and Hans Von Sponeck, so courageously resisted and finally resigned from the United Nations as a matter of principle, calling them by what they really were: genocide. The United States and Britain maliciously and criminally imposed genocidal sanctions on the people of Iraq, that killed approximately 1.5 million Iraqis, all of whom were innocent civilians.

And when U.S. Ambassador to the United Nations and later Secretary of State Madeleine Albright was asked about the five hundred thousand dead children, she said that she thought "the price was worth it."[3] Now, I could have taken that statement to the International Court of Justice, and filed it against the United States as evidence of genocidal intent against the people of Iraq in violation of the 1948 Genocide Convention. And indeed I offered to do so to the then president of Iraq, but for whatever reasons he decided not to take these claims to the International Court of Justice.

And now, as you see, he is on trial in a total kangaroo court proceeding in Baghdad that is completely controlled and dominated by the United States government. So 1.5 million Iraqis died as the result of these genocidal sanctions. And then came September 11. And we know for a fact that the Bush Junior administration knew that a major terrorist attack was going to be launched on the United States. And they let it happen anyway deliberately and on purpose. Why? They wanted a pretext for war. And not just one war but for a "long war" which they are talking about today.

Indeed, from my research the war plans drawn up by the Pentagon for the war against Afghanistan were formulated as early as 1997. Enormous military forces fielded by that same U.S. Central Command were already in and around and surrounding the Persian Gulf and the Indian Ocean before September 11. This war had been long-planned against Afghanistan, and armed, equipped, supplied, trained, and war-gamed and ready to go. They just needed the pretext and that was September 11. Why? The United States wanted access to the oil and natural gas of Central Asia.

That had been a Pentagon objective since at least before the collapse of the Soviet Union in 1991. And the 9/11 attack gave them the pretext to make this major grab for the oil and gas of Central Asia. And they are there today with their bases, with their troops, in the surrounding countries in Central Asia. And of course in the process, obliterated, we don't even have an estimate of the Muslims in Afghanistan who were killed in the air bombardment, twenty, twenty-five thousand, maybe more, and tens of thousands of others starved to death and still suffering today.[4]

But that, as we know from all the records was only the first step in the process. They wanted to finish the job in Iraq. And so immediately after September 11, Bush ordered Rumsfeld to update and operationalize the plans for attacking and invading Iraq. It had nothing at all to do with weapons of mass destruction. We in the peace movement in America had been saying that all along. The United Nations had determined there were no weapons of mass destruction in Iraq. These were lies designed to scaremonger the American people and Congress into supporting an illegal war of aggression, a Nuremberg crime against peace, against Iraq. And they told whatever lies and broke what international laws they had to break in order to attack Iraq.

And today the estimate, again we don't know, perhaps two hundred thousand people in Iraq had been killed outright by the United States, Britain, their allies. And again, most of them civilians. Clearly if you add up what United States government has done to Iraq from August of 1990, when it imposed the genocidal economic embargo until today, the United States and Britain have inflicted outright genocide on the Muslim and Christian people of Iraq and they are predominately Muslim as we know.

Now comes the third step in the Pentagon's preexisting plan, to control and dominate the oil and gas resources of the Persian Gulf and Central Asia. It sounds a bit like the plan that Hitler and the Nazis had in the 1930s, does it not? First go into Austria, then go into Czechoslovakia, then go into Poland. So first Afghanistan, then Iraq, and now Iran. Iran is going to be the next victim of these outright criminals unless you and I can stop them.

Right now there are three aircraft carrier task forces in the Persian Gulf. And whenever they had put three aircraft carrier task forces over there, it's always to prepare for an attack. And according to Seymour Hersch, the award-winning journalist, it will probably be an aerial bombardment, along the lines of what they did to Yugoslavia in 1999. As you remember there, seventy-eight days of aerial bombardment by the United States and NATO with no authorization from the Security Council. Clearly illegal. Killing again, we don't know the exact number, outright four to five thousand innocent civilians. And targeting civilian infrastructure, all up and down, from which the people still suffer today. The use of depleted uranium ammunitions, with consequent outbreaks of cancer are documented today.

So this is what is being planned right now as we speak: an attack upon Iran. Using jet fighter aircraft, fighter bombers, on these three aircraft carrier task forces, using cruise missiles on submarines. Of course, Israel will be involved and have a role to play, doing exactly what the Americans tell them to do. In addition, it appears that if they attack Iran, they will also attack Syria. Yesterday, if you heard President Bush's press conference in Vienna, he threatened Syria, right? There's no other word for it. He threatened Syria.

These neoconservatives want to take out Syria as a favor to Israel. Remember, many of these neoconservatives are affiliated personally and professionally with the Likud Party in Israel and Ariel Sharon, the Butcher of Beirut, the man who exterminated twenty thousand Arabs in Lebanon; most of them, not all of them, were Muslims. And in addition, slaughtered two thousand completely innocent Palestinian women, children, and old men at Sabra and Shatila. Ariel Sharon, the man who went to Haram Al-Sharif, the third holiest site in Islam, where Muhammad (Peace Be Upon Him) ascended into heaven, and desecrated the Haram on September 28, 2000, and deliberately provoked the start of the Al-Aqsa Intifada and has inflicted death and destruction on the Palestinian people since then. Close to thirty-seven hundred Palestinians since then alone have been killed . . . most of them shot down like dogs in the street, and what has the Muslim world done about this?

My Palestinian friends tell me that they are worried that the government of Malaysia might recognize Israel and establish diplomatic relations with Israel. I certainly hope this is not true. We must treat the criminal apartheid regime in Israel the same way the world treated the criminal apartheid regime in South Africa.

If the United States attacks Iran, they will probably attack Syria with the Israeli air force and they will attack Lebanon to take out the Islamic resistance movement in southern Lebanon—Hezbollah—that defended the legitimate rights of Lebanon and the Lebanese people and expelled the invading long-standing occupying Israeli army that had the full support of the United States government for over twenty years.

So they could attack Iran, Syria, southern Lebanon, and inflict yet another round of ethnic cleansing on the suffering Palestinian people. Remember Sharon and Likud believe that Jordan is Palestine. And they want to drive as many Palestinians as possible out of their homes and into Jordan.

So if the United States, as reported by Hersh and other reliable sources, goes ahead and attacks Iran, we could see warfare erupt all the way from Egypt to the border with India. This whole area convulsed in warfare. And who will be the primary victims of this war? Muslims. The United States could not care less about Muslim life. Look at the demonization and victimization of Muslims that we have seen inflicted by the United States and its surrogate, Israel. Look at Guantanamo, where six hundred Muslim men have been treated like dogs in a kennel. Pretty much the way the Nazis treated the Jews. Look at Abu Ghraib and the sadism and sexual exploitation and perversion of Muslims by their American captors. And the same thing has been done in Bagram in Afghanistan. And when Professor Cherif Bassiouni, the U.N. special rapporteur, filed the Report with the Security Council against U.S. practices in Afghanistan, the Americans had Kofi Annan fire him. Just as they had Kofi Annan fire Mary Robinson, the U.N. High Commissioner for Human Rights, when she protested what was going on down in Guantanamo.

The United States could not care less about Muslim life. And the same is true for the genocidal apartheid regime in Israel. They would be happy to use nuclear weapons against Iran. They would be happy to break the taboo of Hiroshima and Nagasaki against Muslims in Iran. It would create no problem at all for them. Indeed, I went to school with these neoconservatives at the University of Chicago. Wolfowitz was there, Chalabi, Khalilzad, Shulsky, all the rest of them. I went through the exact same program. Their mentor was Professor Leo Strauss. And who was his teacher in Germany and his sponsor? Professor Carl Schmitt who went on to become the most notorious Nazi Law Professor of his day, justifying every atrocity that the Nazis inflicted on everyone, including the Jews. We must understand that these neoconservatives are in fact Neo-Nazis. They have espoused the Nazi doctrine of Schmitt and Strauss and Machiavelli and Nietzsche, the "superman." They are the supermen, and the Muslims are the scum of the earth.

Now I do not believe the United States will initially start bombing Iran with nuclear weapons. But if things get out of control they are fully prepared to use tactical nuclear weapons. And here in our materials, you have the Pentagon's *Joint Publication 3-12*, which you can get on the internet . . . just do a Google search and read it. And you will see there, dated March 15, 2005, that tactical nuclear weapons have been fully integrated into United States conventional forces.

So if Iran were to defend itself, human wave attacks, whatever, they will be happy to use nuclear weapons, tactical nuclear weapons against Iran. Remember, these Neo-Nazis, Neo-Cons want to break the taboo of Hiroshima and Nagasaki. They want to use tactical nuclear weapons, to be able to say to the rest of the world: you do what we tell you to do or else look what we did to the Iranians!

It's a very serious situation. And this could even get further out of control. Remember that before Bush invaded Iraq, President Putin of Russia said that if he invaded Iraq he could set off World War Three. Well, I interpreted that as an implicit threat. Even the famous American news broadcaster Walter Cronkite said that if Bush invaded Iraq he could set off World War Three. Two weeks ago we had the meeting of the Shanghai Cooperation Organization: China, Russia, and Iran. So again, if Bush were to attack Iran, he very well could set off a Third World War, a nuclear war. Thank you.

Arab Strategy Forum
Political Systems in the Arab World in 2020:
Moving towards Reform and Development

by Professor Francis A. Boyle
December 13, 2004
Dubai, UAE

This is the Opening Statement I made in my debate against Professor Fouad Ajami of Johns Hopkins University Nitze-SAIS School of International Affairs over the Bush Junior doctrine of so-called "democracy promotion" at the request of the Crown Prince of Dubai Sheikh Hamdan bin Mohammed Al-Maktoum before his Davos-style Conference from December 13 to 15, 2004:

In the name of God, the Compassionate, the Merciful

Your Royal Highnesses, Distinguished Excellencies, Ladies and Gentlemen.

The demand by the Bush Junior administration and its Zionist neoconservative operatives for democratization in the Arab world is a joke and a fraud that is designed to pressure, undermine, and destabilize Arab governments and states at the behest of the genocidal Israeli apartheid regime, and to pursue America's continuing campaign for outright military control and domination of the Gulf oil and gas resources that the United States government launched in direct reaction to the Arab oil embargo of the West in 1973. For over the past three decades American foreign policy toward the entire Middle East has been determined by oil and Israel, in that order.

The United States government will seek direct military control and domination of the hydrocarbon resources of the Arab and Muslim world until there is no oil and gas left for them to steal, using Israel as its regional "policeman" towards that end. Oil and Israel were behind both the Bush Senior and Bush Junior wars against Iraq. And now Bush Junior is threatening to attack Syria, Lebanon, and Iran in conjunction with the genocidal apartheid regime in Israel. As the oil and gas in the Arab and Muslim world proceed to run out, the United States and Israel will become even more predatory, aggressive, destructive, and genocidal toward Arab and Muslim states and peoples.

The Bush Junior administration and its Zionist neoconservative operatives could not care less about democracy in the Arab world. In fact, Bush Junior and his Neo-Cons are all trying very hard to build a Police State in the United States of America that we lawyers are vigorously opposing. What the Bush Junior administration and its Zionist neoconservative operatives really want in the Arab world are quisling dictators who will do their dirty work for them and the genocidal Israeli apartheid regime against the wishes and prayers of the Arab people for democracy, human rights, the rule of law, constitutionalism, as well as for the liberation of Palestine and Al Quds.

Those will be the predominant facts and trends that the Arab world will have to confront between now and 2020. It was not my assignment here today to advise Arab states and the Arab people how to counteract this anti-Arab and anti-Muslim agenda by the United States and Israel. But certainly the sacred *Koran* and the divinely inspired teachings of the Prophet Mohammed—May Peace and Blessings Be Upon Him!—shall guide you and protect you during this most difficult period in the history of the Arab Nation, the Arab People, Arab States, and Islam.

Shukhran.

NOTES

1. Boyle, *Destroying World Order*, 53–91.
2. Samuel P. Huntington, *The Clash of Civilizations and the Remaking of World Order* (New York, NY: Simon & Schuster, January 28, 1998).
3. Madeline Albright with William Woodward, *The Mighty and the Almighty: Reflections on America, God, and World Affairs* (New York, NY: HarperCollins, 2006), 55.
4. Francis A. Boyle, *The Criminality of Nuclear Deterrence* (Atlanta, GA: Clarity Press, 2002), 16–39; Boyle, *Tackling America's Toughest Questions*, 16–38.

Chapter 8

Hillary Clinton Is a Psychopath and a War Criminal

I gave the following interview to Dialogos Media in Greece for broadcasting there during the week of February 18 to 19, 2016, when Hillary Clinton was heavily favored to win the upcoming primary campaign for the 2016 U.S. presidential nomination by the American Democratic Party:

DM: Joining us today on Dialogos Radio and the Dialogos Interview Series is international lawyer and professor of international law at the University of Illinois Dr. Francis Boyle. Boyle has served as legal counsel to the Palestinian Authority, to Hawaiian independence groups, and served on the legal team which led to the conviction of George W. Bush and Dick Cheney for war crimes. Professor Boyle, welcome to our program today.

FB: Well, thank you very much for having me on, and my best to all my friends in Greece. Great country, great people. I spent about two weeks traveling around in 1974, and another two weeks traveling around in 1982.

DM: Wonderful . . . well, let's get started by talking about the Kuala Lumpur War Crimes Commission and the case which led to the conviction of George W. Bush, Dick Cheney, Donald Rumsfeld, Alberto Gonzalez, and others in absentia for war crimes. Tell us about this Commission, and about this case that you were a part of, and its aftermath.

FB: Well, there were two different proceedings. The first one was against Bush and Tony Blair, for their war of aggression and Nuremburg crime against peace against Iraq. I was part of the team that helped get a unanimous conviction there. And then, the second proceeding was against Bush, Cheney, Rumsfeld, Rice, Gonzalez, and several others, for torture and war crimes. Again, I was part of the team that helped get a unanimous conviction, both for torture and for war crimes. Those materials have been filed with the International Criminal Court, and I'm doing the best I can to follow up on my own, tracking these people and staying in touch with all the lawyers to see if we could get them apprehended.

Now Bush was about to go to Switzerland, and a Swiss parliamentarian aware of my work demanded that the Swiss prosecutor-general apprehend and prosecute Bush for torture and war crimes, under the domestic implementing legislation for the Rome Statute of the International Criminal Court. So when word got back to Bush, he didn't go to Switzerland. So that's the way I'm proceeding, and other international human rights experts—I'm not the only one out there, I know the Center for Constitutional Rights in New York is involved, I believe Amnesty International is involved, and there's some other human rights lawyers I stay in contact with around the world—we'll keep after these people the best we can.

DM: Now, let's look more closely at the role of United States foreign policy, its military, and the role of NATO in the world today . . . almost eight years ago, President Obama came to office promising to shut down Guantanamo Bay, promising to right the wrongs of the Bush administration, but instead we've seen Guantanamo remain open, we've seen U.S. military involvement in Iraq and Afghanistan and the Middle East continue and, in fact, intensify, and we've seen the growth of military operations using unmanned drones in Yemen and elsewhere. How does international law view the actions of the Obama administration and the United States today?

FB: Well, actually I wrote a book that comprehensively covered all the violations of international law, human rights, the laws of war, and United States constitutional law by the Bush Junior administration, called *Tackling America's Toughest Questions* (2009), and in the Conclusion I wrote three weeks after Obama was inaugurated, I said it looked like we very well might be getting a third Bush term, and that's what we've got here, two more Bush terms under Obama. He's pretty much continued the Bush policies, both abroad and here at home, compounding and continuing the Bush police state here in the United States. At some point I guess I'll get around to writing a book on the Obama administration's violations of international law, but in the meantime you can read my book on the *Bush violations, Tackling America's Toughest Questions*, and he's basically continued the same policies.

DM: We are on the air with international law expert Francis Boyle here on Dialogos Radio and the Dialogos Interview Series . . . Years ago, you had written about the plans of the United States, the European Union, and NATO for the Ukraine and indeed for the world, with a stated goal of destroying specific states and listing seven countries that were slated to be taken over. What were those plans, and have they come into fruition?

FB: Yes, they have. In my book *The Criminality of Nuclear Deterrence*, I have in there a statement by Deputy Secretary of Defense Wolfowitz, made right after 9/11/2001, that the United States government was going to get into the business of "destroying" states, and I analyze that sentence. It's genocidal. And then soon thereafter, NATO General Wesley Clark was in the Pentagon and he was told they had a list of seven Muslim states that they were going to destroy.

Basically, they've all been taken out now except for Iran. They've destroyed Afghanistan, Syria, Libya, Somalia, Yemen, Lebanon has been pretty much paralyzed, and they lopped off South Sudan from Sudan. So that process continues, and now they're moving towards the Ukraine and China. They're moving towards Russia from Ukraine, and also China. They're moving directly to confront China.

DM: Is there, in your view, any political candidate, any political force in the United States at the present time that can put an end to this foreign policy and to the U.S. military machine overseas? For instance, there's many progressives who have placed their hope in Bernie Sanders as the man to do this. Is this hope misguided, in your view?

FB: Well I'm not going to criticize Senator Sanders here, I've dealt with him personally, but everyone had the same hope about Obama during his campaign. Now, Obama was behind me at Harvard Law School, and he moved to the Hyde Park area in Chicago with the University of Chicago there, where I was an undergraduate. So I had my own sources up there in Chicago, and they told me not to trust Obama, so I never have. Indeed, I didn't vote for him two times in a row. I was not deluded by Obama, which is why I said, three weeks into his administration, in my book, *Tackling America's Toughest Questions*, it looked to me like we were going to get a third Bush term. You know, hope springs eternal. Maybe Bernie Sanders will actually do something, I don't know.

Hillary Clinton is a psychopath and a war criminal, [who said] "we came, we saw, he died," mimicking Julius Caesar and laughing hysterically after Colonel Kaddafi, my former client, was sodomized with a knife and beaten to death.[1] She's a certified psychopath and war criminal. As for the Republicans, none of them look very good at all, between you and me, so I guess maybe Senator Sanders might make a difference. The last time around I did support Jill Stein of the Green Party, I thought she was the best candidate and they had the best platform, but unfortunately the Greens, with all due respect to them, didn't really get themselves organized and accomplish everything. So there we are here in America, what can I say?

DM: We are on the air with international law expert Francis Boyle here on Dialogos Radio and the Dialogos Interview Series . . . The ongoing and worsening conflict in Syria and all across the Middle East has led to a tremendous wave of refugees fleeing their homelands and traveling, under treacherous conditions, to Europe, with Greece often serving as the European entry point for these refugees. What do you make of the European Union's stance towards the refugee crisis and the stance of the international community, and what does international law foresee in such circumstances?

FB: All these refugees are fleeing because the United States government has been destroying their states, as we've already discussed. Syria, Afghanistan, Somalia, Yemen, and Libya account for most of them, so that's why they are fleeing, the outright terror of the aggression, war crimes, genocide, crimes against humanity that the United States government is inflicting upon them. With respect to Europe, everyone there in Europe, all the states are parties to the U.N. Refugees Convention that's the international law. Unfortunately, it appears that they're going to be making Greece the scapegoat for all of this and confining all of these refugees in Greece, if you're reading the plans here, which is completely unfair. I don't know exactly how to advise Greece as to how to deal with the situation. The Refugees Convention is there, but you're being made the scapegoat for American policies here, and Europe is going along with it.

DM: You have written and spoken extensively about growing Israeli belligerence in the Middle East and about the Palestinian right of return. How does international law view Israeli actions in the region, such as the continued construction of settlements, and how can the Palestinian people defend their homeland and their sovereignty, from a legal point of view?

FB: Well I've written three books, including *Palestine, Palestinians, and International Law; Breaking All the Rules*; and *The Palestinian Right of Return Under International Law*. So I'm not going to go through all that. But basically what we have here is outright genocide being perpetrated by Israel against the Palestinians, with the full support of the United States government. And that is what confronts us today as citizens of the world community. Israel wants all of Palestine and they don't want any Palestinians there, so it's going to get worse. I gave the best advice I can to the Palestinian leadership, I've worked with them to get them up to the point where they are now a United Nations Observer State, I have devised a means whereby they can overcome Obama's threatened veto of their membership, full-fledged state membership in the United Nations, and I have also offered to sue Israel at the International Court of Justice in The Hague, the World Court, for inflicting genocide against them and trying to stop the settlements, the genocidal siege of Gaza. So the Palestinian leadership has my recommendations and offer to help. In the meantime, I'm doing everything I can . . . I was the one who set off the Israeli divestment/disinvestment campaign of November of 2000, and then in 2005 the Palestinian civil society contacted me and asked me if I would go in with them on a BDS campaign, which I agreed to do. So the BDS campaign has taken off now all over the world, and I would encourage your listeners to work with the Palestinian BDS campaign for sure. It's having an impact.

DM: We are on the air with international law expert Francis Boyle here on Dialogos Radio and the Dialogos Interview Series . . . Having mentioned Israel and the Middle East, this past summer, the Greek government signed an agreement with the armed forces of Israel, a so-called "status of forces" accord, which Israel has apparently signed with only one other country in the world, the United States. What does this accord mean and what do you make of the Greek government's efforts to forge closer ties with Israel?

FB: Well, I haven't read this document, so I don't think I should comment on a document I haven't read. But it is very unfortunate to see Greece move towards working hand-in-glove with Israel, when you did have a previous history there of supporting the Palestinians. I think the Greek people need to make it clear to the current Syriza government that you're not going to accept this at all, and you want the Greek government to go back and support the Palestinians.

DM: You used to be a member of the Board of Amnesty International USA, back in the late 80s and early 1990s. However, you have since turned into a fierce critic of NGOs such as Amnesty International. Describe for us the relationship that exists between such NGOs and power structures in Washington and elsewhere.

FB: Yes. These western NGOs, and you probably have some of them in Greece, all operate on the basic principle he who pays the piper calls the tune. There's nothing objective, neutral, or dispassionate about any of them, including and especially Human Rights Watch, the Red Cross, I could go down an entire list of these NGOs. So they're really not there to help you and the people of Greece. You might have your own internal Greek NGOs that get money from Greek sources, but that's a different matter. You have to be very careful with these NGOs. For example, this summer Amnesty International adopted a resolution to the effect that it was going to promote the sex industry and sex trade on a worldwide basis, which I did my best to stop. I read the documents in support of this, and it all went back to George Soros documentation. So it seems that Soros must have made a very big contribution to Amnesty International to get this reprehensible policy rammed through their headquarters in London, and then Amnesty worldwide. I take it that Soros must have some type of investments in the sex industry—you know, he's a hedge fund manager—and Soros gave $100 million to Human Rights Watch, so you can figure it out from there. It's true of all of these Western NGOs.

DM: We are on the air with international law expert Francis Boyle here on Dialogos Radio and the Dialogos Interview Series . . . Your outspoken criticism of U.S. foreign policy, against Israel, also issues such as being in favor of independence for Hawaii and for many other issues has put you on the radar of the FBI and other intelligence agencies. Describe for us an encounter you had with the FBI about a decade ago.

FB: One day, two agents of the FBI and the CIA showed up at my office, misrepresented to my secretary who they were, what they were about. I let them in to my office. They proceeded to interrogate me for one hour and tried to get me to become an informant against my Muslim clients, which I refused to do, repeatedly refused. So they went out then and put me on all the United States government's terrorist watch lists. According to my lawyer, there's six or seven of them and as far as he can figure out, I was put on all of them. You know, what can I say? My lawyer did appeal, but he was told I would remain on all of these watch lists until the FBI and CIA take me off, which course is not going to happen in my lifetime. He did make it possible for me to travel, but there we are.

DM: Now let's turn to Greece one more time . . . over the past six years, successive Greek governments, including the supposedly leftist Syriza government, have signed a series of memorandum agreements which have not only imposed harsh economic austerity, which have not only resulted in the privatization and sell-off of key public assets, but which have also essentially signed away, at least on paper, Greece's sovereignty. The EU and the Troika have final approval rights over key legislation that is brought before the Greek parliament, while the memorandum agreements have been placed under the legal authority of the United Kingdom and Luxembourg. Are such agreements valid under international law, and what could Greece do to restore the country's sovereignty? Are there any precedents in international law that Greece could turn to?

FB: It does appear that Syriza has abandoned and betrayed the Greek people and the promises it had made originally to get elected. You know, you're asking me this question for the first time, but certainly one could use an argument of economic duress and threats of coercion under the Vienna Convention on the Law of Treaties, to try to claw back some of these agreements that Syriza has made. As for this debt, there is a well-known doctrine under international law known as "odious debt" that I think Greece could consider repudiating a good deal of this debt. I haven't studied the elements of the Greek debt, but it does appear there are more than enough elements there that could be repudiated as "odious debt." And then finally, clearly Germany owes massive reparations to Greece for the Nazi occupation and war crimes in Greece during World War II. They still have not paid up, and I think the Greek government and the Greek people need to insist on that, and that gives you a lot of leverage against Germany, which is really the most powerful country in Europe right now and is pretty much calling all of the shots here. I think the Greek people understand this. So you have a lot of leverage, but the Syriza government has to use it.

DM: Are the examples of countries such as Iceland or Argentina possible precedents that could be used in the case of Greece?

FB: Well Iceland's pretty small . . . yes, you could look at Argentina, and then also Malaysia, when it was threatened by Soros with his hedge-fund's attack on the "Asian Tigers." Malaysia was able to pull through that.

DM: We are on the air with international law expert Francis Boyle here on Dialogos Radio and the Dialogos Interview Series . . . We live in a global society today that is marked by increased government surveillance, police violence, an increasingly neoliberal and authoritarian world. In light of this, what can ordinary people do to not only stand up for human rights and the rule of law, but to also identify political and social movements that will truly stand up for their rights and not betray them?

FB: Well, you just had a general strike in Greece. I thought that was great, it really shows the Greek people have had enough. Everyone taking to the street, I think we need to see more of that in Greece, and then some type of leadership emerge out of those general strikes. It seems to me they're really in contact with the people. Syriza has forfeited, in my opinion, its right to lead the Greek people. They're working in cahoots with the IMF, the World Bank, the European Central Bank, Brussels, and Berlin.

DM: Professor Boyle, thank you very much for taking the time to speak with us today here on Dialogos Radio and the Dialogos Interview Series, and for sharing your insights and experiences with our listeners.

FB: Thanks for having me on, and I look forward to coming back to Greece sometime when I can fit the trip in. Great country, I learned so much from your people and the history and the culture.

DM: Thank you once more, greatly appreciated.

NOTE

1. Boyle, *Destroying Libya and World Order.*

Chapter 9

International Criminal Court

The White Man's Court

I filed a Complaint with the International Criminal Court against former president George Bush Junior, Vice President Richard Cheney, Secretary of Defense Donald Rumsfeld, CIA director George Tenet, Secretary of State Condoleezza Rice, Attorney General Alberto Gonzalez, and some of their lawyers for their policy and practice of "extraordinary renditions," which was really a euphemism for the two primary ICC statutory crimes of the enforced disappearance of human beings and their consequent torture, inter alia. My *Letter of Transmittal* for this Complaint sent to the first ICC prosecutor Luis Moreno-Ocampo that sets forth in detail the grounds justifying their prosecution and in particular why the International Criminal Court had jurisdiction to prosecute these U.S. government officials despite the fact that the United States was not a contracting state party to the Rome Statute for the International Criminal Court was already reprinted above in the chapter on Trump's CIA Director "Bloody" Gina Haspel.[1] I continued to supplement my ICC Complaint with numerous written submissions tracking, documenting, and arguing against the latest significant public revelations and developments on their "extraordinary renditions" policy and practice.

Then on November 20, 2017, the second ICC prosecutor Fatou Bensouda announced that she was requesting authorization from the ICC to open an investigation into war crimes and crimes against humanity in Afghanistan including: "War crimes by members of the United States ('US') armed forces on the territory of Afghanistan, and by members of the US Central Intelligence Agency ('CIA') in secret detention facilities in Afghanistan and on the territory of other States Parties to the Rome Statute, principally in the period of 2003–2004." With respect to prosecuting these CIA officials, Ms. Bensouda articulated a theory of jurisdiction for their prosecution identical to that set forth in my ICC Complaint of January 10, 2010. Better late than never!

There matters stood until September 10, 2018, when President Trump's neoconservative National Security Advisor John Bolton publicly threatened dire sanctions for anyone at the International Criminal Court who was involved in opening a formal investigation into alleged international crimes committed by officials of the U.S. government and by officials of America's allied governments such as Israel. With respect to Israel, in reaction to its latest genocidal massacre of about 1,400 Palestinians in Gaza pursuant to Israel's so-called "Operation Cast Lead" that had commenced in late December 2008, I was the one who had originally advised Palestinian president Mahmoud Abbas to accept the jurisdiction of the International Criminal Court on behalf of the State of Palestine under article 12(3) of the Rome Statute on January 21, 2009, and then to file a Complaint against the highest-level Israeli government officials for the commission of these and future anticipated and predictable international crimes. These and other matters concerning the Palestinians will be analyzed in more detail below in two later chapters of this book.

The United Nations Organization (UNO) has receded far distant from the positive role it used to play in Africa from the late 1950s to the 1980s when the UNO worked vigorously for the decolonization of Africa from the White racist Western colonial imperial powers. Today what we are witnessing instead is the United Nations basically helping the White racist Western colonial imperial powers recolonize the continent of Africa. I personally would not believe anything that the United Nations Organization is saying or doing in Africa. UN secretary general Ban Ki-Moon was a flunky for the United States. The Americans gave him the job. He did whatever the United States told him to do. Africans are well advised to be extremely skeptical of the United Nations Organization as well as of its specialized agencies and affiliated organizations operating anywhere in Africa.

To be sure, technically the International Criminal Court (ICC) is not an organ of the UNO. Legally, both the ICC and the UNO are supposed to be independent of each other. But both international organizations operate in accordance with that well-known "Piper Principle" of international political science: He who pays the piper calls the tune! The same White racist Western colonial imperial powers call the tune for both the International Criminal Court and the United Nations Organization, including all of the latter's specialized agencies and affiliated organizations. Western money talks, international law and human rights walk—especially in Africa.

When it supported the right of self-determination under international law in Africa, the United Nations overturned the historical legacy of the Berlin Conference of 1884–1885, under which auspices the White racist Western imperial powers commenced their colonial division of the African continent, robbed Africa of its natural resources, and proceeded to inflict outright genocide upon Africans. By contrast, under the influence of Third World countries that fought for independence against the West, the United Nations supported a decolonization campaign that culminated in the independence of Namibia and the dismantling of the White racist criminal apartheid regime in South Africa. In theory, Africa was then legally free. But economically Africa was still dependent upon and subordinate to the Western Powers because of their continued imposition of neocolonial economic control and political domination.

What we are seeing now is an attempt by the United States and the European States—collectively organized into the NATO Alliance—to actually recolonize Africa outright and *in toto*. The opening shot of this process was the 2011 U.S./NATO war of aggression and genocide against Libya that was sanctioned by the United Nations Security Council. This UN-authorized U.S./NATO military operation clearly had the objective of stealing all of Libya's oil and gas resources. Up to 50,000 Africans were brutally exterminated in this process of the United States/NATO reconquering Libya after Muamar Gaddhafi had previously expelled the United States and the United Kingdom. Thanks to the United States/NATO, Libya has now become Somalia on the Mediterranean with waves of African refugees drowning on their way to Europe.

Libya is scheduled to become a de facto base and staging area for the United States/NATO to project power southward into the heart of the African continent in order to steal the abundant natural resources of Africa. As demonstrated in Libya, the White racist Western colonial imperial powers that control NATO and the United Nations Organization will pay no attention whatsoever to the 1948 Genocide Convention when it stands in their rapacious path of invading, bombing, exploiting, persecuting, murdering, and occupying African states and Peoples of Color in order to steal their natural resources. This is what the new "scramble for Africa" is all about by the White racist Western colonial imperial powers along the lines of the old Conference of Berlin. Now implemented today by means of the latest Western high-tech weapons systems such as genocidal drones.

France has always been one of the West's major colonial imperial powers in Africa. Today France is deeply involved in consolidating the entire geopolitical space between the Mediterranean and the Gulf of Guinea for the United States/NATO as most recently demonstrated by its ousting the government of Cote D'Ivoire and its invasion of Mali using Guinea as a staging area for the attack. In fact, France never really left Africa. France still maintains garrison forces all over Africa to exert continued French control and domination upon these Black African States, governments, peoples, leaders, and resources. I am of French ancestry: *Vive La France!* But not in Africa!

Regretfully, with respect to many African leaders, the situation still remains analogous to what Frantz Fanon described in his classic book *Black Skin, White Masks* (1952). You have leadership elites throughout Africa who do the bidding of the United States and the NATO states against the wishes and interests of their own people. The second and current ICC Prosecutor Madame Fatou Bensouda from Gambia is a classic case of *Black Skin, White Masks*. The White racist Western colonial imperial powers who control the ICC put her into office in order to deceive African states and peoples into believing that the ICC works for them rather than against their interests on behalf of the United States/NATO.

In this process of the modern Western recolonization of Africa the ICC at The Hague functions as the White Man's Court. The ICC enables the White racist Western imperialist states to pursue and neutralize African leaders who do not do their bidding. Admittedly, some of the implicated African leaders have unsavory reputations. But so far every suspect the ICC has gone after has been from Africa. This is no coincidence. In fact, and in law, these African tin-pot dictators are small fish compared to the genocidal monsters of White racist United States/NATO/Israel.

The ICC refused to do anything about bringing to justice Tony Blair despite the fact that British lawyers filed a perfectly correct Complaint against him for his numerous international crimes in Iraq. Likewise for the Complaint I filed with the ICC in January 2010 against George Bush, Dick Cheney, Donald Rumsfeld, George Tenet, Condoleezza Rice, Alberto Gonzales, and their lawyers because of their criminal policy and practice of "extraordinary renditions," which is a euphemism for the enforced disappearances of human beings and their torture and thus constitute crimes against humanity in accordance with the ICC's Rome Statute. So far, the ICC has refused to do anything to serve justice upon these Bush-era American international criminals. Ditto for President Obama and his administration for their drone murder policy and practices being run out of occupied Afghanistan that is an ICC member state.

Right after Israel's genocidal Operation Cast Lead against Gaza from December 2008 to January 2009, I recommended to Palestinian president Mahmoud Abbas that Palestine accept the jurisdiction of the International Criminal Court, which President Abbas did do. And what happened? The first ICC Prosecutor Moreno-Ocampo threw it out on the bogus grounds that it was not for him to determine whether Palestine is a State. He reached this disingenuous conclusion despite the facts that Palestine then had de jure diplomatic state relations with about 130+ states and also possessed state membership in UNESCO, a UN specialized agency. This coward and hypocrite Moreno-Ocampo had the gall to toss aside Palestine's acceptance of the jurisdiction of the International Criminal Court like a piece of Kleenex, and refused to investigate Israel for war crimes, crimes against humanity, and genocide against the Palestinians. Moreno-Ocampo would not lift even one finger to help the Palestinians in their moments of dire desperation. He is truly a despicable human being! So far, his successor, Ms. *Black Skin, White Masks* Bensouda, has demonstrated no propensity either for doing justice for the Palestinians against the White racist Israeli genocidaires who have the full support and backing of the racist American genocidaires against Palestine and the Palestinians.

The ICC will not touch White racist American, British, Canadian, European, and Israeli perpetrators of war crimes, crimes against humanity, and genocide against Peoples of Color around the world. So far, the ICC has refused to prosecute any of the U.S./NATO officials for their international crimes against the Afghan people despite the fact that Afghanistan is a party to the ICC Rome Statute. Estimates run from one million to four million Afghans exterminated by White racist Western colonial imperial powers since September 11, 2001. The ICC has also refused to prosecute the White racist leaders of the United States/NATO states for war crimes, crimes against humanity, and genocide against Africans in Libya. The ICC will not bite the White racist Western colonial imperial hands that feed it.

I originally supported the establishment of an International Criminal Court because I figured it might serve as some minimal deterrent to the U.S. government inflicting aggression, genocide, war crimes, and crimes against humanity all over the world, including and especially against Peoples and states of Color in the Third World. I proved wrong in my estimations. I was naïve about the realities of American power ready, willing, and able to subvert and to pervert from the get-go an international institution that it never intended to join in the first place.

Of course, the United States could never have permitted a real, independent, and effective International Criminal Court to come into existence! Otherwise, its highest-level civilian and military officials would be—and should be—sitting behind bars in a Hague jail cell today. Instead we now witness the ICC White Man's Court stinking up The Hague.

My good faith advice today to Third World states who are not yet parties to the Rome Statute is *not* to join the International Criminal Court. And if Third

World states are already parties to the ICC Rome Statute, again my good faith advice to them is to pull out now before the White racist Western colonial imperial powers sic the ICC after them as their pet attack dog. The ICC is the West's rottweiler against Africa and Asia!

NOTE

1. See Chapter 6 *infra*.

Chapter 10

Trump's Lethal Decision on Jerusalem

President Trump has won praise from Christian Zionists and many staunch supporters of Israel for declaring Jerusalem Israel's capital, but critics say it only makes peace a more distant goal, reports Dennis J. Bernstein.

Protests have broken out across the Middle East against President Trump's recognition of Jerusalem as Israel's capital—and Western critics complain that the move adds one more brick in the wall against the prospects for peace. Professor Francis Boyle, who teaches international law at the University of Illinois College of Law and served as a longtime legal adviser to the Palestine Liberation Organization (PLO), calls Trump's announcement a "symbolic but still critical step in Israeli designs to control not just Jerusalem, but all of historic Palestine." I spoke with Boyle on December 6, 2017.

Dennis Bernstein: What was your initial response to the announcement by President Trump that the United States will be moving its embassy to Jerusalem?

Francis Boyle: It is always a sad day when you know that people are going to die. It is a defeat for the human spirit. In the last intifada (September 2000–February 2005), about 3,000 Palestinians died and 1,000 Israelis. I don't know what will happen this time. The Palestinians have called for "three days of rage." Trump could very well set off a third intifada here.

Dennis Bernstein: Trump says this doesn't get in the way of the U.S. being an honest broker, that the vision is for peace. From the legal perspective, how do you see this?

Francis Boyle: First of all, the United States has never been an honest broker here. I was legal advisor to the Palestinian delegation to the Middle East Peace Negotiations from 1991, when they began, to the signing of Oslo. It was very clear that the United States was always serving as Israel's lawyer. You had Miller, Ross, and Kurzer, all three American Jews, two of them Orthodox.

The Palestinians had to go hat-in-hand to present their case to American Jews. Nothing has changed: We now have Kushner, Greenblatt, and Friedman, all three of whom are Orthodox Jews. The whole thing has been preposterous from the beginning. We have always been in favor of Israel, using lies, threats, and intimidation to force the Palestinians to accept whatever the Israelis are giving them. That is international diplomacy for you, conducted by the United States, not only in the Middle East but all over the world.

Dennis Bernstein: Would you say that what is going on here is not just Israel trying to control Jerusalem but all of Palestine?

Francis Boyle: That has always been Israel's policy. I had a conversation with the Chair of the Palestinian Delegation to the Middle East peace negotiations. [Dr. Haidar Abdul Shaffi.] He told me that the Zionists have not changed their position since the Basle Conference of 1897. They want all of Palestine. What is happening now in Jerusalem is a step in that direction.

If you look at the recently leaked so-called peace plan that was presented to [Palestinian President Mahmoud] Abbas in Saudi Arabia, he was basically given an ultimatum to either accept some tiny Bantustan or forget it. It is very clear that they want all of Palestine, all of the West Bank, all of Jerusalem. They want the Golan Heights and maybe even some more of Syria.

Dennis Bernstein: We have revelations now that Jared Kushner, our chief peace negotiator in the Middle East, failed to disclose in ethics filings his role as director of a family foundation that funded Israeli settlements. Do you think that is a problem?

Francis Boyle: Of course, because basically he is aiding and abetting war crimes and crimes against humanity in Palestine.

Dennis Bernstein: Is the United States participating in illegal actions in Israel, or doesn't it matter anymore?

Francis Boyle: For most of the Arab and Muslim world, it matters. Here in the United States, apart from the BDS movement, we have basically thrown in our lot with the Israeli government. Congress has been bought and paid for by the Israel lobby. During his campaign, Trump made explicit promises in order to secure Jewish funding and votes.

We arm, equip, supply, and train Israel. What is going on in Gaza right now is a form of genocide. They are being strangled to death. The 1948 Genocide Convention, to which both Israel and the United States are parties, says that "deliberately inflicting on a people conditions of life calculated to bring about their physical destruction in whole or in part" is genocide. That is exactly what is going on in Gaza today.

Dennis Bernstein: How would you assess the situation now? Is a two-state solution at all viable?

Francis Boyle: That is for the Palestinians to decide. Their right of self-determination is at stake here. As of today, their official position is two states with their capital in East Jerusalem. There have been hints that they might go back to the one-state solution, which was their position before the Palestinian Declaration of Independence of November 15, 1988, when they officially accepted a two-state solution. Since then they have gotten nothing. Every day Israel just steals more land and drives out more Palestinians.

Dennis Bernstein: Are there any options for the Palestinians in the international arena, for example, at the United Nations?

Francis Boyle: I have advised them to invoke the "Uniting for Peace" Resolution adopted by the UN General Assembly in 1950, so that they can be admitted to the UN General Assembly as a full-fledged UN member state, recognizing their capital as East Jerusalem. And, as you know, after Palestine became a UN Observer State, you and I discussed the concept of a Legal Intifada that the Palestinians could pursue.

My advice to the Palestinians is a full-court press in all specialized United Nations agencies and affiliated organizations, using all available legal mechanisms. This would include suing Israel at the International Court of Justice, which I have offered to do for them. And of course they have filed a complaint against Israel for war crimes and crimes against humanity before the International Criminal Court. According to press reports, they are meeting right now to decide what to do and President Abbas will soon be addressing the Palestinian people.

Dennis Bernstein: I suppose it is important to emphasize the fact that this could turn very violent.

Francis Boyle: I am afraid so. This could turn into the third intifada. The First Intifada, which took place in 1987, was spontaneous. The Second Intifada [September 2000–February 2005] was provoked when Ariel Sharon went to the Al-Aqsa Mosque with a couple hundred soldiers. Eventually, about 3,000 Palestinians lost their lives as a result.

Now we have Trump provoking the situation. His people, including Bannon and Flynn, know exactly what they are doing. They believe in Sam Huntington's concept of "the clash of civilizations." They truly believe that they are leading a crusade against the Muslim world. This is being done very deliberately.

THE PALESTINIAN LEGAL INTIFADA

On November 29, 2012, the UN General Assembly overwhelmingly approved a resolution to upgrade the Palestinian Authority's observer status to a non-member state. According to various sources, the UN General Assembly voted to recognize Palestine as a sovereign state, despite threats by the United States and Israel that the Palestinian Authority would be punished by withholding much needed funds for the West Bank government. It was reported that Britain threatened to abstain from the vote for enhanced Palestinian status at the UN unless the Palestinians agreed not to take the Israelis to various international courts.

As the vote was in progress, Dr. Francis A. Boyle, Professor of International Law at the University of Illinois College of Law, and the author of *The Palestinian Right of Return Under International Law* (2011), spoke about why the United States was making such dire threats of economic retaliation against the Palestinians if they continued to pursue recognition by the UN. Professor Boyle was advisor to the Palestinian Liberation Organization and its chairman, Yasser Arafat, on the Palestinian Declaration of Independence of November 15, 1988. Boyle said today, "This can be the start of a legal intifada by Palestinians against Israel!"

DB: Professor Boyle, welcome back to *Flashpoints*. Can we begin with your understanding of why the U.S. would threaten to cut off Palestine, and why the Brits are so upset?

FB: No member state of the United Nations Organization has ever been destroyed or eliminated. Some of them have broken off into constituent units, but they have never been extinguished. Israel would like all of Palestine—the West Bank, and East Jerusalem—without the Palestinians. So it's important, as they see it, not to have recognition of Palestinian statehood by the United Nations Organization. It's that simple.

I've been working with the Palestinians and their peace initiatives since 1987 and was Legal Advisor with the Palestinian delegation to the Middle East peace negotiations. The Israelis never demonstrated even one iota of good faith when negotiating a two-state solution with the Palestinians. The Zionists have always wanted all of Palestine, going back to the Basle Conference of 1897. Nothing has changed. That is still their agenda, and why they are vigorously fighting against recognition of Palestine by the UN. Last year they fought against our admission as a member state to the U.N. This is an existential battle going on now for 115 years, and it's not about to end tomorrow.

DB: What are the implications in terms of international law? We know that Israel—supported by the U.S. and many countries in Western Europe—has violated international law with an illegal, ongoing, brutal occupation. We've seen two slaughters in the last four years where Israel went after the Gaza Strip and people couldn't even run—they didn't even have the possibility of becoming refugees again. There's a lot at stake if the international community recognizes the Palestinians. You present six legal remedies the Palestinians would have available if this becomes a reality. What are they?

FB: Obviously Palestinians could barely defend themselves because the U.S., the most powerful military power in the world, has given Israel over and over again every type of high-tech weapons systems possibly imaginable. So their strong suit is international law. I already recommended to them, in Ramallah, that they consider implementing these steps, which I call a Legal Intifada.

First is becoming a party to the Rome Statute for the International Criminal Court. After Operation Cast Lead One, I advised President Abbas to accept the jurisdiction of the International Criminal Court (ICC) under Article 12, paragraph 3, which he did. Then he filed a long complaint with the ICC prosecutor over Operation Cast Lead One. The ICC prosecutor, Moreno Ocampo, announced that he was going to investigate two issues: Did Palestine have the capacity to accept the jurisdiction of the ICC under Article 12, paragraph 3? And did Israel commit war crimes and crimes against humanity against the Palestinians during Cast Lead? The Goldstone Commission Report answered the second question in the affirmative; Israel had inflicted war crimes and crimes against humanity against the Palestinians.

As to the first point, just before he left office, Moreno-Ocampo announced that he did not believe Palestine had the capacity to accept the jurisdiction of the ICC under Article 12, paragraph 3. In any event, he said it was not for him to determine whether Palestine was a state. This, despite the fact that Palestine was admitted as a full-fledged member state of UNESCO (United Nations Economic and Social Council), which is a UN specialized agency. Basically, Moreno-Ocampo copped out. If he hadn't, there's a good chance Israel would not have repeated what I call Cast Lead Lite, which occurred for eight days in November. In his press conference, Moreno-Ocampo said, "But of course, Palestine could ratify the Rome Statute and then proceed as a member state, and that would solve the jurisdictional problem." All Palestine has to do once it becomes a UN member state is accede to the terms of the Rome Statute and file that with the UN Secretary General, which is the depositary for the Rome Statute. The Secretary General will be obligated to accept that instrument of accession, and then Palestine can simply reactivate the complaint that's already there and add in Cast Lead Lite for November 2012. If they want to, they can also add the current settlements policy.[1] The International Court of Justice ruled in its Advisory Opinion on the Wall, that all the settlements in the West Bank and East Jerusalem violate the Fourth Geneva Convention of 1949. Of course, such violations are a war crime, and when they are widespread or systematic, which they certainly are both in the West Bank and East Jerusalem, they become a crime against humanity.

DB: The British foreign secretary says the Palestinians are not going to get their support unless they agree to pledge not to sue Israel for war crimes. There it is.

FB: Yes. And he doesn't understand that they already did that, so these are obviously highly technical matters that their international law staff will follow. They already filed that complaint, so they just need to reactivate the complaint they have filed. This would put them in the driver's seat with the settlements policy issue in the dock.

Britain created this problem in the first place with the Balfour Declaration. They've always been against us, so it doesn't surprise me that the Brits are still taking this position. They were behind the partition resolution sixty-five years ago.

It's not just Palestine. The Brits did the same to my country, Ireland—they partitioned us. The British partitioned the Indian subcontinent into India and Pakistan, creating a monumental human rights tragedy that's still going on. Britain also partitioned the Republic of Bosnia and Herzegovina, which remains a problem. It's a joke that the British say they are for peace. They've created so many of the problems that we confront today: India, Pakistan, Palestine, Ireland, Bosnia, the Falklands/Malvinas, for starters.

DB: What could happen about the illegal siege of Gaza under the International Court of Justice?

FB: Once it becomes a UN Observer State, Palestine can then accede to the terms of the Statute of the International Court of Justice (ICJ), which is the World Court of the UN system. Palestine will—across the board on all these issues—be following the precedent of Switzerland, which did not join the UN until about five years ago. But during that period of time it had UN Observer State status, and in that capacity Switzerland had most of the rights it needed to do whatever it wanted to do. Switzerland became a party to the ICJ Statute. Palestine, I'm sure, will too. Palestine, by taking the Swiss instrument and filing it with the World Court, would be able to sue Israel at the ICJ. I've offered to President Abbas and the PLO Executive Committee to file this lawsuit and try to break the genocidal siege of Gaza that is still going on today, as we speak. President Morsi of Egypt, despite all the rhetoric, still hasn't done anything about it. It's on a list of things the Palestinians can do once the dust settles.

Third, Palestine could then join the Law of the Sea Convention and get legal access and a legal right to these enormous gas supplies right off the coast of Gaza, which Israel has access to. Lebanon, Cyprus, and Turkey all have their claims in, but Palestine has a claim too. Indeed, a pretty substantial claim. If Palestine gets access to that gas, it can become economically self-sufficient, so this is a very important issue.

Palestine can become a party to the International Civil Aviation Organization and get legal, sovereign control over their own air space. By becoming a member of the International Telecommunications Union, they will get control of their airwaves, phone lines, band widths for internet and satellite access.

Those are some of the immediate consequences. Of course, Palestine would also become a High Contracting Party to the Four Geneva Conventions of 1949. Back in 1989 I recommended this step to President Arafat as a purely humanitarian measure. The U.S. government applied massive pressure to the Swiss government not to accept our instrument of accession. So what the Swiss did, again—they copped out back in 1989—was say, "Well, we're not in a position to determine whether or not Palestine is a state, but we will treat their declaration as binding." And they still carry us as a footnote.

Palestine will be upgraded to a High Contracting Party like all the 193 states in the world, with the right to demand that they all act to protect it as a fellow High Contracting Party under common Article 1 to the Four Geneva Conventions, where they have an obligation not only to respect the Conventions themselves, but to ensure respect by Israel.[2] These are the six steps, in terms of priority, that Palestine could get to work on tomorrow.

DB: If the Law of the Sea Convention were applied, are the offshore gas fields so extensive they could perhaps help bring Palestinians out of poverty? How big is that battle? We don't hear much about the battle around resources; it's seen as a religious war.

FB: This isn't a religious war. I've spent a lot of time in the Middle East and dealt with Palestinians, Christians, Muslims, and Jews. This is a war over land, resources, and water—that's what is going on here. Israel believes it's in its best interest to present this as a religious war, but it simply is not. Those gas supplies under the Mediterranean are enormous. The financial literature, including the *Wall Street Journal* and the *Financial Times*, have extensive discussions about how much natural gas is there. It certainly would be enough to make Palestine economically self-sufficient, along with the capacity of its people, who are highly educated and highly motivated. Israel would be entitled to its share as well. If you read the debates over the gas fields, of course no one mentions the Palestinians and their legitimate claim to the gas fields. Palestine, Israel, Lebanon, Cyprus, and Turkey would have to sit down among themselves within the framework of the Law of the Sea Treaty and negotiate some type of equitable sharing of these gas supply fields which in turn would be based upon the delimitation of their continental shelves.

That is where it stands. If this could not be resolved by negotiations, Palestine would have access to the UN's Law of the Sea Tribunal in Jamaica. There are hundreds of billions of dollars' worth of gas there. We really don't know precisely how much there is, but it's enormous, and it would help the Israeli people too. Right now, there is some gas being pumped out, but given the disputed status of the title, it's not much. So if there is massive exploitation of this gas, certainly Israel has a very long coastline there on the Mediterranean, but so does Gaza, and the Palestinians are entitled to their cut.

DB: So when the Israelis fire at the Gaza Strip from the water offshore in Gaza, they are firing over these very extensive oil resources? When these Israeli warships intercept boats coming from Turkey and other places trying to break the siege on Gaza, they attack the boats. The Israelis are killing international activists over the waters where these resources exist, which is a rather obvious attempt to defend the resources they want to steal.

FB: That's correct. In theory it could be possible for the stakeholders, primarily Israel, Palestine, Lebanon, and to a lesser extent Cyprus and Turkey, to sit down and establish an equitable but lawful sharing of these gas supplies. But Israel doesn't want to share it with anyone. Cyprus and Turkey seem to be enforcing what they believe are their claims, and Lebanon is doing the same, which means that all these conflicting claims to these resources make it difficult to agree on a viable exploitation of those resources.

This isn't only going on in Gaza. Israel is staking a *de facto* claim to these tremendous gas resources, which would probably make Israel energy interdependent as well. Israel currently has no domestic sources of energy supplies there at all. I've read estimates that there may be resources for the next hundred years, but that's cutting the Palestinians out of the picture. Now they get their oil and gas from Egypt but that's been disrupted—they have to scramble to get it somewhere else.

This is a very important factor in the equation, together with the water. Most of the water—the aquifers—is on the West Bank. This is Palestinian water and the settlers are stealing it. I once saw a Palestinian village literally thirsting to death because it had no water. I followed the pipeline upstream to Ariel, a settlement on the West Bank, where I could see the water being diverted from the village so the settlers could have an Olympic-sized swimming pool. Since then, I've read that they have two Olympic-sized swimming pools in Ariel. This is outrageous—unacceptable. It's clearly plunder of Palestinian water resources.

In today's resolution submitted by the Palestinians at the UN they made it quite clear that any final settlement is going to have to involve water because it is their water that is being stolen by Israel. We see Israel stealing and plundering natural resources, certainly water on the West Bank, and now they're going after the gas fields in the Mediterranean. The Israelis have a valid claim, but it's not all theirs. They are going to have to sit down with Lebanon and Palestine and, to a lesser extent, Cyprus and Turkey, which have laid claims to some of these gas fields.

NOTES

1. The Palestinians have now done these things.
2. Today Palestine is recognized as a High Contracting Party to the Geneva Conventions and Protocols.

Chapter 11

Stopping Zionist Genocide against the Palestinians

The Boycott, Divestment, and Sanctions (BDS) Campaign

This is a public lecture I gave at the request of the Campus Chapter of the Students for Justice in Palestine at the University of Illinois at Urbana-Champaign on March 1, 2018, as part of their Israeli Apartheid Week:

> Palestinians have been victims of genocide as defined by the 1948 Genocide Convention since the founding of the State of Israel. I say that because of my practical experience. I single-handedly won two World Court Orders for the Republic of Bosnia and Herzegovina against Yugoslavia to cease and desist from committing all acts of genocide against the Republic of Bosnia and Herzegovina in 1993. This was the first time ever that any lawyer, let alone government, had won two such World Court Orders in one case since the World Court was founded in 1921.

If you are interested all of my oral and written submissions to the World Court on genocide for winning those two World Court Orders overwhelmingly in favor of Bosnia can be found in my book *The Bosnian People Charge Genocide!* (1996).

Article II of the Genocide Convention defines the international crime of genocide in relevant part as follows: "In the present Convention, genocide means any of the following acts committed with intent to destroy, in whole or in part, a national, ethnical, racial, or religious group, as such: (a) killing members of the group;(b) causing serious bodily or mental harm to members of the group;(c) deliberately inflicting on the group conditions of life calculated to bring about its destruction its physical destruction in whole or in part."

That is exactly what Israel is doing today to the 1.8 million people of Gaza: deliberately inflicting on the group conditions of life calculated to bring about their physical destruction in whole or in part. The Zionists have been doing this since they imposed their siege on Gaza starting in 2007. I have been all up and down and back and forth over Gaza. Gaza is just like the Dachau concentration camp that I have also visited myself.

As documented by Israeli historian Ilan Pappe in his seminal book *The Ethnic Cleansing of Palestine* (2006), Israel's genocidal policy against the Palestinians has been unremitting, extending from before the foundation of the State of Israel in 1948 and is ongoing even now and especially intensifying against the 1.8 million Palestinians living in Gaza. As Pappe's analysis established, Zionism's final solution to Israel's much-touted and racist and genocidal demographic "threat" allegedly posed by the very existence of the Palestinians has always been genocide, whether slow-motion or in bloodthirsty spurts of violence as we have seen more recently in Operation Cast Lead and Operation Protective Edge—both euphemisms for Zionist genocide against the Palestinians and the people of Gaza.

Indeed, the very essence of Zionism requires ethnic cleansing and acts of genocide against the Palestinians. Concerning Operation Cast Lead in 2008–2009, UN General Assembly president Miguel d'Escoto Brockmann, who had been the foreign minister of Nicaragua during Reagan's contra-terror war against them, condemned it as genocide. At that earlier time, I was down in Nicaragua myself and for many years helped the Nicaraguan people against the Reagan contra-terror war against them that was soundly condemned by the International Court of Justice. You can read about this in my book *Defending Civil Resistance under International Law* (1987).

Israel and its predecessors-in-law the Zionist agencies, forces, and terrorist gangs have committed genocide against the Palestinian people that started on or about May 15, 1948—Nakba Day. You will note that President Trump has decided to stick it to the Palestinian people by illegally moving the U.S. Embassy from Tel Aviv to Jerusalem on Nakba Day 2018 and has already illegally recognized Jerusalem as the capital of Israel for the first time ever. In my book *Palestine, Palestinians, and International Law* (2003), I have an entire chapter on the legal status of Jerusalem under international law. It is quite interesting that the last time we had an official statement on Jerusalem by the United States government was by George Bush Senior when he was the United Nations Ambassador. He correctly pointed out the reasons why the United States government had not previously recognized Jerusalem as the capital of Israel and kept the U.S. Embassy in Tel Aviv. Prior to President Trump!

I have been to that U.S. Embassy in Tel Aviv in order to complain vigorously about the war crimes that Israel has inflicted against the Palestinians.

You know what they told me? That this was an "internal affair" of Israel! In other words, the United States government was not going to get involved, was not going to do anything at all about it, and if I didn't agree with that decision I could take it up with the State Department in Washington DC. Well, of course, I knew that would be a waste of time and so I did not.

Israel and its predecessors-in-law the Zionist agencies, forces, and terrorist gangs certainly committed genocide against the Palestinians that started on Nakba Day 1948 and continues apace until today in violation of Genocide Convention Articles II(a) and (b) and (c) that I quoted to you already. For over the past seven decades the Israeli government and its predecessors-in-law the Zionist agencies, forces, and terrorist gangs have ruthlessly implemented a systematic and comprehensive military, political, religious, economic, and cultural campaign with intent to destroy in substantial part the national, ethnical, racial, and different religious group (Jews versus Muslims and Christians) constituting the Palestinian people. Just last week we saw that the Christian denominations in charge of the Church of the Holy Sepulcher had to shut it down because the Zionists are trying to tax it out of existence in violation of the Hague Convention of 1907, the Fourth Geneva Convention of 1949, and other rules of customary international law binding upon Israel.

The Zionists could not give diddly-squat about international law! I have been up against them for decades, both in Israel and here and all over the world. I've debated them, I've argued with them, I've opposed them. They all lie! Every one of them that I have ever dealt with personally lies and that includes the American Zionists at the U.S. State Department.

It was so bad that when I was the Lawyer for the Palestinians at the Middle East Peace Negotiations, the State Department would lie to them, literally lie to them, about documents that they had drawn up for the Palestinians to sign in English. The Palestinians would bring them back to me with the notes as to what the State Department said these documents meant. I said, well, that's a lie, this is a lie, the other thing is a lie, etc. Just bald-faced lies by the U.S. State Department to the Palestinians.

The United States has never been an "honest broker" when it comes to the Palestinians. I have been there from the outset of the Middle East Peace Negotiations in 1991 with my client and friend the late great Dr. Haider Abdul Shaffi from Gaza itself, Head of the Palestinian Delegation and of the Palestinian Red Crescent Society there. It's a shocking disgrace what the U.S. government has done to the Palestinians from the very outset of these negotiations in 1991 and still continuing today under Kushner, Greenblatt, and Friedman. Do you really think we are going to get peace between Israel and the Palestinians from three Orthodox Jews? Of course not!

And to show you how bad it was back in 1991 at the beginning of these peace negotiations, Bush Senior put three American Jews in charge of the process: Ross, Miller, and Kurzer. They even later admitted they served as Israel's lawyer. That is true, I was there up against them. Notice nothing has changed from 1991 until today. It's still three American Jews in charge of these so-called peace negotiations serving as lawyers for Israel. I remember telling my client and friend at these peace negotiations Hanan Ashrawi that this was un-American. She smiled very politely looking at me and I could tell what was on her mind: No, this is typically American! Typically American when it comes to the Palestinians. I can tell you that because I've been there for a long time dealing with these American Zionists and opposing them for the Palestinians ever since I entered Harvard in 1971.

This Zionist-Israeli campaign has consisted of killing members of the Palestinian people in violation of Genocide Convention Article II(a). This Zionist-Israeli campaign has caused serious bodily and mental harm to the Palestinian people in violation of Genocide Convention Article II(b). This Zionist-Israeli campaign has deliberately inflicted on the Palestinian people conditions of life calculated to bring about their physical destruction in substantial part in violation of Article II(c) of the Genocide Convention. Particularly in Gaza today as we speak, 1.8 million Palestinians are being treated almost as if they were Jews at Dachau.

Apologists for Israel have argued that since these mass atrocities are not tantamount to the Nazi Holocaust against the Jews, therefore they do not qualify as genocide. Previously I had encountered and refuted this completely disingenuous, deceptive, and bogus argument against labeling genocide for what it really is when I was the Lawyer for the Republic of Bosnia and Herzegovina arguing their genocide case against Yugoslavia before the International Court of Justice. There the genocidal Yugoslavia was represented by Shabtai Rosenne from Israel. Think about that! Israel's top international lawyer was representing the Yugoslav genociders against the Bosnians. Indeed in these proceedings Rosenne listed himself as Ambassador-at-Large from Israel. Why? Israel was supporting the Yugoslav war of extermination against the Bosnians, including against the Bosnian Jews who were my clients as well. I acted to protect them all at the World Court: the Bosnian Jews, Bosnian Muslims, Bosnian Croats, and others.

Rosenne from Israel proceeded to argue to the World Court that since he was an Israeli Jew, what Yugoslavia had done to the Bosnians was not the equivalent of the Nazi Holocaust against the Jews and therefore did not qualify as genocide within the meaning of the 1948 Genocide Convention. You can see the live transcript of the oral arguments and debates between Rosenne and me in my book *The Bosnian People Charge Genocide!* (1996). I rebutted Rosenne by arguing to the World Court that you do not need the equivalent to the Nazi Holocaust against the Jews in order to find that wholesale atrocities against a civilian population constitute genocide in violation of the 1948

Convention. Indeed the entire purpose of the Genocide Convention was "to prevent" another Nazi Holocaust against the Jews. That is why Article I of the Genocide Convention clearly provided: "The Contracting Parties confirm that genocide, whether committed in time of peace or in time of war, is a crime under international law which they undertake to prevent and to punish." Let me repeat that: "to prevent." That's what the Palestinian BDS Campaign is all about. That is why we are here tonight: "to prevent" the Zionist genocide against the Palestinians that is still going on today, including and especially in Gaza.

In support of my successful 1993 genocide arguments to the International Court of Justice for Bosnia, I submitted to the World Court that Article II of the Genocide Convention expressly provided: "In the present Convention, genocide means any of the following acts committed with the intent to destroy, in whole or in part, a national, ethnical, racial, or religious group, as such." Let me repeat: "or in part." In other words that to be guilty of genocide a state did not have to intend to destroy the whole group as the Nazis intended to do with the Jews. Rather a state can be guilty of genocide even if it intends to destroy a mere part of the group: "in whole or in part."

Yugoslavia certainly intended to exterminate all the Bosnian Muslims if they could have gotten away with it as proven by their subsequent mass extermination of 7,000+ Bosnian Muslim men and boys at Srebrenica in July of 1995. I would later become the Attorney of Record for the Mothers of Srebrenica and Podrinja as well as for the Women of Srebrenica at the International Criminal Tribunal for the Former Yugoslavia (ICTY). In that capacity I convinced the ICTY Prosecutor Carla del Ponte to indict Yugoslav president Slobodan Milošević for almost every crime in the ICTY Statute for atrocities he inflicted upon the Bosnians, including two counts of genocide: one count of genocide for Bosnia in general and the second count of genocide for Srebrenica in particular. Notice 7,000+ was enough to constitute genocide as far as the ICTY Prosecutor was concerned. Milošević died while on trial in The Hague after the ICTY itself denied his Motion to Dismiss these charges after the close of the Prosecution's case and sustained all of the charges against him, including and especially the two counts of genocide: genocide in general in Bosnia, and genocide in particular against the 7,000+ Bosnian Muslim men and boys at Srebrenica.[1]

I argued to the World Court that at that point in time the best estimate we had was that Yugoslavia had exterminated about 250,000 Bosnians out of a population of about 4 million Bosnians, including therein about 2.5 million Bosnian Muslims. Therefore, I argued to the World Court that these dead victims constituted a "substantial part of the group" and the appropriate interpretation of the words "in part" set forth in Article II of the Genocide Convention should be interpreted to mean a "substantial part."

The World Court agreed with me overwhelmingly and emphatically rejected Rosenne's specious, reprehensible, and deplorable arguments. So they issued their first Order to me on April 8, 1993, that Yugoslavia must cease and desist from committing all acts of genocide against the Bosnians, both directly and indirectly by means of their Serb surrogates. This was the international equivalent of the U.S. domestic temporary restraining order and injunction combined. The same was true for the second World Court Order with three additional measures of protection that I won for Bosnia and Herzegovina against Yugoslavia on September 13, 1993. The same was true for an Article 74, paragraph 4 Order I won for Bosnia against Yugoslavia from the World Court on August 5, 1993.

In its final *Judgment* on the merits in the Bosnia case issued in 2007, the World Court definitively agreed with me once and for all time that in order to constitute genocide a state must only intend to destroy a "substantial part" of the group as such. The state did not have to intend to destroy the entire group as Rosenne had argued, but only a "substantial part" as I had argued in 1993. So in other words based on these World Court rulings and also rulings by the International Criminal Tribunal for the Former Yugoslavia, to find Israel guilty of genocide against the Palestinians it is not required to prove that Israel has the intention to exterminate all Palestinians. Rather all that is necessary is to establish that Israel intends to destroy a substantial part of the Palestinians. The Zionists have certainly done that: more recently, the first Intifada, the Al-Aqsa Intifada, Operation Cast Lead, Operation Protective Edge, etc. Furthermore, in paragraphs 293 and 294 of its 2007 *Bosnian Judgment* the World Court found that you did not even need 250,000 exterminated Bosnians to constitute genocide, let alone six million dead Jews. Rather even the 7,000+ exterminated Bosnian Muslim men and boys at Srebrenica were enough to constitute genocide.

Starting in 1948 Israel obliterated 500 Palestinian villages from off the face of the earth, literally reducing them to rubble now scattered across the Palestinian countryside in order to prevent their ethnically cleansed inhabitants from ever again returning to their homes because their homes no longer exist. I have been all up and down Palestine and Israel myself. I have seen the ruins of these villages with my own eyes.

I protested such atrocities to the highest-ranking legal officer in charge of the military occupation of Palestine on the West Bank in his own office. When I said these are Nuremberg crimes that you are inflicting on the Palestinians, he pleaded the so-called defense of "necessity." I responded that the "necessity" defense was rejected at the Nuremberg Tribunal in 1946 when the lawyers for the Nazis made those arguments at that time. Do you know what he told me? His words were: "We have public relations people in the United States and they take care of these matters for us"! So in other words he didn't disagree with anything I was saying. He basically conceded it, but that it was all a matter of public relations here in the United States. Then I met with the Legal Adviser to the Foreign Ministry of Israel in his office. He gave me the exact same answer! Finally, I met with the relevant lawyer for the Ministry of Injustice in Israel in his office and he gave me this exact same answer too. They didn't refute my arguments. Basically, they conceded them: What Israel is doing to the Palestinians are Nazi crimes! But all the Zionists care about is public opinion here in the United States. That is where you people come in. You must change public opinion here in the United States and BDS is the most effective way to do this!

The list of Zionist genocidal massacres of Palestinians is quite extensive. I won't go through them all here today. To just name a few of Israel's most notorious acts of genocide against the Palestinians: Deir Yassin, Tantura, Sabra and Shatila. I was the attorney for several women who were next-of-kin of the 3,500 Palestinian old men, women, and children who were exterminated at Sabra and Shatila surrounded by the Israeli army and acting under the command of Israeli General Yaron whom I later sued for them.[2] Even the UN General Assembly determined that the massacre at Sabra and Shatila was genocide.

To continue this Zionist list of genocide: Jenin, Nablus, and again repeatedly and continuously in Gaza. The Zionists are now threatening another series of acts of genocide against the people of Gaza as we speak today. To repeat: Israel is now deliberately inflicting on the 1.8 million Palestinians in Gaza conditions of life calculated to bring about their physical destruction in whole or in part in gross and flagrant violation of Genocide Convention Article II(c) and the United States government supports this. Even the great Obama who was behind me at Harvard Law School supported it and did nothing to stop it. Of course, the word Trump speaks for itself!

Article I of the Genocide Convention requires: "The contracting parties confirm that genocide, whether committed in time of peace or in time of war, is a crime under international law which they undertake to prevent and to punish." And that is why we are here tonight: "to prevent" Zionist genocide against the Palestinians. It is clear that Netanyahu and his gang of criminals are trying to provoke yet another Intifada by the Palestinians so that they can slaughter them again just like the Zionists did in the Al-Aqsa Intifada.

Now that being said let me briefly review the history of the BDS Campaign. The Al-Aqsa Intifada was deliberately provoked by that war criminal and genocider Ariel Sharon at the Al-Aqsa Mosque. I have been on the Haram al-Sharif with Holy Al-Aqsa and the Dome of the Rock where Mohammed ascended to heaven. Sharon went up there with the approval of Prime Minister Barak and provoked the Palestinians and deliberately shot dead many of them trying to save and rescue Al-Aqsa.

As we speak here today the Palestinians at the Haram are trying to defend Al-Aqsa day in and day out from these fanatical Zionist Jewish settlers and religious fanatics who want to go in there and destroy Al-Aqsa and build their so-called Third Temple. This is a very dangerous situation. I kid you not! Now that Trump is president anything could happen. We could lose Al-Aqsa and the Dome of the Rock and the Haram to these fanatical religious Zionist Jews. That would have the full support of President Trump. I know of no restraint on this administration when it comes to the Palestinians!

So it seemed to me that with the provocation of the Al-Aqsa Intifada, even as determined and condemned by a UN Security Council Resolution, that the so-called peace process was over that I had started out with in 1991 with Dr. Haidar Abdul Shaffi. I can assure all of you that Dr. Abdul Shaffi was tough as nails at these peace negotiations. He would not compromise with the Zionists in terms of selling out the basic rights of the Palestinians under international law. Yes, we were prepared to make compromises but not at the expense of the basic rights of the Palestinians under international law. That story is told in my book *Palestine, Palestinians, and International Law* (2003). Dr. Abdul Shaffi kindly gave me permission to write about it. That analysis has been updated in my book *Breaking All the Rules* (2008). In addition, in my book *The Palestinian Right of Return under International Law* (2011) you will see press conferences by both Dr. Abdul Shaffi and Hanan Ashrawi that I moderated in Washington DC on the Palestinian Right of Return under Resolution 194, which Trump has said, "We're going to take that off the table just as we've now taken Jerusalem off the table." Well, if you read the Oslo Accords you will see that they state quite clearly that all "final status" issues remain open for negotiation, including the Right of Return and Jerusalem. It is not for Trump to take any of these issues off the table. Even Israel signed the Oslo Accords under Rabin.

So it was clear to me that for both Labor and Likud—Tweedledum versus Tweedledee, I've dealt with lawyers and officials on both sides, and there's no difference between the two—the peace negotiations were dead as a doornail. The second Al-Aqsa Intifada was on. My friend Professor Jamal Nassar, who at that time was Chair of the Political Science Department at Illinois State University, asked me to give a public lecture on this whole series of events, which I did do. In that lecture on November 30, 2000, I publicly issued an appeal for the establishment of an international campaign of divestment and disinvestment against Israel on the grounds and for the same reasons that we had a campaign of divestment and disinvestment against the criminal apartheid regime in South Africa. I was involved in large numbers of cases in this Campaign against South Africa defending anti-apartheid resisters. You can read about it in my book *Defending Civil Resistance under International Law* (1987), including obtaining the first acquittal ever of anti-apartheid protesters up in Chicago at the South African Consulate, *Chicago v. Streeter* (1985). We even made the *New York Times* on that one. I know apartheid when I see it. I've litigated it all over this country!

I issued this appeal for divestment and disinvestment against Israel for the same reasons we had against the criminal apartheid regime in South Africa, and what was going on by Israel was far worse than that. Now I won't go through all the history here except to say the next major development was that the President of Harvard University—where I have three degrees—the die-hard Zionist Larry Summers publicly condemned those of us involved in the Harvard divestment/disinvestment campaign as anti-Semitic. What a coward and hypocrite!

Of course Summers is a die-hard Neo-Con Zionist and tried to impose his Neo-Con Zionist agenda on Harvard. Indeed, Harvard is so bad that my friend Edward Said was offered Harvard's top honcho Chair in Comparative Literature and was not going to take it. So the Palestinians asked me to meet with Edward and convince him to take Harvard's top honcho Chair in Comparative Literature. Edward had gotten his PhD in Comparative Literature from Harvard. I spent an entire evening at a Chinese restaurant on the campus of Columbia University trying to convince Edward to take Harvard's top honcho Chair in Comparative Literature. Most professors would give their right arm for any Chair at Harvard. I spent a whole evening arguing with Edward. I can be quite persuasive. I got nowhere. Finally, Edward said to me that based on his personal experience at Harvard, that Harvard is so anti-Palestinian that it would thwart his intellectual creativity to go to Harvard! Now think about that! Edward Said, one of the great intellectuals in the world, saying Harvard was so anti-Palestinian that it would thwart his intellectual creativity to go there. Of course Edward was right! And Harvard has become even more anti-Palestinian since Edward and I were students there decades ago.

So after Summers condemned me and the rest of us as anti-Semitic, WBUR Radio station in Boston, which is the NPR affiliate in Boston, called me up and asked me, "Would you be willing to debate Summers for one hour live on the radio with call-ins?" I said, "Sure, I'd be happy to." They then called up Summers. He refused to debate me! He did not have the courage and the integrity and the principles to debate me. Well, later Harvard fired Larry Summers for imposing his Zionist Neo-Con agenda even further on Harvard and his other scurrilous charge that women are dumber than men when it comes to math and science. Well, as a triple Harvard alumnus I say good riddance to Larry Summers!

Then WBUR asked me, "Would you debate Dershowitz?" I said, "Sure, I'm happy to debate Dershowitz." So Dershowitz and I had this debate. It was September 25, 2002. There is still a link on there on WBUR dealing with this scurrilous charge that those of us involved in the Harvard divestment/

disinvestment campaign were anti-Semitic. Dershowitz is supposed to be the best lawyer the Zionists have to offer. I clobbered him. It was so bad that during the debate Dershowitz admitted that I was the expert on international law and human rights. Well, at least Summers was smart enough not to debate me—unlike Dershowitz! By the way, Dershowitz is a war criminal. Yes, he admitted in an interview he gave to Law Professor Ali Khan that he was a member of an Israeli Committee that approves the murder and assassination of Palestinians. The murder and assassination of Palestinians violates the Geneva Conventions. It is a war crime. So the next time you see Dershowitz up there on TV just remember: one, I clobbered him; and two, he is a war criminal. Our WBUR debate on September 25, 2002, is the best debate out there refuting scurrilous charges that people involved in the BDS Campaign are anti-Semitic.

Now I won't go through the rest of this history here except to say that in 2005 Palestinian Civil Society leaders contacted me and said they wanted to set up a Boycott, Divestment, and Sanctions (BDS) Campaign along the lines of the successful Campaign against apartheid South Africa. Would I go in with them? I said I would. So today we have the BDS Campaign: Boycott, Divestment, and Sanctions. I am *D* in BDS and I'm happy to be here speaking with you this evening. As you know two weeks ago the BDS Campaign was nominated for the Nobel Peace Prize by a Norwegian Parliamentarian and the Nobel Peace Prize is given out in Norway. I think the BDS Campaign has at least an inside track perhaps on winning that Nobel Peace Prize. It's always a crap shoot who wins those things. Maybe they will come through for the BDS Campaign. I don't know.

But that brings us here today and tonight. What can you do here on the BDS Campaign for the University of Illinois and this surrounding community? We had a very active Campaign against the criminal apartheid regime in South Africa when I arrived here in 1978 and I immediately joined it. Again, I won't go through the whole history of that here, including three of our students who were maliciously prosecuted by the University of Illinois simply for holding up signs in the Illini Union saying: "Divest Now!" Then they were subjected to a kangaroo court criminal prosecution over here in Champaign County by Judge Townshend. But that was it. Only three of them. They declined our offer to appeal. I thought we had a good chance to win on appeal. Instead they did some community service, were graduating seniors, and moved on with their lives. Indeed there was a law student also involved in the protests and the fascist dean of our law school instituted disciplinary proceedings against him. I had to go in there and help defend him so that he could continue on with his legal career.

But in 1987 the University of Illinois Board of Trustees divested from the criminal apartheid regime in South Africa. Now think about that: 1987!

There was a campaign. There was a struggle. But eventually we got the University of Illinois Board of Trustees to divest from the criminal apartheid regime in South Africa. And divestment took place all over the country. Northwestern University—I was involved in helping defend those students up there. Harvard partially, selectively divested. I was involved in helping defend the Harvard alumni there. The University of Chicago—my Disalma Mater where I got my undergraduate degree—a gang of die-hard racist bigoted Zionists for sure: they refused to divest and were proud of it. Certainly don't go to the University of Chicago for any reason. Believe me!

But we divested here because of the student struggle. Well, we did it before, we can do it again! My advice to you all then: set up a Committee. Go out! Read the back pages of the *Daily Illini* that covered our struggle against the criminal apartheid regime in South Africa here at the University of Illinois starting at least when I showed up in 1978 until 1987. Study the strategy and tactics that were used by the students for that struggle. It's all there in the *Daily Illini*. And then come up with your own strategy and tactics to apply here, and those of you who graduate from here who go elsewhere use it there.

This is not a case of anyone reinventing the wheel here. We already have the wheel. Indeed, the legal arguments against the criminal apartheid regime in South Africa are all here in my book *Defending Civil Resistance under International Law* (1987), including the brief we filed in *Chicago* v. *Streeter*. And all the arguments against the genocidal apartheid regime in Israel are in my three books here: *Palestine, Palestinians, and International Law* (2003); *Breaking All the Rules* (2008); *The Palestinian Right of Return under International Law* (2011). So the legal arguments are all there. But we need you. We need organization. We need a strategy. We need action. Remember the 1.8 million Palestinians living in Gaza today are at risk. They are counting on us to come through for them! Thank you.

ANSWERS TO QUESTIONS

Refuting Charges of Anti-Semitism

During my career, Zionists have accused me of being everything but a child molester. It just comes with the territory. My response is that Zionists are more loyal to Israel than they are to the United States. That has been my experience since I entered the die-hard Neo-Con Zionist University of Chicago in 1968. So that is my usual response. Except if you wish you can hear this debate between Dershowitz and me. You know Dershowitz is Israel's go-to-guy here in the United States. Whenever they want dirty work done they ask Dershowitz to do it. So you can hear that debate if you want. You're going to have to develop the hide of the rhinoceros. Don't let anyone intimidate you because of what's at stake. If Zionists attack you, you say: You people are more loyal to Israel than you are to the United States! I'm a loyal American citizen. I'm exercising my First Amendment Rights. If you don't like it, you can stuff it! Go to Israel!

Zionist Opposition to BDS

It's too little and too late. I let this genie out of the bottle in 2000. I knew at that time it was going to spread like wildfire all over the United States and the world. So after many years of just ignoring the BDS Campaign, finally they've decided to set up a Ministry over there in Israel and launch this lawfare campaign. But they're not winning. They're losing across the board. So I think that you just need to keep soldiering on. Yes, you will be threatened. Indeed a group of Zionist members of the U.S. Congress filed a formal complaint with the Department of Commerce demanding that I be investigated and prosecuted just for exercising my First Amendment rights here as a U.S. citizen to set up that divestment/disinvestment Campaign. Nothing came of it.

You just have to be comfortable with who you are and move forward. Because right now I'm afraid that BDS is all the Palestinians have with Trump weighing in against them. It does not look good at all. The reports I have read of whatever his so-called Peace Plan is, it's basically going to be a Surrender Plan. It's sort of like the Godfather making an offer you can't refuse with Luca Brasi pointing a gun at your head and saying either your name will be on that paper or your brains will be on the table. I'm afraid that's what they're going to do to President Abbas. As we all know, that's not going to work. I don't think it's going to work.

End of the Middle East Peace Process

I do want to say that based on my work at the Middle East Peace Negotiations from 1991 to 1993, we could have had peace. I was advising both the Palestinians and the Syrians. The Jordanians—everyone knew they wanted peace with Israel but they couldn't go first and eventually there was a peace treaty with Jordan. Fine. At that time regretfully Lebanon was occupied by Syria courtesy of President Bush Senior, so the Lebanese did what the Syrians told them to do. But I knew both the Palestinian and the Syrian positions. Indeed I was drafting their papers. We could have had peace!

When Prime Minister Rabin came in, he signed the Oslo Accords and then he moved to negotiating a comprehensive peace treaty with Syria. That peace treaty was modeled on the peace treaty with Egypt: that is, full peace for full withdrawal from the territories Israel stole in 1967. That peace treaty was ready to go at the end of 1995, but Rabin held it back from the Knesset because an election was coming up. He did not want to make it part of an election issue. As you know he was murdered and assassinated by a religious fanatic with the support of Netanyahu and others of his ilk at that time. That was the end of the peace process. There has been no further development to speak of since Rabin's murder and assassination. President Arafat said he lost his partner for peace when Rabin was murdered.

We Have Truth and Justice on Our Side!

As I see the BDS Campaign, we have Truth and Justice on our side! We just need to keep arguing Truth and Justice and bring it out to the American People. That's what we did in the Campaign against the criminal apartheid regime in South Africa. We brought our arguments and our activities out to the American People.

As we all know Congress has been completely bought off by the Zionist Lobby, and the White House too these days as we now see it. So there's no hope there either. We have to take our Campaign out to the American People and educate them. It's hard work. That's true. And not just education but also organization, action, protest, demonstrations.

Just look at how the students here at the University of Illinois accomplished this to get the University of Illinois Board of Trustees to divest. I can assure you that that criminal apartheid regime in South Africa that I was up against for all those years, they hired some of the top law firms and lobbying firms in this country to oppose what we were doing. But eventually they lost because we had Truth and Justice on our side. Today there is no apartheid regime in South Africa. Sure, they have their problems—we have a lot of problems here—but apartheid isn't one of them. But it still is going to take a lot of hard work for us to get to that point for Israelis and Palestinians.

NOTES

1. See my forthcoming book *Stopping Serb Genocide Against the Bosnians!* (Sarajevo: Bosnia-Herzegovina, 2020).
2. *Memorandum on the Yaron Case*, 5 Palestine Y. B. Int'l L. 254, 257 (1989).

Chapter 12

The Criminality of Nuclear Deterrence Today

This is a keynote address I gave before the XVIIIth Conference *Mut Zur Ethik: Direkte Demokratie* in Feldkirch, Austria, on September 5, 2010, on the occasion of Verlag Zeit-Fragen publishing the German-language translation of my book *The Criminality of Nuclear Deterrence* (Clarity Press: 2002) under the title *Das Verbrechen der atomaren Abschreckung*:

> I am very happy to be speaking with you this evening. I want to express my gratitude to Zeit-Fragen for publishing the German-language edition of my book *The Criminality of Nuclear Deterrence* (Clarity Press, 2002), which comes out now on the anniversary of the end of the Second World War. At this time sixty-five years ago, Japan surrendered to the United States after the atomic bombings of Hiroshima and Nagasaki and the incineration of 250,000 completely innocent human beings.

My father was a Marine who invaded Saipan, Tinian, and Okinawa, and was preparing to invade Mainland Japan. I was brought up to believe that the bombings of Hiroshima and Nagasaki had saved my father's life and thus made mine possible, although my father never raised me to be anti-Japanese or anti-German. But when I came to study international relations, I realized: this simply was not true. Indeed it was total propaganda by the United States government to justify nuclear terrorism and the mass-extermination of a quarter of a million human beings. Even Justice Pal in his dissent to the *Tokyo Judgment* said that the Japanese war criminals had done nothing to their discredit as the bombings of Hiroshima and Nagasaki, which you can only compare to Nazi acts.

Today the world is at a precipice of another world war. The United States government has committed acts of aggression against Afghanistan, Iraq,

Pakistan, Somalia, Yemen, and has authorized, armed, equipped, and supplied Israel to commit acts of aggression, crimes against humanity, and outright genocide against Lebanon and Palestine. Today the United States government is threatening to attack Iran under the completely bogus pretext that they might have a nuclear weapon, which the International Atomic Energy has said is simply not true. If they attack Iran with the Israelis, a British think tank has predicted they could exterminate 2.8 million Iranians! They are fully prepared—the Americans and the Israelis—to use tactical nuclear weapons.

Indeed today tactical nuclear weapons have been fully integrated into U.S. armed forces and tactical training and programs. I have read the Manual myself. Nukes are now treated—starting with the Bush Junior administration—as if they were just another weapon.

We must remember when President Putin was in Iran and he said he did not believe the Iranians had a nuclear weapon, President Bush Junior publicly got up and threatened World War III. Remember that threat! He threatened World War III! I cannot recall in my lifetime a threat of this nature. You would have to go back to Hitler and Mussolini and Tojo to find high-level government officials threatening a world war.

What did this threat mean? It was saying to Russia, "You had better stand back if we attack Iran." It wasn't a threat to Iran; that would not produce a world war attacking Iran, but just a slaughter. But saying to Russia, "You had better stand back, we are prepared to risk World War III if you don't let us get our way with Iran." An attack on Iran would set this entire region of the world on fire, from Egypt over to India, from Uzbekistan down to Diego Garcia. And as my friend and my colleague, Hans von Sponeck, pointed out yesterday with his map: We see the counter-alliance to NATO—Russia, China and the so-called Central Asia Collective Security Organization. If you read about the origins World War I or World War II an attack on Iran could clearly set off World War III—remember Bush threatened it. And it could easily become nuclear. I kid you not on the dangers we are facing us all as human beings today!

We stand on a nuclear precipice, and any attempt to dispel this ideology of nuclearism and its myth propounding the legality and morality of nuclear weapons and nuclear deterrence must come to grips with the fact that the nuclear age was conceived in the original sins of Hiroshima and Nagasaki. These weapons have always been criminal! Remember they were developed to deal with the Nazis, out of fear that the Nazis would get them first. And yet for some reason they used them on the Japanese to make a point, to terrorize the rest of the world.

The atomic bombings of Hiroshima and Nagasaki constituted war crimes and crimes against humanity as defined by the Nuremberg Charter of August

8, 1945—right after the United States bombed Hiroshima, and the day before they bombed Nagasaki—that condemned the wanton destruction of cities, towns, and villages; and applied it to the Nazi leaders, but of course never applied it to themselves. In my book *The Criminality of Nuclear Deterrence*, there is an entire chapter on the criminality of the bombings of Hiroshima and Nagasaki and I list all the legal violations there, up to and including the United States Department of War Field Manual 27-10 (1940). So these bombings and also the firebombing of Tokyo, exterminating 100,000 civilians, were war crimes. Even as recognized officially by the United States government itself.

The start of any progress towards resolving our nuclear predicament as human beings must come from the realization that nuclear weapons and nuclear deterrence have never been legitimate instruments of state policy but have always constituted instrumentalities of internationally lawless and criminal behavior. And those states that wield nuclear weapons, their government officials are criminals in accordance with the Nuremberg Charter, Judgment, and Principles, and the Tokyo Charter and Judgment that the Allies applied to the Nazi war criminals and the Japanese war criminals after World War II. So I'm not talking here about applying any principles of law that the United States government and the other victors of World War II applied to their enemies to hold them accountable.

The use of nuclear weapons in combat is contemplated now by the United States and Israel against Iran. How many times have we heard U.S. government officials involved in the Bush Junior administration and now the Obama administration say, "All options are on the table." They mean it: not just the use the force but the use of nuclear weapons as well. These are prohibited by conventional and customary international law, including the Genocide Convention of 1948, designed to prevent a repetition of the Nazi Holocaust against the Jews, the Poles, the Russians, the Ukrainians. The use of nuclear weapons would also violate resolutions of the UN General Assembly that repeatedly condemned their use as an international crime. We must understand that when dealing with nuclear weapons and nuclear deterrence: They are not simply immoral, they are not simply illegal, but they are criminal across the board!

The Swiss Foreign Ministry commissioned a study of nuclear deterrence by three American authors, I read it, and I agree with what they said. They pointed out that the critical factor is the delegitimization of nuclear weapons in the minds of the people. Having litigated nuclear weapons protest cases in the United States, Canada, Britain, and elsewhere since 1982, for me the critical factor in winning these cases is to explain to the common, ordinary people on juries that nuclear weapons and nuclear deterrence are criminal. Not simply illegal, not simply immoral, but criminal!

Yet the government officials in all the nuclear weapon states, not just the United States—they are the worst of them—but also Russia, France, Britain, China, India, Pakistan, Israel, North Korea: They are the criminals! For threatening to exterminate all humanity! For threatening Nuremberg crimes against peace, crimes against humanity, war crimes, and genocide. That's what nuclear deterrence really is: threatening mass extermination. And in the Advisory Opinion by the International Court of Justice on nuclear weapons, the World Court ruled that the threat stands or falls on the same legal grounds as the actual use. If mass extermination of human beings is a crime, then the threat to commit mass extermination is also a crime.

It is as if the leaders of the nuclear weapon states have all taken out a gun, cocked the trigger, and held it at the heads of all humanity! In any system of criminal justice today that activity is criminal! In the United States it would be attempted murder, and you would be prosecuted for it. Yet today U.S. government officials threaten murder to millions of people around the world. And now especially in Iran.

According to the Nuremberg Judgment soldiers would be obliged to disobey criminal orders to launch and wage a nuclear war. And yet, how many soldiers have been educated to understand these principles? A few have educated themselves, acted on it, and have been prosecuted by the United States government. I have helped to defend them, with a good deal of success, but not complete success. You can read about this in my latest book, *Protesting Power: War Resistance and Law* (Rowman & Littlefield, 2008). How we defended military resisters in our all-volunteer armed forces who refused to fight in illegal, criminal wars waged by the United States government, going back to Gulf War I by Bush Senior, Haiti by Clinton, Gulf War II by Bush Junior, etc.

All government officials and military officers who might launch or wage a nuclear war would be personally responsible for the commission of crimes against peace, crimes against humanity, war crimes and genocide. And such individuals—whether statesmen or high-level military personnel—would not be entitled to any defenses of superior orders, act of state, *tu quoque*, self-defense, presidential authority, etc. All those defenses were made by lawyers for the Nazi defendants at Nuremberg and they were rejected. And yet today in the United States of America starting with the Bush Junior administration and now continuing with Obama you will hear international lawyers working for the government, and many in the private sector, making Nazi arguments to justify what the United States government is doing around the world. That's how desperate the situation is!

The whole Bush Doctrine of preventive warfare, which is yet to be officially repealed by Obama now after eighteen months, was made by the Nazi lawyers for the Nazi defendants at Nuremberg, and it was rejected.

And the argument by Nuremberg was: There is no such thing as preventive self-defense or things of this nature. What is self-defense can only be determined by reference to international law. And the test is clearly: the necessity of self-defense must be instant, overwhelming, leaving no choice of means, no moment for deliberation. Certainly not Afghanistan or Iraq or Lebanon or Palestine or Iran or Somalia or Yemen or Pakistan. And yet all victims of this Nazi doctrine of preventive self-defense that is now justified by all these prostituted international lawyers on the payroll of the United States government, leaving government service, now they infiltrate into American academia where they likewise try to justify and teach these doctrines and policies that were condemned as criminal at Nuremberg.

Article 2, paragraph 4 of the United Nations Charter prohibits both the threat and the use of force except in cases of legitimate self-defense. And there is a standard for self-defense: Article 51 of the UN Charter, and as supplemented by Nuremberg, that clearly rejects the wars against Afghanistan as aggression—explained in my book in greater detail—against Iraq, against Pakistan, which by the way has nuclear arms. The Obama administration has now escalated to a war against Pakistan, trying to set off civil war and destabilize Pakistan, just as they did in Yugoslavia, just as they did in Iraq, just as they did in Afghanistan. As we lawyers say, "The modus operandi is the same."

The Empire does not change from one administration to the next! In America the government is run by elites who are either liberal imperialists, conservative imperialists, or reactionary imperialists, like the Neo-Cons. But they are all imperialists! And they believe in the God-given right to the American Empire. That's the way America started. Remember, how did the United States of America start? White European settlers coming over to North America, exterminating millions of indigenous people, and robbing their land, and building an Empire. The process just continues today as we speak.

The threat to use nuclear weapons, what we call "nuclear deterrence"—I would call instead "nuclear terrorism"—constitutes ongoing international criminal activity: planning, preparation, solicitation, and conspiracy to commit Nuremberg crimes against peace, crimes against humanity, war crimes, and genocide. These are what we lawyers call inchoate crimes, not the substantive offences themselves, but crimes leading up to the commission of the substantive offences. They were made criminal at Nuremberg in order to establish a bright line and that we would punish even walking up to that bright line as criminal.

In the case of nuclear weapons, once a nuclear war starts I doubt very seriously we are going to be having another war crimes tribunal for anyone. So what that means then is that it is up to us citizens of the world to stop and prevent a nuclear war, and to stop and prevent the threat, conspiracy, solicitation of the use of nuclear weapons. "Everything is on the table"—clearly a threat to use nuclear weapons, clearly a criminal threat under the World Court Advisory Opinion, against Iran.

As I explain in more detail in my book, the design, research, testing, production, manufacture, fabrication, transportation, deployment, installation, storing, stockpile, sale, and purchase and the threat to use nuclear weapons are criminal under well-recognized principles of international law. And I know the German government has finally asked the United States, NATO, to take its nukes out of Germany. And Mrs. Clinton has said, "We don't support it." Well, is the German government going to cave in? Or will it use law and international law and the Nuremberg Charter, Judgment and Principles to get American criminal nukes out of Germany? I guess we will find out this fall.[1]

Those government decision-makers in all nuclear weapon states with command responsibility for nuclear weapons are responsible today for personal criminal activity under the Nuremberg Principles for this practice of nuclear deterrence/nuclear terrorism, that they inflict on all states and peoples in the world today. And in particular counter-ethnic targeting for the United States, destroying Russians just because they are Russian.

Also counter city-targeting! When I worked on the case of the U.K. nuclear weapons in Scotland we established that the entire purpose of the U.K. nuclear weapons force, under the control and allocated to NATO, was to destroy the city of Moscow, seven million human beings! It had no other purpose. Needless to say, once we did that we got all of our defendants off for four counts each of malicious destruction of property when they destroyed a tender servicing the U.K. Trident II nuclear weapons submarines with these weapons of mass extermination. They might have destroyed the tender, but they did not act maliciously. They acted for the perfectly lawful reason to stop the nuclear extermination of seven million human beings![2]

So I argue in my book, the simple idea of the criminality of nuclear weapons and deterrence can be used to pierce through the ideology of nuclearism, to which so many citizens in the nuclear weapon states and around the world have succumbed—by means of propaganda techniques, propagated by the governments, going back to the bombings of Hiroshima and Nagasaki. At the time of the bombings of Hiroshima and Nagasaki the U.S. government tried to present this as positive to the American people and in particular that it was necessary to end a war to avoid an invasion of Japan, which of course was not going to happen, because the Japanese were already defeated and were trying desperately to negotiate a surrender.

It is with this simple idea of the criminality of nuclear weapons that people can easily comprehend the illegitimacy and fundamental lawlessness of these policies that their governments pursue in their names—or allied governments as well. And to those living in the NATO states today: Their leaders are all accomplices; they go along with nuclear policies as well. They send their generals over to NATO headquarters to be integrated into NATO's strategy.

I remember after the Berlin Wall fell, the German Branch of International Association of Lawyers Against Nuclear Arms had a big conference in Berlin and I gave the keynote address along these lines. And they asked the German General of the Bundeswehr in charge of liaison with NATO on nuclear weapons to respond to me. And he got up and he said, "Well, we all know that Nuremberg is soft law!"

I had two reactions to that. One: "Mister General, we hanged your predecessors at Nuremberg, under the Nuremberg laws. How can you say it is soft law?" Not that I support the death penalty even for major war criminals like Bush Junior and Tony Blair.

But the second reaction I had to this notion of "soft law" like Joe Nye's "soft power": "Soft law," I said, "you know, he got that from us." So we Americans have convinced German generals that Nuremberg is "soft law" in order to pursue our nuclear policies with the cooperation of the next generation of German generals whose predecessors we hanged at Nuremberg.

After the public speech I discussed this matter with him, and he agreed with me but he said, "Look, we have no alternative but to do what the Americans tell us to do." And I quoted to him a passage from the Bible saying, "Yes, and the blind shall lead the blind." And the German General said, "We have to trust that the Americans are doing the right thing." Right over the nuclear precipice! The German people have to stand up here and say, "Enough! We want your nukes out of Germany for sure and we are no longer going to cooperate with you on nuclear weapons policies!"

Humankind must abolish nuclear weapons before nuclear weapons abolish humankind! Nevertheless, there are a small number of governments in the world that continue to maintain their nuclear weapons systems despite the rules of international criminal law to the contrary. I would respond in a very simple way: Since when has a small gang of criminals—the leaders of the nuclear weapons states—been able to determine what is illegal or legal for the rest of the world by means of their own criminal behavior? What right do nuclear weapons states have to argue that by means of their own criminal behavior—nuclear deterrence/nuclear terrorism—they have made criminal acts legitimate? No civilized state would permit a small gang of criminal conspirators to pervert its domestic legal order in this way. Indeed both the Nuremberg Tribunal and the Tokyo Tribunal made it clear that a conspiratorial band of criminal states has no right to opt out of the international legal order by means of invoking their own criminal behavior as the least common denominator of international deportment. It's a basic rule of international law: Right cannot arise out of injustice! *Ex iniuria ius non oritur*!

The entire human race has been victimized by an international conspiracy of ongoing criminal activity carried out by the nuclear weapons states and their leaders under this doctrine of nuclear deterrence, which is really a euphemism for nuclear terrorism. And the expansion of NATO has now drawn in almost all of Europe. They have broken down—the United States and NATO—even the traditionally neutral states. Sweden today acts as if it were a de facto, but not yet de jure, member of NATO. Finland has basically abandoned its neutrality. Austria, with a constitutional obligation to be neutral, has basically abandoned its neutrality. Even Ireland, little bitty Ireland—I have dual-nationality with Ireland. The Americans have forced and compelled Ireland to join up to the Partnership for Peace (PFP) which is one step away from NATO membership, and have forced Ireland then under PFP to put some troops in Afghanistan to help them wage an illegal and criminal war of aggression against Afghanistan.

The only state in Europe still holding out is Switzerland. Yes, it signed up for Partnership for Peace which it should never have done. But at least Switzerland is holding out; it has no troops in Afghanistan or Iraq. And Switzerland must continue to hold out. And that is exactly why it has been subjected to so much pressure! Including an attack on its banking and financial system to bring Switzerland into line with NATO and the United States, exactly as every other country in Europe has done and succumbed to. That is really what's at stake here. Are you, the Swiss, going to join up—either de facto or de jure—with NATO and the Americans, so that if and when they attack Iran and perhaps set off a new world war, you and your children will get sucked into it? Switzerland avoided the last two world wars. I certainly hope Switzerland will avoid the next one by having nothing to do with the United States and NATO. And somehow working your way out of Partnership for Peace.

This international criminal conspiracy of nuclear deterrence/nuclear terrorism is no different from any other conspiracy by a criminal gang or band. They are the outlaws. We are the sheriffs—the citizens of the world. So it is up to us to repress and dissolve this international criminal conspiracy by whatever non-violent means are at our disposal and as soon as possible. As I said: If we all don't act now, Obama and his people could very well set off a Third World War over Iran, that has already been threatened publicly by Bush Junior.

Every person around the world has a basic human right to be free from the criminal practice of nuclear deterrence/nuclear terrorism, and its specter of nuclear extinction. All human beings in our capacities as creatures of God possess the basic right under international law to engage in civil resistance for the purpose of preventing, impeding, or terminating the ongoing commission of these international crimes.

And this is not civil disobedience. It's civil resistance! We have disobeyed nothing! We are obeying the dictates of international law! It is the government officials in the nuclear weapons states and their allied states that are disobeying international law. They are the criminals! We are the sheriffs! And it is up to us to stop them!

Every citizen of the world community has the right and the duty to oppose the existence of nuclear weapons systems by whatever non-violent means are at his or her disposal. Otherwise the human race will suffer the same fate as the dinosaurs. And the planet earth will become a radioactive wasteland. And it very well could happen in our lifetime.

The time for preventive action is now! And civil resistance by all of us human beings is the way to go. Thank you.

KING'S BAY PLOWSHARES FACE 25 YEARS FOR ACTION AT U.S. NUCLEAR SUBMARINE BASE

Seven Catholic plowshares activists entered Kings Bay Naval Submarine Base in St. Mary's, Georgia on April 4, 2018. They went to make real the prophet Isaiah's command to "beat swords into plowshares." The seven chose to act on the fiftieth anniversary of the assassination of the Rev. Dr. Martin Luther King, Jr., who devoted his life to addressing what he called the "triple evils of militarism, racism and materialism." Carrying hammers and baby bottles of their own blood, the seven attempted to convert weapons of mass destruction. They hoped to call attention to the ways in which nuclear weapons kill every day, by their mere existence and maintenance.

Kings Bay Naval base opened in 1979 as the navy's Atlantic Ocean Trident port. It is the largest nuclear submarine base in the world. There are six ballistic missile subs and two guided missile subs based at Kings Bay.

The activists went to three sites on the base: The SWFLANT administration building, the D5 Missile monument installation, and the nuclear weapons storage bunkers. The activists used crime scene tape, hammers, and hung banners reading: "The ultimate logic of racism is genocide - Dr. Martin Luther King," "The ultimate logic of Trident is omnicide," and "Nuclear weapons: illegal/ immoral." They also brought an indictment charging the U.S. government for crimes against peace.

The activists at the nuclear weapons storage bunkers were Elizabeth McAlister, 78, of Jonah House, Baltimore; Fr. Steve Kelly SJ, 69, of the Bay Area, California; and Carmen Trotta, 55, of the New York Catholic Worker.

At the Strategic Weapons Facility Atlantic Administration building were Clare Grady, 59, of the Ithaca Catholic Worker; and Martha Hennessy, 62, of the New York Catholic Worker.

At the Trident D5 monuments were Mark Colville, 55, of the Amistad Catholic Worker, New Haven, Connecticut; and Patrick O'Neill, 61, of the Fr. Charlie Mulholland, Catholic Worker, Garner, North Carolina.

This is the latest of 100 similar actions around the world beginning in 1980 in King of Prussia, Pennsylvania.

The King's Bay Plowshares face up to 25 years of incarceration in a U.S. Federal penitentiary for their action of courage, integrity, and principles. It was my great honor and privilege to submit the following two Declarations to the U.S. Federal District Court in the King's Bay Plowshares case on behalf of Elizabeth McAlister—a great leader and hero of the American Peace Movement since the darkest days of the Vietnam War that she resisted with her late husband Philip Berrigan and his late brother Daniel Berrigan, S.J.. R.I.P. The other King's Bay Plowshares have also used my two Declarations and advice to defend themselves in court.[3]

UNITED STATES DISTRICT COURT
SOUTHERN DISTRICT OF GEORGIA
BRUNSWICK DIVISION

USA
v NO. 2:18-CR- 22
Elizabeth McAlister

Declaration of Francis A. Boyle

Pursuant to 28 USC 1746, Francis A. Boyle declares under penalty of perjury:

1. I am a Professor of Law at the University of Illinois College of Law at Champaign, Illinois. I hold both a Doctor of Law Magna Cum Laude from Harvard Law School and an A.M. and Ph.D. in Political Science from the Harvard Graduate School of Arts and Sciences, Department of Government, where I specialized in International Political Science and its relationship to International Law. I graduated from the exact same Harvard Ph.D. Program that produced Henry Kissinger, Zbigniew Brzezinski, Samuel Huntington et al. before me. My resume is attached to this Declaration and is hereby incorporated by reference.
2. I am an expert in International Law and Foreign Policy. I have studied, read, and written extensively in these areas, and have been qualified as an Expert Witness in several courts across the country and abroad. In particular, with respect to these proceedings concerning the Laws of War with respect to nuclear weapons, I have been qualified as an Expert on the Laws of War and testified in U.S. military court-martial proceedings

involving (1) U.S.M.C. Corporal Jeff Paterson (1990); (2) U.S. Army Captain Doctor Yolanda Huet-Vaughn (1991); (3) U.S. Army Captain Lawrence Rockwood (1995); (4) U.S. Army Reserve Staff Sergeant Camilo Mejia (2003); and (5) U.S. Army First Lieutenant Ehren Watada (2006).

3. Currently valid U.S. Army Field Manual 27-10 (1956) on *The Law of Land Warfare* was drafted for the Pentagon by then Major Richard R. Baxter. Professor Baxter later taught me his course on *The Laws of War* at Harvard Law School. I was the top student in his class and Professor Baxter recommended me for my current position as a law professor. Professor Baxter was later elected a Judge on the International Court of Justice, the so-called World Court of the United Nations System. While he was alive Professor Baxter was generally considered to be the world's leading Expert on the Laws of War, and even by the United States Government itself. The United States Government chose Professor Baxter to head-up the American Delegation for the negotiation and the drafting (1974–1977) of Additional Protocols I and II of 1977 to the Four Geneva Conventions of 1949 dealing with the Laws of War and International Humanitarian Law. I was his student at that time and personally studied these Geneva Protocols under him while he was negotiating them for the United States Government.
4. I currently teach a course on *The Constitutional Law of U.S. Foreign Affairs*. Previously, I had taught the course here on *Criminal Law* for several years before I moved over to teach *International Human Rights Law*, which includes therein International Humanitarian Law and the Laws of War. I also currently teach our course on *International Law*.
5. In 1983 the United States Military Academy at West Point invited me to Lecture and Debate before their 21st Senior Conference on *Nuclear Deterrence* on the subject of *Nuclear Deterrence and International Law*. The audience consisted of about 200 high-level officials from the United States Government in charge of supervising U.S. nuclear weapons and U.S. nuclear deterrence policies. Sitting in the audience for my West Point Lecture and Debate were among other Generals the Three-Star General in charge of War-operations at the Pentagon, the Three-Star General Commandant at West Point, the Director of the Defense Nuclear Agency, the U.S. Air Force's Special Assistant for Nuclear Targeting, former White House National Security Advisor Brent Scowcroft, former United States Undersecretary of State George Ball, the Developer of the American Hydrogen Bomb Richard Garwin, etc. My West Point Paper was later published by the United States Military Academy in *The Nuclear Debate: 21st Senior Conference Proceedings* (West Point: 1983) and later in Volume 4 of the *New York Law School Journal of*

International and Comparative Law, No. 2 (1983). I am uniquely qualified to testify in this case concerning the relevance of international law and in particular the Laws of War to U.S. nuclear weapons and U.S. nuclear deterrence policies.

6. I offer this Declaration based upon personal knowledge of the allegations against these particular Defendants named herein as set forth in the Indictment; my personal knowledge of the past protest activities, cases and actions filed both by and against these named Defendants, and their strongly held religious beliefs. I further offer this Declaration in support of Defendants in this matter in establishing the content and application of the Laws of War to elements of the offenses charged and in support of justification defenses, including necessity, and crime prevention, and their absence of criminal intent.
7. I am aware that expert opinion on points of law is ordinarily not permitted in court. However, opinion of published international legal scholars is an important exception to that rule. The Statute of the International Court of Justice provides that questions of international law shall be determined by resort, inter alia, to "the teachings of the most highly qualified publicists of the various nations. . ." Id., Art. 38 (1) (d). An integral part of the United Nations Charter, which is a treaty and thus equivalent to a Federal statute as the Supreme Law of the Land under Article VI of the United States Constitution, this rule of evidence is applicable in Federal court. The Supreme Court expressed the same opinion in *The Paquete Habana*, 175 US 677, 700 (1900), which directly concerned the Laws of War at Sea. Cf. Fed. R. Crim. P. 26.1 (ordinary Rules of Evidence do not apply to determination of foreign law). I have written extensively on the Laws of War at Sea and the Laws of War on Land and the International Laws of Neutrality during Wartime in my book *Foundations of World Order* (Duke University Press: 1999). Volume XXI, No. 3 of the prestigious *The International History Review* (September 2000) reviewed my book as follows: ". . . *Foundations of World Order* is a major contribution to this reinterrogation of the past, and should be required reading for historians, political scientists, international relations specialists, and policymakers." Id. at 667-68.
8. In the implementation of foreign policy, the current Administration, at the Kings Bay Naval Station continues to plan, prepare and conspire for threat or use of many W-76 and W-76-1 nuclear warhead weapons, each capable of unleashing 100 kilotons of heat, blast and radiation, and many of the W88/Mk-5 warheads which carries 455 kilotons of nuclear weapons. Any planning, preparation, conspiracy for threat or use of even one of these nuclear warheads was and is unlawful, that is illegal and criminal. This conclusion is elaborated in paragraphs 9-15 below.

9. The body of Federal law which governs these matters includes rules and principles of international law including therein the Laws of War. International law is not "higher" or separate law; it is part and parcel of the structure of Federal law. The Supreme Court so held in the landmark decision in *The Paquete Habana*, 175 US 677, 700 (1900), that was recently reaffirmed in *Hamdan v. Rumsfeld*, 548 US 557 (2006). Federal statutes must be interpreted and applied consistently with international law. See e.g. *U.S. v Flores*, 289 US 137, 159 (1933); Jordan J. Paust, *International Law as Law of the United States* (2nd ed. 2003) at 99, 120, 124-25. Thus international law including treaties and customary international law and the Laws of War must be considered along with Congressional statutes, Constitutional law, administrative law, Federal common law, Rules of Court, military law such as U.S. Army Field Manual 27-10 (1956), incorporated state law and any other pertinent body of law, whenever it applies according to the pertinent rules of supremacy, parallel construction, and choice of law.
10. International law, as part of US law, includes the Laws of War. This body of positive law as applied to threat or use of nuclear weapons is summarized most authoritatively by the International Court of Justice, *Legality of the Threat or Use of Nuclear Weapons*, 8 July 1996 (ICJ Op). The London Charter (1945) establishing the Nuremberg Tribunal and the Nuremberg Judgment (1946) made it clear that those rules and principles preempt contrary domestic law. Particular prohibitions of law are directly incorporated into the US criminal code as war crimes (18 USC 2441) or genocide (18 USC 1091–1093) and binding US treaties that are "the supreme law of the land" (U.S. Constitution, Article VI, clause 2), US Military Manuals including the Naval Commanders' Handbook and U.S. Army Field Manual 27-10 (1956), and universally binding "intransgressible" rules of humanitarian law. The fundamental rules and principles of humanitarian law include: a) "States must never make civilians the object of attack and must consequently never use weapons that are incapable of distinguishing between civilians and military targets" (ICJ Op., § 78). A corollary is that it is prohibited to use weapons that cause uncontrollable effects [1977 Protocol I to the Geneva Conventions, Art. 51(4)]. Use of the Trident II system where most of the above described nuclear warheads are deployed for threat or use is unlawful per se because if targeted at military objects, the effects still are indiscriminate and uncontrollable. b) "It is prohibited to cause unnecessary suffering to combatants; it is accordingly prohibited to use weapons causing them such harm or uselessly aggravating their suffering" [ICJ Op., § 78; 1907 Hague Convention IV, Art. 23(e)]. "If an envisaged use of weapons would not meet the requirements of

humanitarian law, a threat to engage in such use would also be contrary to that law" (ICJ Op., § 78). The United States is bound as a party to each of these treaties. Because of the known and intended effects of the explosion of the nuclear warheads, each of these rules prohibits their planning, preparation, threat or use. In addition, any use of the warhead would also violate the international law of armed conflict by causing widespread, long-term, and severe damage to our common environment and contaminating neutral states, and violate the right to life and other non-derogable human rights, rights that cannot be suspended even in a state of emergency.

11. As further explained in my book *The Criminality of Deterrence* (2002), thermonuclear warheads such as those on Trident II are in a category of nuclear weapons that are, ipso facto, incapable of distinguishing between civilian and combatant, are uncontrollable in space or time and cause unnecessary suffering. Thus any planning, preparation, threat or use of these warheads was and is both illegal and criminal.
12. The London Charter for the Nuremberg Tribunal made explicit that violations of the Laws of War are criminal and that individuals are punishable for committing war crimes. In addition, the Nuremberg Charter defined crimes against peace and crimes against humanity as well as war crimes. The former basically consist of waging a war of aggression or a war in violation of a treaty or other international obligation. It is also important to reiterate that the Nuremberg Charter articulates inchoate crimes as well, such as the planning or preparation and conspiracy to commit a crime against peace, a crime against humanity, or a war crime. My teacher Professor Baxter expressly incorporated these Nuremberg Principles of international criminal law and the Laws of War into Paragraphs 498, 499, and 500, inter alia, of U.S. Army Field Manual 27-10 (1956) *The Law of Land Warfare* for the Pentagon where they still are as of today.
13. These provisions apply equally in times of formal peace as in times of war.
14. The various scenarios developed by the United States Government for the use of nuclear weapons cannot be accomplished without violating international law, including the Laws of War as incorporated into U.S. law. The plans for targeting of U.S. nuclear weapons were found in the Single Integrated Operational Plan ("SIOP"), which is now renamed the Operations Plan ("OPLAN") which lists the targets to be destroyed in a number of nuclear and non-nuclear countries. To employ these weapons, as is currently planned, would clearly violate the Nuremberg Principles, in that the concept of a crime against humanity specifically prohibits such wanton destruction, including and especially the Nuremberg War Crimes

themselves of (1) the "wanton destruction of cities, towns, or villages"; and (2) "devastation not justified by military necessity."

15. I am aware from my reading and study, including the Nuclear Posture Review (February 2018) as well as contracts let to "upgrade" or "extend the lives of" nuclear warheads that U.S. nuclear weapons policies include on-going threats of a "first-strike" made "believable" by maintaining the Trident II missiles and submarines in order to deliver the nuclear warheads prepared for launch on extremely short notice. I am further aware from my reading and study that a high degree of accuracy of the Trident II missiles is crucial to a first strike and cannot ameliorate the indiscriminate and uncontrollable effects.
16. Any first strike use of the Trident II missiles with nuclear warheads would, ipso facto, violate the United Nations Charter and the Hague Convention of 1907, prohibiting the opening of hostilities without a formal declaration of war or reasoned ultimatum. And any use of even one of the warheads in any circumstance whether in response or defense would violate the principles of necessity and proportionality because it cannot be used within the intransgressible rules and principles of international humanitarian law.
17. Since the threat or use of the Trident II is inherently criminal under international and US law, anything used to facilitate its operation is an instrument of a crime.
18. The Judgment of the Nuremberg International Military Tribunal meted out severe punishment in 1946 against individuals who, acting in full compliance with domestic law but in disregard of the limitations of international law, had committed war crimes and crimes against peace as defined in its Charter. 6 FRD 69 (1948). That Charter has been enacted as a law of the United States, 59 Stat. 5144 (1945) and as War Crimes 18 USC 2441. By implication, the Nuremberg Judgment privileges all citizens of nations engaged in war crimes to act in a measured but effective way to prevent the continuing commissions of those crimes. The same Nuremberg Privilege is recognized in Article 38 of the Statute of the International Court of Justice ("General Principles of Law Recognized by All Civilized Nations") which has been adopted as a Treaty by the United States. In my opinion, such action certainly includes non-violent exposure and inspection of sites of ongoing war crimes.
19. In the present day, there has been a breakdown in the Constitutional principle of checks and balances which implements the separation of powers; most notably neither Congress nor the courts have been willing to ensure that the Executive Branch act within the laws that limit methods and means of the threat or use of military force. The fact that the U.S. Government continues to use nuclear warheads and that their

use is actively threatened on high alert reflects the stubborn refusal of the U.S. Government to abide by its own fundamental Laws of War and to proceed with negotiations for nuclear disarmament in all its aspects as required by the 1968 Nuclear Non-Proliferation Treaty to which the United States is a contracting party. In spite of years in which these Defendants have participated in citizens petitions, letters, referendums, civil cases, requests for criminal prosecution and the recent decisions on these questions with the full participation of the United States Government before the International Court of Justice, the U.S. government flouts its responsibility to abide by the Laws of War, laws to which we are fundamentally bound. Under these circumstances, where redress within traditional channels is refused and ineffective, domestic criminal law coincides with the "Nuremberg Privilege" mentioned in the preceding paragraph to afford a justification for seeming violations of domestic criminal laws in an effort to prevent the war crimes outlined above.

20. In my opinion the charges brought against these Defendants in these circumstances must be dismissed. The prosecution of this case cannot go forward because all charges brought contain elements directly related to the production and processing of nuclear materials for nuclear warheads for active threat or delivery. These statutes as applied in this case are all promulgated pursuant to the War Powers of Congress, can only be and must be interpreted consistent with the Laws of War and international law in general. Any alleged installation must be for a purpose that comports with the Laws of War. Clearly the Trident II missiles can never be planned, prepared, threatened or used within the Laws of War and any instrumentalities or property furthering that planning, preparation, threat or use is illegal and criminal. All charges must be dismissed because the court may not apply conspiracy or protection of property statutes in a way that ignores or abrogates the fundamental Laws of War. In these circumstances, where the alleged "property" is part of ongoing planning, preparation for illegal and criminal threat of or use of the most grotesque weapons of mass destruction these Defendants acted lawfully and reasonably to prevent egregious and fundamentally prohibited of all crimes, war crimes. The gas showerheads at Auschwitz were instrumentalities of crimes. The same principle of international criminal law holds true for Trident II missiles.
21. I declare under penalty of perjury that the foregoing is true and correct. I am prepared to testify under oath and answer questions on these and related matters.
22. It is my opinion that these Defendants undertook non-violent, symbolic action to attempt to disarm the Kings Bay Naval base.

23. It is further my opinion that these actions described in the Indictment are in full compliance with the laws, treaties, and legal principles outlined herein and served a legal purpose.
24. It is my further opinion that for all the reasons discussed above that are generally known to these unique Defendants, they did not possess the criminal intent required to establish any of the crimes for which they have been indicted.
25. Pursuant to the requirements of the United States Supreme Court set forth in *Mullaney v Wilbur,* 421 U.S. 684 (1975) and *In Re Winship*, 397 U.S. 358 (1970), the United States Government must prove beyond a reasonable doubt the criminal intent and all facts necessary to constitute the crimes for which these Defendants have been indicted. I respectfully submit that this Declaration of today's date creates a reasonable doubt with respect to all the crimes for which the Defendants have been indicted. Therefore all charges against them must be dismissed.

Signed this ______ day of
June, 2018 at Champaign, Illinois

____

Francis Anthony Boyle
Professor of Law
University of Illinois
College of Law
Massachusetts Bar No. 052540

UNITED STATES DISTRICT COURT
SOUTHERN DISTRICT OF GEORGIA
BRUNSWICK DIVISION

USA
v NO. 2:18-CR- 22
Elizabeth McAlister

SUPPLEMENTAL DECLARATION OF FRANCIS A. BOYLE

Pursuant to 28 USC 1746, Francis A. Boyle declares under penalty of perjury:

1. I submitted a Declaration in this matter dated June 25, 2018. This Declaration supplements that original Declaration and should be read in light of that document.

2. I am an expert in International Law and Foreign Policy and my credentials are set out in the previous Declaration.
3. It was my conclusion in June 25, 2018, for the reasons set out at length in that document, that the existence, threat, or use of any of the Trident thermonuclear weapons at Kings Bay is absolutely illegal and criminal under the laws of the United States and international law.
4. Recent events have made the existence, threat, or use of those weapons of mass destruction like the Kings Bay Tridents even more horrific and the possibility of nuclear war even more likely.
5. In October of 2018, President Donald Trump and his U.S. National Security Advisor John Bolton declared it is the intention of the U.S. to withdraw from the Intermediate Range Nuclear Forces (INF) Treaty.
6. The INF Treaty was signed on December 8, 1987 by President Ronald Reagan of the United States and General Secretary Mikhail Gorbachev of the Soviet Union.
7. The INF Treaty barred both the United States and Russia from deploying nuclear and conventional ground launched ballistic missiles and cruise missiles with a range of 500 to 5500 kilometers or 300 to 3400 miles.
8. As a result of the INF Treaty, the U.S. and the Soviet Union destroyed a total of 2,692 short, medium, and intermediate range missiles by June 1, 1991.
9. Reactivating Intermediate Range Nuclear Missiles will make the world and the United States a much more dangerous place and will greatly exacerbate the current violations of U.S. and international law which I discussed in my initial Declaration.
10. New Intermediate Range Nuclear Missiles, combined with the Trident missiles, give the United States an even more obvious and effective illegal and criminal offensive first-strike nuclear weapons capability against both Russia and China.
11. Intermediate Range Nuclear Missiles will be able to reach Russia in as little as 3 minutes from launch in Eastern Europe and the Tridents can reach Russia in around 15 minutes.
12. The Intermediate Range Nuclear Missiles would primarily target strategic nuclear weapons command centers in Russia, while the Tridents will be targeted at all other civilian population centers and infrastructure locations and nuclear forces.
13. U.S. INFs in Europe will provide Russia with an enormous incentive to "use it or lose it" by launching a pre-emptive strategic nuclear attack upon the Continental United States in the event of a crisis or an accident or a computer malfunction or a radar misinterpretation or human error. These phenomena have repeatedly happened before.

14. According to President Trump's National Security Adviser John Bolton, one of the other reasons for pulling the United States out of the INF Treaty is so that the United States can deploy INFs against China and thus better threaten China with an illegal and criminal offensive first-strike nuclear weapons attack.
15. The Intermediate Range Nuclear Missiles would primarily target strategic nuclear weapons command centers in China, while the Tridents will be targeted at all other civilian population centers and infrastructure locations and nuclear forces.
16. U.S. INFs in Asia will provide China with an enormous incentive to "use it or lose it" by launching a pre-emptive strategic nuclear attack upon the Continental United States in the event of a crisis or an accident or a computer malfunction or a radar misinterpretation or human error. These phenomena have repeatedly happened before.
17. These actions announced by the Trump administration further violate the international law obligations of the United States under the Nuclear Non-Proliferation (NPT) Treaty which is designed to achieve nuclear disarmament as interpreted by the International Court of Justice Nuclear Weapons Advisory Opinion, as I discussed in my earlier Declaration and as I discussed in my book *The Criminality of Nuclear Deterrence* (Clarity Press: 2002).
18. These actions announced by the Trump administration are further violations of the laws of war and international humanitarian law.
19. These actions announced by the Trump administration are further violations of criminal law under U.S. and international laws. They can only result in genocide and are threatening to commit genocide.
20. The Trump administration pulling out of the INF Treaty seriously jeopardizes the renewal of the 2010 New Strategic Arms Reduction Treaty (New START) between the United States and Russia that imposes severe constraints on the offensive strategic nuclear weapons systems of these two nuclear superpowers. Non-renewal of the New START Treaty would set off a frantic nuclear arms race between the United States and Russia as well as by the other acknowledged nuclear weapons states such as China, Britain, France, India, Pakistan, Israel, and North Korea.
21. These developments would lead to the unraveling, dissolution, and nullification of the seminal Nuclear Non-Proliferation Treaty itself and the research, development, testing, production, and deployment of nuclear weapons by every state in the world with a nuclear power plant. Currently 30 countries in the world have operational nuclear power plants – that figure is 31 if Taiwan is considered separately from China. See *Operational & Long-Term Shutdown Reactors*, Int'l Atomic Energy

Agency, https://pris.iaea.org/PRIS/WorldStatistics/OperationalReactorsByCountry.aspx (last updated Oct. 28, 2018).

22. The non-violent symbolic disarmament actions of Defendants in this matter take on greater and compelling urgency in light of the announcement by the United States that it will withdraw from the INF Treaty.
23. I repeat my opinion that the charges against these Defendants should be dismissed. The Court must recognize that the possession, preparation for use, threat of use or use of Trident nuclear weapons at Kings Bay is illegal and criminal.
24. The non-violent, symbolic disarmament actions by Defendants in this matter are in full compliance with the laws, treaties, and principles of U.S. and international law and served a lawful purpose: preventing the ongoing commission of genocidal international and U.S. domestic crimes.
25. The very existence of humanity is at risk!
26. I declare under penalty of perjury that the foregoing is true and correct. I am prepared to testify under oath and answer questions on these and related matters.

Signed this ____ Day of __________, 2018 at Champaign Illinois.

____

Francis Anthony Boyle
Professor of Law
University of Illinois
College of Law
Massachusetts Bar Number 052540

NOTES

1. U.S. nuclear weapons are still in Germany.

2. George Monbiot, "Our Nuclear Programme Is Illegal," *Guardian*, September 20, 2000, https://www.theguardian.com/comment/story/0,3604,374144,00.html.

3. After a kangaroo court proceeding, they were all found guilty. Their sentencing has been delayed because of the Covid-19 pandemic.

Chapter 13

U.S. Biowarfare Programs Have 13,000 Death Scientists Hard at Work

Author of U.S. Biowarfare Act Says
America's $100 Billion Germ Warfare
Industry a "Criminal Enterprise,"
By Sherwood Ross

The American legal authority who in 1989 drafted the law Congress enacted to comply with the 1972 Biological Weapons Convention says the U.S. today [October 11, 2015] is in flagrant violation of that Convention.

"Since Sept. 11, 2001, we have spent somewhere in the area of $100 billion" on offensive biological warfare, charges Professor Francis Boyle of the University of Illinois, Champaign.

Boyle said an estimated 13,000 "death scientists" in 400 laboratories in the United States and abroad are employed making new strains of offensive killer germs that will be resistant to vaccines.

For example, Dr. Yoshihiro Kawaoka's group at the University of Wisconsin has found a way to increase the toxicity of the flu virus by 200 times! Boyle says Kawaoka is "the same death scientist who resurrected the genocidal Spanish Flu virus for the Pentagon for offensive biowarfare purposes."

As for fighting flu, the National Institutes of Health in 2006, a typical year, got only $120 million from Congress to fight flu, which kills an estimated 36,000 Americans annually. By contrast, Congress gave NIH $1.76 billion for "biodefense," even though the anthrax outbreak in 2001 killed just five persons.

"'These distorted budgetary allocations' (spending 15 times as much for germ warfare as for fighting flu) demonstrate that the priority here is not the promotion of the public health of American citizens but rather to further develop the U.S. offensive biowarfare industry that will someday 'blowback' upon the American people with a catastrophic pandemic," Boyle said.

Boyle went on to say the Pentagon and Central Intelligence Agency (CIA) are "ready, willing, and able to launch biowarfare when it suits their interests . . . They have a super-weapons-grade anthrax that they already used against us in October 2001."

Boyle here was referring to the anthrax pathogens mailed to two U.S. Senators (Tom Daschle, of South Dakota and Patrick Leahy, of Vermont) and others after 9/11 that were traced back to the Government's biowarfare lab at Fort Detrick, Maryland.

Boyle's remarks came in response to written questions from Sherwood Ross, a Miami, Florida-based columnist. Asked if the recent outbreaks of Ebola in Sierra Leone and Liberia could be from U.S. government–backed facilities, Boyle replied:

"These Ebola vaccines were experimental U.S. biowarfare vaccines that were being tested out in West Africa. It was a result of testing out of the U.S. biowarfare vaccines at our lab in Kenema, Sierra Leone, that created the West African Ebola pandemic in the first place."

Boyle warned that the Galveston National Laboratory in Texas, a high-containment research lab, has been seeking for potential biowarfare agents in the wild in other parts of the world "in order to turn them into biological weapons."

Boyle said, "They should shut down Galveston as an ongoing criminal enterprise along the lines of the S.S. and the Gestapo—except that Galveston is far more dangerous to humanity than Hitler's death squads ever were."

Boyle added, "American universities have a long history of willingly permitting their research agenda, researchers, institutes, and laboratories to be co-opted, corrupted, and perverted by the Pentagon and the C.I.A. into death science. These include Wisconsin, North Carolina, Boston U., Harvard, M.I.T., Tulane, University of Chicago, and my own University of Illinois, as well as many others."

(Sherwood Ross formerly reported for the *Chicago Daily News* and was a columnist for UPI [Magazines in Review] and Reuters (Workplace.)

BOYLE CHARGES U.S. WITH GERM WARFARE PROGRAM IS "CRIMINAL ENTERPRISE" Q. AND A. WITH FRANCIS A. BOYLE ON BIOWARFARE

Francis A. Boyle is a leading American professor, practitioner, and advocate of international law. He was responsible for drafting the Biological

Weapons Anti-Terrorism Act of 1989 (BWATA), the American implementing legislation for the 1972 Biological Weapons Convention. His BWATA was passed unanimously by both Houses of the U.S. Congress and signed into law by President George Bush Sr. The story is told in his book *Biowarfare and Terrorism* (Clarity Press: 2005). He served on the Board of Directors of Amnesty International USA (1988–1992) and represented Bosnia-Herzegovina at the World Court. Professor Boyle teaches international law at the University of Illinois College of Law in Champaign. He holds a Doctor of Law Magna Cum Laude as well as a PhD in political science, both from Harvard University.

Q: To get some idea of the magnitude of U.S. biological warfare research involving deadly diseases now going forward, the federal government is said to be funding 400 laboratories globally. These labs purportedly are concocting new strains of lethal microbes for which there is no cure. Right off the bat, I'd like to ask you, "Is this a criminal enterprise whose dimensions are being concealed from the American public?"

A: Of course it is! Since September 11, 2001, we have spent somewhere in the area approaching $100 billion on biological warfare. Effectively we now have an Offensive Biological Warfare Industry in this country that violates the Biological Weapons Convention and my Biological Weapons Anti-Terrorism Act of 1989. We have reconstructed the Offensive Biological Warfare Industry that we had deployed in this county before its prohibition by the Biological Weapons Convention of 1972 that was described by Sy Hersh in his groundbreaking exposé of it in his book *Chemical & Biological Warfare America's Hidden Arsenal* (Bobbs-Merrill, 1968). Our putative adversaries around the world such as Russia and China have undoubtedly reached the same conclusions I have derived from the same open and public sources and have responded in kind. So what the world now witnesses is an all-out offensive biological warfare arms race among the major military powers of the world: United States, Russia, Britain, France, China, Israel, inter alia. The Biological Weapons Convention has become the proverbial "mere scrap of paper." But my BWATA still remains the law of the land in the United States with a penalty of life-in-prison for violators. That is why the self-styled "synthetic biologists" proposed to repeal my BWATA so that they can use synthetic biology to manufacture new classes of biological weapons more efficiently.

Q: Exactly what is biowarfare?

A: Biological warfare involves the use of living organisms for military purposes. Such weapons can be viral, bacterial, and fungal, among other forms, and can be spread over a large geographic terrain by wind, water, insect, animal, or human transmission. Toxins—living organisms such as fungi—are also used.

Q: Which are the most dangerous?

A: Today several USG labs are at work on Anthrax, Tularemia, Plague, Ebola, Botulism, and the genocidal Spanish flu virus.

Q: What do they do with these pathogens?

A: Using DNA genetic engineering, U.S. death scientists are concocting new strains of lethal microbes for which there are no cures. Bacteria, for example, can be made resistant to vaccines, made more virulent, easier to spread, and harder to eradicate. Right now, U.S. death scientists are scouring the biosphere around the world to locate any bioagent in nature that they can exploit and pervert into offensive biowarfare purposes.

Q: USA Today has done some fine reporting on this subject. Among other things, their reporters have exposed massive incidents of lax security conditions at USG labs and university labs funded by USG. What might the consequences be of this disregard for safety?

A: This is a biocatastrophe waiting to happen here in the United States. In fact, it has already happened in West Africa with the Ebola pandemic there. It is only a matter of time before we have a similar pandemic at home here caused by U.S. biowarfare programs. In this regard you should watch the excellent award-winning documentary by *Coen & Nadler entitled Anthrax-War* (Transformer Films 2009) in which I appear and served as a consultant on.

Q: Recently, thirteen cases of plague were reported in Arizona, California, Colorado, Georgia, New Mexico, Oregon, and Utah, resulting in three deaths. Could these deadly plague pathogens (infectious agents) have come from the U.S. government's (USG) germ warfare labs?

A: I suspect they might have. But proving it is another matter. Any time you see some mysterious and widespread outbreak of an exotic disease around the country, you have to factor into the analytical explanatory equation that it could be the result of some illegal U.S. biowarfare program.

Q: Is it a fact, as alleged, that the Anthrax pathogens mailed to two U.S. Senators and others after 9/11 trace back to the USG biowarfare lab at Ft. Detrick, Maryland? You have written that Senators Daschle and Leahy, both Democrats, had opposed the Patriot Act, which gives USG unprecedented powers and abolishes Americans' traditional personal liberties. If the Anthrax was sent by the Pentagon, was it to intimidate the Senators?

A: Yes! I have written about this in my book *Biowarfare and Terrorism* (Clarity Press, 2005). More recently my friend and colleague Professor Graeme MacQueen from McMaster University in Canada has also written about this in his book *The 2001 Anthrax Deception* (Clarity Press, 2014). You are free to read these two books, draw your own conclusions, and see if you agree with us. Over the years there are numerous interviews I have given on this matter that you can obtain by Googling my name and adding the word "anthrax" to their search engine. The twin purposes of these October 2001 anthrax attacks were (1) to scaremonger the American People and Congress into adopting the totalitarian and Orwellian USA Patriot Act and (2) to wage an offensive war of aggression against Iraq. As President George Bush Junior proudly boasted "Mission accomplished!"—on both counts.

Q: Recently, there have been outbreaks of Ebola in Sierra Leone and Liberia. You have raised the possibility that USG may be illegally experimenting with these diseases on citizens of those African nations. Could you please elaborate?

A: These Ebola vaccines were experimental U.S. biowarfare vaccines that were being tested out in West Africa. It was a result of testing out of the U.S. biowarfare vaccines at our lab in Kenema, Sierra Leone, that created the West African Ebola pandemic in the first place. I have given numerous interviews to support my conclusion here in more detail. These can be located by Googling my name and adding the word "Ebola" to their search engine.

Q: Is such germ warfare development work illegal under the BWC Treaty of 1972? (Dr. Boyle was the American attorney who wrote the implementing legislation for the U.S. that passed Congress without a single negative vote.)

A: Yes. The U.S. is a party to the 1972 Biological and Toxic Weapons Convention which bans "development, production, stockpiling and use of microbes or their poisonous products except in amounts necessary for protective and peaceful research. . ." Colonel David Huxsoll, Commander of the Army's Medical Institute of Infectious Diseases, has admitted that offensive research is indistinguishable from defensive research.

Q: Although Russia said it scrapped its germ warfare program after the Communists lost power in 1991, the U.S. budget for this purpose has increased. Are there any countries or terrorist groups that might realistically attack the U.S. with such weapons? One critic has said USG's biowarfare push resembles "a dog chasing its own tail."

A: The truth of the matter is that the United States government has been pursuing the development of an offensive biowarfare program and industry since the Reagan administration and his Neoconservatives came to power in 1981. I set forth this earlier biowarfare documentation on Reagan and his Neo-Cons in my previous book *The Future of International Law and American Foreign Policy* (Transnational Publishers Inc., 1989), Chapter 8, "The Legal Distortions Behind the Reagan Administration's Chemical and Biological Warfare Buildup." Interestingly enough, the Department of Defense itself reprinted my study as Current News Special Edition CHEMICAL WEAPONS, NO. 1586 (28 May 1987) and distributed it to thousands of high-level DOD civilian and military officials all over the world.

Q: It sounds fantastic, I know, but scientists once paid by the USG to cure cancer are now being paid to develop deadlier strains of anthrax, dengue, Japanese encephalitis, tularemia, Q fever, and other dreaded diseases. Comment?

A: On the relationship between cancer research and bioweapons you should have a look at the book by Dr. Len Horowitz, *Emerging Viruses AIDS and Ebola – Nature, Accident, or Intentional?* (Tetrahedron Inc., 1996).

Q: You have written that Dr. Yoshihiro Kawaoka's group at the University of Wisconsin has found a way to increase the toxicity of flu virus by 200 times. What is the purpose of this horrible-sounding research and why should UW support it?

A: This is the same U.S. death scientist who resurrected the genocidal Spanish flu virus for the Pentagon for offensive biowarfare purposes. Like all U.S. universities, Bucky Badger U. gets a cut out of all research funds brought in from the outside. Here at *Chief Illiniwak University* they publicly admitted that they take 51 cents out of every research $1 Buck brought in from the outside and charge it off to "overhead." At most American Universities today, money talks and principles walk. My Disalma Mater Harvard is no better, no worse, and no different.

Q: During the 1980–88 Iraq–Iran war, the Reagan White House okayed the Pentagon's sale of weapons-specific biological agents and poison gas to Iraq that Saddam Hussein used against Iran and his own Kurdish minority? At least 5,000 Kurds were gassed. And, according to *Time* magazine of January 20, 2014, the CIA reckoned Iran suffered 50,000 deaths. Doesn't this prove the White House has used biological agents offensively?

A: Certainly chemical weapons were used illegally. In addition, the Reagan administration shipped weapons-specific biowarfare agents to Saddam Hussein in Iraq in the hope and expectation that he would weaponize them and use them against Iran. He did weaponize them. So far I have not seen evidence that he used bioweapons against Iran or the Kurds. But these biowarfare weapons that Saddam Hussein produced thanks to Reagan and his Neo-Cons did "blowback" upon U.S. armed forces when they invaded Iraq in 1991. This "blowback" played a causative role in the Gulf War Syndrome that afflicted U.S. soldiers who participated in Gulf War I under President Bush Sr. I discuss this in my book *Destroying World Order* (Clarity Press, 2004) and in the British TV documentary *The Dirty War* (1993) produced by and shown on Britain's Independent Television Network TV4 that I consulted on and appear in.

Q: You have pointed out that the Galveston National Laboratory in Texas, a high-containment research lab, admits to seeking for potential biowarfare agents in the wild in other parts of the world "in order to turn them into biological weapons."

A: Right! They should shut down Galveston as an ongoing criminal enterprise along the lines of the S.S. and the Gestapo—except that Galveston is far more dangerous to humanity than Hitler's death squads ever were. They say their work with Ebola is for a vaccine, but the same technology can also be weaponized. Galveston is working to aerosolize Ebola just as Ft. Detrick worked to aerosolize Anthrax. Aerosolization of a biowarfare agent is always the tip-off to the development of a weapon to be delivered by air to human beings who will breathe it in. Ft. Detrick should be shut down as well because it too is an ongoing criminal enterprise.

Q: Besides Ft. Detrick and Galveston, are there any other biowarfare laboratories you believe should be closed?

A: All of them. Since 1981, the Pentagon has been gearing up to fight and "win" biological warfare without prior public knowledge and review. What's more, American universities have a long history of willingly permitting their research agenda, researchers, institutes, and laboratories to be co-opted, corrupted, and perverted by the Pentagon and the CIA into death science. These include Wisconsin, North Carolina, Boston U., Harvard, MIT, Tulane, University of Chicago, and my own University of Illinois as well as many others.

Q: Biological warfare development requires highly sophisticated technology and safe laboratories. No so-called "terrorist" group is known to possess anything like the requisite facilities. Besides America, what countries have operative biowarfare labs?

A: U.S., U.K., Russia, France, China, Israel, for sure. There are several other countries that the U.S. has established satellite biowarfare labs in.

Q: Is there any published data on USG's expenditures for biowarfare since 9/11? I assume it has taken off like other Pentagon outlays.

A: Yes, there are published figures on this in the open record. The last time I did a calculation from them the sum was approaching $100 billion. By comparison, in 2012 dollars we spent $30 billion on the Manhattan Project to develop the atom bombs that were then used to destroy Hiroshima and Nagasaki. You can see my book *The Criminality of Nuclear Deterrence* (Clarity Press, 2002), Chapter 2, "The Lessons of Hiroshima and Nagasaki." So that historical precedent and analogy is a pretty good indication that the U.S. offensive biowarfare industry is intended for use on human beings somewhere. The momentum behind the money propels inexorably towards use of the weapons.

Q: Does the recent Pentagon mail-out of live anthrax virus to eighty-six laboratories here and to seven nations abroad, bear out your prior criticism of USG's careless handling of these pathogens?

A: Of course. But I don't believe there was anything "careless" or "accidental" about any of this. The Pentagon knows exactly what they are doing. They are not "incompetent" at the Pentagon. This was deliberate. Just like the anthrax attacks of October 2001 were deliberate.

Q: You contend that the American pharmaceutical industry and the World Health Organization (WHO) are dumping dangerous vaccines in West Africa where the publics are already suffering from Ebola. Why would WHO get involved in this? Can you elaborate?

A: First, to make money. WHO is a front organization for Big Pharma. Second, to reduce the numbers of Black West Africans—genocide.

Q: It's been estimated that 36,000 Americans are dying every year from flu. By contrast, only five Americans died from an Anthrax attack and that was back in 2001. Yet, the National Institutes of Health (NIH) in 2006, a typical fiscal year, received only $120 million from Congress to fight flu but $1.76 billion for "biodefense"?

A: Right! These distorted budgetary allocations demonstrate that the priority here is not the promotion of the public health of American citizens but rather to further develop the U.S. offensive biowarfare industry that will someday "blowback" upon the American people with a catastrophic pandemic.

Q: Scientists who oppose the Pentagon's activity insist that germ-warfare defense is clearly impractical; that every person would have to be vaccinated against every harmful biological agent. Since that likely is clearly impossible isn't the only application of a defensive development in conjunction with offensive use?

A: We are currently stockpiling vaccines to immunize our civilian and military leadership elites for if and when they decide to wage offensive biowarfare. *Pace the Constitution*, "We the People of the United States" will have to fend for ourselves as best we can with our grossly underfunded and inadequate public health services that have been deliberately starved of money in order to feed the U.S. offensive biowarfare industry beast.

Q: Recently, Defense Secretary Ashton Carter told a St. Louis audience of government employees, "You're some of the nation's most innovative and inventive physicists, chemists, and geneticists . . . molecular biologists," etc. Yes, indeed. How many employees does the Pentagon now have in germ warfare work and how much is it costing the American people?

A: Overall I have read a figure that there about 13,000 death scientists in America today doing dirty biowarfare work who perversely call themselves "life scientists." Doctor Mengele would be proud of them all! As Doctor Strangelove said, "Mein Fuhrer, I can walk!" Seventy years after World War II ended the Nazis have won.

Q: Given all of the above, does it appear conceivable to you the Pentagon is developing a massive germ warfare weapon as a means of intimidating the world? After all, it has positioned itself in about 900 bases around the globe from which it can, and does, strike using conventional weapons, and it has used illegal radioactive ammunition in its war against Iraq.

A: Of course. But not just intimidation. The Pentagon and the CIA are ready, willing, and able to launch biowarfare when it suits their interests. They already attacked the American people and Congress and disabled our Republic with super-weapons-grade anthrax in October 2001. A fortiori they will do so again to foreign states and peoples when deemed convenient. Us too! They have a stockpile of that super-weapons-grade anthrax that they already used against us in October 2001.

Q: Thank you, Professor Francis Boyle.

A: Thanks so much for doing this interview.

Chapter 14

The Mass Rape of the Bosnian Women Was Genocide!

I delivered this public lecture at the request of the Women's Law Society at the University of Illinois College of Law on March 9, 2016, in honor of International Women's Day:

> I want to express my gratitude to the Women's Law Society for asking me to speak here today and especially in honor of International Women's Day. The WLS organizers asked me to talk about a problem related to women and human rights. Over my career since coming here in 1978—both practicing and teaching international human rights law—the most daunting problem I ever confronted was being the Lawyer for all the raped women of Bosnia and Herzegovina. I was the Attorney of Record for at least 20,000+ raped women of Bosnia before the International Court of Justice in The Hague, the World Court of the United Nations System. All 20,000+ of these raped Bosnian women were my Clients. I had originally figured 20,000 was a gross underestimate since rape is always underreported—especially during war time. When the war and the genocide were over, the United Nations got into Bosnia in order to investigate. I have read that the current UN estimate is that about 40,000 Bosnian Muslim women were raped during that war and genocide.

The Bosnian President Alija Izetbegović appointed me their General Agent with Extraordinary and Penitentiary Powers to represent the Republic of Bosnia Herzegovina before the International Court of Justice. That meant I was their Attorney of Record and their Ambassador to the World Court with responsibility to argue their case for genocide and to stop the genocide against the Bosnians. This lawsuit was the most important international human rights case ever filed at the World Court since it was founded in 1921. All I am going to do here is discuss one critical element of the case when

I argued to the World Court that the mass rape of the Bosnian women was genocide. I was given complete authority by President Izetbegović to argue this case as I saw fit, and the mass rape of the Bosnian women was a decisive component of this genocide lawsuit as I saw it.[1]

Even the Nazis during World War II did not engage in the mass and systematic rape of women as a technique of warfare, though the Japanese came very close to it against Chinese women during the Second World War. Bosnia was appalling! It seemed to me that what was going on there was not just rape—which in times of war is a war crime—but that what was going on there was genocide. Outright genocide! So I decided to argue that the mass rape of the Bosnian women was genocide to the World Court.

Now when I argued the case to the World Court I was operating on the basis of multiple and independent reputable human rights sources that what we were dealing with here was somewhere between 20,000 to 25,000 raped Bosnian Muslim women. If you look at the Genocide Convention, I was working with this definition in respect to arguing their case for genocide:

> Article II. In the present Convention, genocide means any of the following acts committed with intent to destroy in whole or in part, a national, ethnical, racial, or religious group, as such…
>
> (b) causing serious bodily or mental harm to members of the group…[2]

Certainly rape causes both serious bodily and serious mental harm to members of the group. In this case, Yugoslavian and Bosnian Serb Christian men were raping Bosnian Muslim women.

But that is only the *actus reus* of the crime of genocide that I just quoted to you. I also had to prove the *mens rea*, and in the case of genocide, this was a specific intent offense. So I had to argue and prove that these women were being raped because of their Muslim religion or because of their Bosnian nationality or because of their Bosnian Muslim ethnicity. So how did I do that? I compiled all the victims' statements we could get from United Nations Organs, the Council of Europe, reputable human rights organizations such as Amnesty International and Human Rights Watch, and put them all together and filed them with the World Court. And what type of evidence did I use to establish their genocidal specific intent by means of rape? Here, I am going to use some graphic language, but, hey, we are all adults here and we are lawyers. So that is just the way I had to argue the case:

I got numerous statements that, while these women were being raped, their rapists and the men surrounding them and oftentimes gang-raping them, said to them while they were in the process of raping and gang-raping them "Fuck Mohammad!" That proved that the rapists and gang-rapists were motivated because of the women's religion. Or the rapists and gang-rapists would yell to their victims while raping them "Fuck your Turkish mother!" Bosnians are not Turks. They are South Slavic people, but because they are Muslims, Serbs derogatively refer to them as Turks. I put that in there to indicate these women were being raped on grounds of nationality and ethnicity. And: "Fuck you, you Balija whore!" Balija is a Serb derogatory term for Bosnian Muslims. Ditto. And: "Fuck Alija!"—in reference to my Client the President of the Republic of Bosnia Herzegovina Alija Izetbegović, who was a Bosnian Muslim. Ditto. Etc.

I compiled all these statements I possibly could obtain and put them into a package and filed them with the World Court. It was not enough just to prove that these women were being raped. It was not enough just to prove that these rapists and gang-rapists were war criminals and sadists. I had to prove that in the process of raping them these Christian Serbs raped the Bosnian Muslim women for religious reasons or national reasons or ethnical reasons as required by Article 2 of the Genocide Convention that says: "committed with intent to destroy, in whole or in part, a national, ethnical, racial, or religious group, as such." I argued to the World Court that Christian Serb men were raping Bosnian Muslim women for national and ethnical and religious reasons.

I also argued to the World Court Article 2, paragraph (d) of the Genocide Convention to establish that the mass rape of the Bosnian women was genocide for a second count of the *actus reus* for genocide: "Imposing measures intended to prevent births within the group." And here, again, I used a multiplicity of victims' statements from all reputable human rights sources and organizations, that while these women were being raped and gang-raped, their rapists and the men surrounding them and their gang-rapists, were saying to them "We're going to give you a good little Serbian baby," or "We're going to give you a good little Serb baby." This is because in this South Slavic culture the ethnicity is deemed to descend from the father. So, technically, if you have a child born of a Bosnian Muslim woman raped by a Christian Serb father, the baby is deemed to be Serb. Also, "We're going to give you a good little chetnik baby!" Chetnik was a term for Serbian partisan resistance fighters during World War II. Nothing wrong with resisting the Nazis. But here these Christian Serb men were invoking the Serb term Chetnik while they were raping these Bosnian Muslim women.

Next, Yugoslavia and the so-called Bosnia Serb Army, which was in fact an arm of the Yugoslav National Army, maintained rape camps for Bosnian Muslim women throughout the Bosnian territories that they occupied. There Bosnian Muslim women were confined and reduced to sexual slavery, repeatedly raped and gang-raped, traded around, sold, and trafficked. If they became pregnant in these rape camps, we had numerous victims' statements that their captor-rapists told them: "We are going to make you stay here to give birth to a chetnik baby so that you do not get an abortion." Yet another violation of Genocide Convention article 2(d) that I filed with and argued to the World Court.

Finally, we had large numbers of Bosnian refugees up in Canada. The Clinton administration—Clinton was such a phony and a hypocrite on Bosnia, I won't go through it all here. But Canada was letting them in, while Clinton was not letting them into the United States on a large scale until after the Dayton Agreement. I called up to Canada and said, "I need five courageous women, victims of rape, willing to give me their statements that I will file with the World Court and they must also be willing to testify at the World Court in front of the entire world what happened to them." They got me the five courageous rape victims, we had their victim statements recorded, translated into English, and I filed them with the World Court.

At this beginning stage of the case I was simply trying to get what is called "an indication of provisional measures of protection." That is the international equivalent of a temporary restraining order and injunction against all acts of genocide. So the proceedings on the merits and the trial itself would come later on down the line. At this stage, I was just trying to stop the genocide and the war and the rapes. I fully intended to call as witnesses before the World Court as many rape victims as I could fit into the schedule for the trial on the merits.

To make a long story short, I won a massive overwhelming Order from the World Court against Yugoslavia. Three measures of protection, the first that Yugoslavia itself should cease and desist from committing all acts of genocide against Bosnia and the Bosnians. I won that measure unanimously. The second, that Yugoslavia must do everything in their power to stop all these paramilitary, military, terrorist groups, and criminal gangs that they had launched upon the Bosnians, including for the purpose of the mass rape of the Bosnian women as techniques of ethnic cleansing and warfare. I won that measure with only the Russian Judge dissenting. And then third, which I had requested, that Yugoslavia do nothing more to further extend or aggravate this dispute over genocide. I won that unanimously too.

So then my Order was transmitted to the United Nations Security Council for enforcement as required by the United Nations Charter. It was for the Security Council to enforce my Order that genocide and the raping be stopped because Yugoslavia did not stop the genocide and raping and indeed they continued it and escalated it. What did the Security Council do with my Order? Nothing! Clinton sabotaged its enforcement together with the British and the French and the Russians. So nothing was done.

Amazingly, instead of enforcing my World Court Order against Yugoslavia, these Great Powers then decided to punish Bosnia and the Bosnians by coming up with the so-called Owen-Stoltenberg Plan. This would have carved up the Republic of Bosnia and Herzegovina into three little chunks of land, destroyed our Statehood under international law, robbed us of our U.N. Membership, and subjected 1.5 to 2 million *more* Bosnians to ethnic cleansing. The Bosnian Apocalypse was staring me right in my face!

So I returned to the World Court asking for a second Order of provisional measures of protection to stop Owen-Stoltenberg. Then the very next day I flew to Geneva where I was the Lawyer for the Republic of Bosnia and Herzegovina at the Owen-Stoltenberg negotiations in order to stop them *in situ*. I sabotaged the whole damn thing right then and there. I made sure it never happened. And then I went back to the World Court and won that second Order—again—a massive overwhelming victory on behalf of the Republic of Bosnia and Herzegovina against Yugoslavia to cease and desist from committing all acts of genocide against the Bosnians, both directly and indirectly by means of their genocidal surrogates. That was the end of the Owen-Stoltenberg Plan.

When the war was over, President Izetbegović gave an interview in which he said, "We almost lost our State in the Fall of 1993," which was correct. I was there. Bosnia almost fell. All of Bosnia would have been turned into Srebrenica, and I later became the Attorney of Record for the Mothers of Srebrenica and Podrinja at the International Criminal Tribunal for the Former Yugoslavia. 8,000+ Bosnian Muslim men and boys were just exterminated, and many women were raped. We would have had at least another 100,000+ more dead Bosnians and another 40,000+ more raped Bosnian Muslim women if Bosnia had fallen in the fall of 1993.

But Clinton, Britain, France, and Russia refused to enforce my second World Court Order at the UN Security Council against Yugoslavia. Even most despicably, Clinton, Britain, France, and Russia sabotaged my strategy and our efforts to invoke the United Nations' Uniting for Peace Resolution (1950) in order to have the United Nations General Assembly enforce my World Court Order against Yugoslavia. And in the fall of 1993 Clinton finally came out of the closet and revealed his genocidal intention to carve up and destroy the Republic of Bosnia and Herzegovina.

Clinton hauled into the White House the Dutch Foreign Minister Kooijmans to serve as his stalking horse in order to do his genocidal dirty work for him. I had already briefed Kooijmans in his office at The Hague on these so-called Bosnian "peace" plans, saying they were all genocidal; that he should have nothing to do with them; and asked him to help us. Instead Clinton and Kooijmans came up with what they called the Contact Group Plan, which, again, would have done the same thing as Owen-Stoltenberg: Carve up the Republic of Bosnia and Herzegovina into three pieces, destroy Bosnia's Statehood under international law, and subject 1.5 to 2 million *more* Bosnians to ethnic cleansing.

So acting pursuant to my advice, President Izetbegović gave me the authority to sue Britain at the World Court for aiding and abetting Yugoslavia's genocide against the Bosnians and the Republic of Bosnia and Herzegovina. We really couldn't sue Clinton. Clinton was guilty as sin and deserved to be sued! But the only hope we had was that Clinton would change his mind. And among the other Permanent Members of the Security Council, the British were certainly the worst against us by far—though I had repeatedly offered to sue France and Russia at the World Court as well. Ditto for Croatia.

I set out to sue Britain to stop this latest Clinton/Kooijmans/Contact Group genocidal carve-up plan. I also set out to sue Britain at the World Court for aiding and abetting the Bosnian genocide, to stop the genocide, including the mass rape of the Bosnian women, and to break the genocidal arms embargo that the Security Council had illegally imposed upon the Bosnians in gross violation of their basic right to self-defense under UN Charter article 51. The Bosnians could not defend their women and their children. The Yugoslav National Army was one of the most powerful armies in Europe. After the Tito–Stalin split, Tito had armed, equipped, supplied, and trained the JNA to repulse an invasion by the Soviet Union. By comparison, the Bosnians had no heavy weapons of their own. They were being slaughtered. I could watch it live on CNN.

In response, the British then threatened the Bosnians to the effect that if they let me argue this genocide case against them at the World Court, we will starve you to death. It was the middle of winter. All the food supplies for the Bosnians came in at Sarajevo airport that was under the control of the British and French troops. The British just threatened to cut off the supplies then and there. So under those circumstances of extreme duress, we had to withdraw that lawsuit against Britain for genocide from the World Court. The British also said, "And by the way, fire Boyle!" The British and everyone else involved knew full well that so long as I was Bosnia's Lawyer at the World Court, I would use all the powers at my command and move heaven and earth to prevent their genocidal carve-up and destruction of my Client the Republic of Bosnia and Herzegovina and the further genocide of my Clients the Bosnians.

Well, alright, I was doing this case free of charge and *pro bono publico*. I wasn't paid a dime by the Bosnian government, whether for expenses or for fees. Indeed, I was eating my own expenses. It cost me $30,000 in out-of-pocket expenses to win those two World Court Orders that I took out of my own bank account and put on my American Express Gold Card. That money was paid back to me by a Bosnian woman living in Canada who took out a second mortgage on her home. So the Bosnian government brought in their own Bosnian lawyer to take my place. And then what happened? Here we get directly into feminist legal studies and international human rights law.

When I was flying back from the World Court to here in Champaign the day after winning my first Order, on that long airplane flight home I contemplated to myself: "Ok. I won this Order but now I'm going to have to prove it at the trial. And here, there's 25,000 raped women. I did win the temporary restraining Order but proving it in Court on the merits is another matter. I want this to be done in a way that would set a precedent for the future of all women. So I am really going to need an expert on both feminist legal theory and international human rights law to conceptualize this entire matter for me on setting up, proving, and winning that the mass rape of the Bosnian women was genocide." So I called up my friend Professor Kathleen Mahoney, who teaches at the University of Calgary Law School in Canada, and I asked her to handle all this for me and in particular to conceptualize how we are going to argue and win that the mass rape of the Bosnian women was genocide from a feminist legal studies perspective. She readily agreed to do it, free of charge and *pro bono publico*, eating her own expenses, and immediately set up a team of women lawyers there in Calgary and went to work on it for me.

What happened? After I was moved off the case, Bosnia's lawyers dismissed Professor Mahoney and her team and dropped the entire issue that the mass rape of the Bosnian women was genocide from the World Court lawsuit. They dropped it all completely from the proceedings. After I had deliberately put it right in there smack dab in the heart of the lawsuit as one of the critical elements of this genocide case right from the very get-go.

And then, when it came to the trial on the merits at the World Court, I was not there, but here. I did follow it from here and as far as I could tell, Bosnia's Lawyers did not have even one Bosnian woman victim of rape testify. I stand subject to correction by someone who actually attended the World Court trial in The Hague, but you had 20,000+ raped women, and Bosnia's lawyers did not call even one rape victim to testify as a witness? And this despite the fact that at the very beginning of these proceedings I had told the World Court that I had at least five rape victims and I was going to call them all to testify at the trial about what happened to them?

So of course in its Judgment on the merits, the World Court basically said, "Well Bosnia made the charge at the beginning of the lawsuit, but they didn't put on any evidence in the Memorial or in the trial to support it."[3] So it was summarily dismissed, and that was that. These 40,000 raped women of Bosnia were abandoned and betrayed by their own government! Likewise, the Mothers of Srebrenica and Podrinja were abandoned and betrayed by their own government! Ditto for the Women of Srebrenica!

Where do we stand now? My argument that the mass rape of women can constitute genocide was ratified by International Criminal Tribunal for Rwanda in the *Akayesu* case decided in 1998. *Akayesu* is the leading source of international legal authority that we have today that the mass rape of women can constitute genocide. As for Professor Mahoney, she and her team took all of their outstanding work and filed it with the International Criminal Tribunal for the Former Yugoslavia where it was used in the *Foca Rape Camp* case. The Serbs established and maintained rape camps. These Bosnian Muslim women were kept in these rape camps, they were repeatedly raped and gang-raped, they were traded around and sold and trafficked. Professor Mahoney and her team successfully argued to the International Criminal Tribunal for the Former Yugoslavia that their sexual slavery was a crime against humanity.

Now, that is a major advance for women in the development of international human rights law and of international criminal law. Up until that ruling, sexual slavery in war time had never been considered anything more serious than a series of war crimes. Thanks to Professor Mahoney and her team, sexual slavery is now a crime against humanity. More serious than a war crime, and just short of genocide.

For example I have tried to help the Sex Slaves in Korea that the male chauvinist pig militarists in Japan still call their "comfort women" that were designated for their own personal sexual "comfort." Well, clearly this is a crime against humanity—what the Japanese did to the Korean women and also to the Chinese women, the Sex Slaves over in China too, during World War II. And Japan still denies it as of today. In both cases, nothing meaningful has really been done to rectify these grave injustices, these crimes against humanity against the Korean women and the Chinese women by Japan. Most of these women have gone to their graves in silence and unvindicated. These Korean women and these Chinese women too have been abandoned and betrayed by their own governments.

Finally, overall, it has just been announced that on March 24, 2016, the International Criminal Tribunal for the Former Yugoslavia will issue its Verdict on Radovan Karadžić. Karadžić had been indicted for almost every crime in the ICTY Statute including two counts of genocide—one count for Bosnia in general and the second count for Srebrenica in particular. During the summer of 1993. I stopped Karadžić, Milošević, Tudjman, Boban, Owen, Stoltenberg, the United Nations, and the European Union from carving up and destroying the Republic of Bosnia and Herzegovina with the most catastrophic consequences for the Bosnians. We were all in Geneva together! And they had the backing of Clinton and Christopher working behind the scenes in Washington, DC in support of their efforts to destroy us. It will certainly be nice to see Karadžić finally get his just desserts after all these years!

Similarly, working on behalf of my clients, the Mothers of Srebrenica and Podrinja, I got the ICTY Prosecutor to likewise indict Slobodan Milošević for almost every crime in the ICTY Statute book including two counts of genocide—one count for Bosnia in general and the second count for Srebrenica in particular. He died while on trial in The Hague taking all his secrets with him.

How convenient for Clinton, Britain, France, Russia, the United Nations, and the European Union. Dead men tell no tales! I will have to study the Karadžić Verdict and figure out what more—if anything—can now be done on behalf of the 40,000 raped women of Bosnia, the Mothers of Srebrenica and Podrinja, the Women of Srebrenica, and the Bosnians. Thank you.

NOTES

1. See my book *The Bosnian People Charge Genocide!* (Davao: Aletheia Press, 1996), and my forthcoming book, *Stopping Serb Genocide Against the Bosnians!* (Sarajevo: Bosnia and Herzegovina, 2020).
2. G. A. Res. 260(III) A, *Convention on the Prevention and Punishment of the Crime of Genocide* (December 9, 1948).
3. *Application of Convention on Prevention and Punishment of Crime of Genocide* (Bosnia and Herzegovina v. Serbia and Montenegro), Judgment, 2007 I.C.J. 191 (February 26, 2007).

Chapter 15

What Is the Future for Bosnia and Herzegovina?

I gave this lecture before the Fisher Forum for the University of Illinois at Urbana-Champaign Russian, East European, and Eurasian Studies, where I am an Associate, on June 15, 2012:

> I served as Legal Advisor to the Republic of Bosnia and Herzegovina (RBIH) Delegation to the Vance-Owen Negotiations in New York in March of 1993. The Vance-Owen (V-O) Plan would have cantonized, paralyzed, and dysfunctionalized RBIH along the lines of Lebanon, but would have kept the existence of RBIH as a state under international law. When the genocidaire Radovan Karadžić rejected the V-O Plan, the Great Powers of the world including the Clinton administration decided to punish RBIH by terminating its existence as a state by means of imposing the Owen-Stoltenberg Plan. Clinton quickly abandoned his 1992 presidential campaign promise of "lift-and-strike": lift the genocidal arms embargo illegally enforced against RBIH by the UN Security Council, NATO, and the Bush Senior administration, while simultaneously launching NATO airstrikes against the Serbian heavy weapons then surrounding and mercilessly bombarding the Bosnian cities, especially Sarajevo. The RBIH Army of citizen-soldiers organized by my friend General Sefer Halilović had no heavy weapons or aircraft. But on April 8, 1993, I procured a NATO no-fly zone over RBIH. The Serbs could no longer murder the Bosnians from the skies!

I was the Lawyer for the entire RBIH Delegation at the Owen-Stoltenberg (O-S) negotiations in Geneva in the summer of 1993. The Owen-Stoltenberg Plan would have carved-up RBIH into three little statelets that would have never survived; destroyed RBIH as a state under international law; robbed RBIH of its U.N. membership; and subjected 1.5 million to 2 million *more* Bosnians to ethnic cleansing. At UN Headquarters in Geneva, the genocidal

O-S lawyer for the United Nations Paul Szasz admitted to me that Karadžić was the real author of the O-S Plan, which was then readily approved by Owen representing the European Union and its member states as well as by Stoltenberg representing the United Nations Organization. Szasz then re-drafted the genocidal O-S documents accordingly. Genocide by word-processor. The Banality of Evil.

I personally made sure that the Karadžić-Owen-Stoltenberg-Szasz genocidal carve-up of RBIH and the Bosnians never happened! In addition, acting pursuant to my advice and under instructions from the RBIH government, I tried to negotiate with O-S for an internal constitutional reorganization of RBIH along the lines of the Constitution for the Swiss Confederation. O-S obstinately rejected the Swiss model because that would have saved BIH as a state and the Bosnians as a people.

Over two years later in the fall of 1995, and following directly in the footsteps of the genocidal Karadžić-Owen-Stoltenberg Plan, the first draft of the Dayton Agreement that Richard Holbrooke gave to the RBIH Delegation would have constituted a de jure carve-up and partition of RBIH into two little statelets that were never designed to survive for very long: the Federation of Bosnia and Herzegovina versus Republika Srpska (RS). When I pointed this out to the RBIH Delegation in Dayton, they rejected it. Instead, Holbrooke imposed upon RBIH a de facto carve-up and partition of RBIH into these two little statelets that nevertheless did preserve BIH as a state and BIH's membership in the United Nations Organization. But that was the end of the Republic of Bosnia and Herzegovina as a legal entity. RIP: RBIH (1992–1995).

Pursuant to the Dayton Accords, on December 15, 1995, the Republic of Bosnia and Herzegovina was carved up in Paris by Richard Holbrooke, the United Nations Organization, the European Union Member States, the United States, and the many other states in attendance, despite the United Nations Charter, the Nuremberg Principles, the Genocide Convention, the Four Geneva Conventions and their two Additional Protocols, the Racial Discrimination Convention, and the Apartheid Convention, inter alia, as well as two overwhelmingly favorable World Court Orders this author had won for RBIH on April 8, 1993, and September 13, 1993. This UN-sanctioned execution of a UN member state violated every known principle of international law and human rights that had been formulated by the international community in the post–World War II era. Bosnia was sacrificed on the altar of Great Power politics to the Machiavellian god of expedience. In 1938 the Great Powers of Europe did the exact same thing to Czechoslovakia at Munich. The partition of that nation state did not bring peace to Europe then. Continued partition of Bosnia and Herzegovina will not bring peace to the Balkans or Europe now.

No thanks to the Butcher of the Balkans Holbrooke, after Dayton BIH was barely alive as a State and put on an international emergency life support apparatus, where it still remains today in a comatose condition. Since then, the Great Powers including the United States have been plotting, planning, and scheming all along to pull the proverbial plug on BIH's statehood under international law and eliminate BIH once and for all time. Holbrooke's genocidal Dayton Constitution was nothing more than a deliberate weigh-station and fig-leaf for the complete disintegration of BIH as a state under international law and its ultimate partition and absorption by Croatia and Serbia as plotted and agreed upon by Tudjman and Milošević at Karadjordjevo in March of 1991.

Pursuant thereto, ten years later in the fall of 2005, the Bosnian ruling Party for Democratic Action (SDA) asked me to give them a Legal Opinion on the advisability of agreeing to the so-called Hays Plan, which was later called the April Package. The SDA sent me the draft Hays Plan, which was then under negotiations among all the BIH political parties at the U.S. State Department, together with their notes on these negotiations. It was clear to me from reading these materials that the U.S. State Department fully intended to accommodate the wishes of the RS Delegation that the Hays/April Package further consolidate and cement the permanent existence of RS as a statelet as the next step towards the final dissolution of BIH as a state. I recommended to SDA in the strongest terms possible that they reject the Hays/April Package.

Immediately thereafter I appeared on a panel sponsored by SDA North America in the Chicago Metropolitan Area on the occasion of the BIH Statehood Day celebrations as their guest. On that SDA panel I publicly recommended against the Hays/April Package in the strongest terms possible in front of many powerful SDA leaders. Appearing on that same SDA panel with me was BIH's former foreign minister Muhamed Sacirbey who publicly agreed with my assessment that the Hays/April Package could prove fatal for the continued existence of BIH as a state.

Needless to say, I was shocked and stunned to learn that President Tihic of SDA then agreed to the Hays/April Package despite my negative advice after SDA had asked me for it and after prominent SDA member Sacirbey had publicly agreed with me before SDA North America. Because of the mortal dangers that the Hays/April Package posed to the very existence of BIH as a state, I proceeded to launch my Campaign against the ratification of the Hays/April Package by the BIH parliament. In this Campaign I was joined by many loyal and patriotic Bosnians with whom I had fought during the war and genocide against Bosnia, including and especially the Party for Bosnia and Herzegovina (SBIH) and its leader Haris Silajdžić.

When I went to bed the night before the vote by the BIH parliament on the Hays/April package, I had assumed we were going to lose the vote and that the final disintegration of BIH as a state would be only a matter of time. I woke up the next morning to the wonderful news that two loyal and patriotic SDA members had voted against the Hays/April Package despite Tihic's orders and therefore the Hays/April Package was dead. Bosnia and Herzegovina would live to fight another day! Silajdžić and SBIH then used this success and the momentum generated by our anti-Hays/April Campaign to trounce Tihic and SDA for the BIH presidency and parliament in the October 2006 national elections.

Holbrooke had founded the 1995 Dayton Agreement upon the basis of the March 1994 Washington Agreements that he had brokered between RBIH and Croatia. At the time someone at the Pentagon publicly admitted that what was really going on here was the slow-motion carve-up of RBIH that would take at most about fifteen years. So, sure enough, arriving right on schedule fifteen years after Dayton, came the 2010 Bosnian national elections that could not produce a government for almost fourteen months while the BIH state further disintegrated right before our very eyes. Under international law one of the most elementary requirements of a state is a government that works: No government, no state! And now it appears that the new BIH coalition government has just fallen apart after a mere five months in office over the pretext of a budgetary dispute in the run-up to the October 2012 elections.

This prolonged and near-terminal deadlock on the reconstitution of a BIH government has resulted in numerous calls by the so-called International Community (IC) and by some domestic Bosnian politicians such as SDA's Tihic for a "revision" or "reform" or "amendments" to the Dayton Constitution along the lines of the previously discredited Hays/April Package. It has been my public advice in Bosnia that under no circumstances must the Bosnians accept any so-called "amendments" to the fatally flawed and genocidal Holbrooke/Dayton Constitution such as a fictively revised Hays/April Package or any of its successors or modifications. That would be the equivalent of painting whitewash on the hull of the good Ship of State *BIH Titanic* as it slowly sinks to the bottom of the Adriatic Sea, to which BIH has access through the town of Neum that I saved for the Republic from Owen, Stoltenberg, Tudjman, and Croatia. Rather, Bosnia must hold out for and insist upon the complete replacement—not amendment—of the genocidal Holbrooke/Dayton Constitution. This replacement Constitution must be freely negotiated by all the representatives of Bosnian civil society along the lines of the Philadelphia Convention that gave the United States of America its Constitution in 1787 that replaced the congenitally defective Articles of Confederation.

Bosnia must convene an All–BIH Constitutional Convention! Bosnia needs a fully effective and functional Constitution for BIH that will regularly produce a BIH government that can actually work for the benefit of all of the citizens of Bosnia and Herzegovina irrespective of their national, ethnical, racial, or religious affiliations, and thus guarantee the existence of BIH as a state for the historical future. Time is of the essence! The clock is ticking. The International Community are systematically extinguishing all the lights in Bosnia. Soon the Great Powers will pull the plug on Bosnia and Herzegovina. We need an Arab Spring for Bosnia starting in Sarajevo! Thank you.

Chapter 16

Interview with Francis Boyle on Bosnian "Peace" [*sic*!] Negotiations

Professor Francis Boyle was General Agent for the Republic of Bosnia and Herzegovina before the International Court of Justice with Extraordinary and Plenipotentiary Powers and a member of the International Expert Team of the Institute for Research of Genocide in Canada.

On behalf of the victims of the aggression against Bosnia and Herzegovina and genocide against its citizens, the Institute for Research of Genocide in Canada thank you Professor Boyle for your contribution to the truth about these crimes and justice for the victims of these crimes. Please answer the following questions for us [on November 12, 2013]:

C: What I got from your background is that before you entered the negotiation, you were active in academics and law. You worked for the PLO and you were involved in the peace negotiations there but also you worked for the International Tribunal for Indigenous Peoples. In what ways would you say that your past experience influenced your work in the Bosnian negotiations?

FB: When the war and genocide against Bosnia started, shortly after its Declaration of Independence on March 6, 1992, I was serving as legal adviser to the Palestinian delegation to the Middle East peace negotiations. I had overwhelming responsibilities there, so I really could not do anything to help the Bosnians although I did monitor the situation. In the late summer, early fall of 1992, the chair of the Palestinian delegation, Doctor Haidar Abdul Shaffi asked me to draft the Palestinian counteroffer of what later became the Oslo Agreement. The whole fall was taken up by that matter. [. . .] Finally, I submitted that counteroffer to the Palestinian delegation in Washington and the PLO leadership in Tunis and President Arafat and then the peace negotiations broke down. It was early December 1992 when Israel deported some Muslims from Gaza into Lebanon. At that point, there was nothing more for me to do.

I felt terrible about the situation of the Bosnians. I did some research on the matter and I sent them a Memorandum of Law, it was mid-December 1992, recommending that they sue Yugoslavia, Russia, Britain, France at the International Court of Justice for violating the Genocide Convention and that we ask for an emergency special hearing of the World Court, where I would get an indication of provisional measures of protection for Bosnia against Serbian acts of genocide. I would try to break the genocidal arms embargo that had been legally imposed on Bosnia and try to stop the carve-up of Bosnia pursued by the Vance-Owen plan. To make a long story short, on March 6, 1993, I had a 45-minute conversation with the Bosnian Vice-president Ejup Ganic and I could hear the artillery shells going off in the background; it was surreal. [. . .] We went through the whole lawsuit and my strategy. At the end of it, he said he would recommend this lawsuit to President Izetbegović and that I should go out to meet him the following week for the start of the Vance-Owen negotiations. I spent the next week drafting the Application for Bosnia against Yugoslavia for genocide [. . .] and also Bosnia's request for provisional measures at the emergency hearing. That took a week. Then I flew out to New York to be with Izetbegović for the V-O negotiations. I advised him on V-O. Then I went through the lawsuit with President Izetbegović. I went through my strategy and approach. [. . .] Then he signed a full-powers for me appointing me as Bosnia's General Agent with Extraordinary and Plenipotentiary Powers before the World Court with instructions to sue Yugoslavia. [. . .] That was the start of my involvement in Bosnia.

C: At that point, what did you identify as the main issue to be addressed in the conflict? Was that ethnicity or nationalism, or socio-economic problems? What was going on in Bosnia according to you?

FB: It was outright genocide by Yugoslavia and Milošević against the Bosnians. They proclaimed independence as was requested by the European Union. The EU put out guidelines and said to Bosnia and Croatia that they needed to have elections. They had elections and they voted for independence and they were hit with genocide and aggression. Again, when that happened on March 6, 1992, there was nothing I could do to help them but a year later, I was in a position to help them.

C: Was that genocide caused by ancient hatred between the ethnic communities, as some would argue?

FB: It had nothing to do with ancient hatred! It was Milošević using nationalism to steal land and ethnically cleanse the Muslims and Croats who were living there, as well as Jews. There was no hatred by the Bosnian Muslims against Serbia or Yugoslavia or the Bosnian Croats or the Bosnian Jews. It was Milošević exploiting nationalism and ethnicity and religion to accomplish his objective of Greater Serbia. Just like Hitler wanted Lebensraum to the east, Milošević wanted Lebensraum to the west. He was using all that and exploiting it.

C: At the time of the Vance-Owen negotiations, the Carrington Plan, which proposed a loose federation of states in which the ethnic communities would be protected by minority rights, and the Cutileiro Plan that divided the country into three ethnic units had been rejected. Were you aware of those plans?

FB: I was aware of Cutileiro beforehand, but that was before I came in. I came in at V-O. That's where I got involved. [. . .] V-O had a lot of problems, as far as I could tell. It would have cantonized Bosnia along the lines of the work that Vance had done in Lebanon. Vance had been involved in the Lebanon negotiations too and he basically came up with a plan there to cantonize Lebanon. It didn't seem to work very well in Lebanon but I gave the President my best assessment of the situation and made it clear that the state would still be there. When I got to the World Court, Yugoslavia's lawyer [Shabtai Rosenne from Israel] argued that V-O had put us out of business as a state. As I correctly pointed out to the World Court, and they agreed with me, all V-O called for was an internal reorganization of our state and at that point in time, Izetbegović accepted it because it would preserve the state. He was willing to make compromises. His most important concern was to preserve the state. It was Karadžić who rejected V-O. The World Court agreed with my interpretation of V-O that it was simply a plan for an internal reorganization of the Bosnian state. What was most critical for President Izetbegović and for me was to keep the state intact; that at the end of the day, there would still be a state of Bosnia-Herzegovina, which there still is today, twenty years later, despite the attempts by the entire world to destroy that state.

C: As you said, V-O specifically tried to prevent Bosnia's partition . . .

FB: It was not a partition, that is correct. It would have cantonized Bosnia along the lines of Lebanon and perhaps it would have paralyzed that state. Indeed, in the Dayton Agreement, basically what Holbrooke did was apply V-O to the Federation and then de facto carve up the rest of it. That is why even the Federation itself has a hard time working. It is pretty much the cantonization of the V-O scheme, based on the Lebanon scheme of Vance, that many of Vance's advisers had worked with him on in Lebanon. That pretty much paralyzed Lebanon during the civil war. But the critical factor was to keep the state. A second point to keep in mind is that V-O also served as the "green light" for Croatia and President Tudjman to invade the Republic of Bosnia-Herzegovina and commence his campaign of ethnic cleansing in western Bosnia, in those areas that were allocated to the Bosnian Croats under Vance-Owen. That is not just my interpretation. That was the interpretation of the ICTY. I was contacted by them and asked to serve as their expert in the prosecution of General Blaskic on all these peace plans which I agreed to do. Their working theory of the case was that V-O really gave Tudjman the "green light" to seize and steal those areas of Bosnia that had been allocated to the Bosnian Croats. I think that is also a correct interpretation of the situation. I don't know if that was Vance's intention, but certainly that is the way Tudjman saw it.

C: In the reasoning behind this solution by V-O, you mentioned Vance's history in Lebanon. Do you think there are certain characteristics or that there is something in their professional background that made them likely to opt for the V-O territorial solution? For example, they had a history in Rhodesia, but also a lot more international negotiators came in at this stage so perhaps there was a focus on the international system rather than on national states. Do you think anything like that mattered?

FB: As I said, I think in trying to be fair to Vance, who is now deceased, Vance was involved in the Lebanon peace negotiations, which I had studied. Lebanon was a multi-ethnic, multi-religious state. I think that he figured . . . not that I discussed it with him, but I think that he and his people figured that they could take the cantonization scheme from Lebanon and apply it to Bosnia. That was my assessment. That is certainly what I had advised President Izetbegović. It was the President's decision, however. I did not advise the President whether or not to accept V-O. That was not for me to decide as I saw it, as long as it preserved the state. It was the President's decision to accept V-O. He did because it would have preserved the state of Bosnia-Herzegovina despite the cantonization.

C: Officially V and O drew their lines not on the basis of ethnicity, expressing the wish to create multi-ethnic cantons. But if you look at the map, ethnicity does come into play . . .

FB: It certainly came into play. There is no question about it. What they said in public was one thing; what they did in private was another. We have to understand that between Vance and Owen, it was Vance running the show. Owen just sort of went along for the ride. Later, with Owen-Stoltenberg, Vance resigned because that was real dirty work and he didn't want anything to do with it. At that point, Owen was running the show. This was really Vance and his people . . . Again, I am not here to criticize Vance. I think he figured that that was the best he could do under these circumstances. I don't know what to say about that.

C: What made them revert to and accept this ethnic separation of Bosnia?

FB: I guess Vance figured it sort of worked in Lebanon, so he would try it in Bosnia. But again, I can only read Vance's mind and the document, because I never discussed it with Vance. President Izetbegović dealt with Vance. I was outside the room, listening to the negotiations. I wasn't in the room with Vance. I was advising the President on elements of the plan and what the consequences might be. That the consequences could be that you would have a government that is paralyzed, as did happen in Lebanon, although the state would still be preserved. As far as President Izetbegović saw it, preserving the state was the most important factor here.

[. . .]

C: What I try to get at is how in this case Vance and Owen came to that decision.

FB: As I said, I think it was primarily Vance. He was running the show. That was clear. He was the de facto representative of the U.S. Government. Everyone knew that. Even though he technically represented the United Nations, everyone knew that Vance was there speaking pretty much on behalf of the U.S. Government. He had been former Secretary of State. That's the way people looked at Vance, that he had the backing of the U.S. Government behind him. Of course, Vance never said that, to the best of my knowledge, but that is the way people looked at Vance.

C: You mentioned that he took a lot of the negotiators that he worked with in Lebanon with him to Bosnia. Would you be able to remember any of the names of those people?

FB: I can't remember. You'd have to research that. But I think he had some of the same staff working with him on Lebanon. [. . .]

C: And after the V-O plan had been rejected, you got Stoltenberg and Owen . . .

FB: What happened then was this Bill Clinton in his 1992 campaign for the Presidency . . . In order to get votes, he said that if he were elected, his policy would be "lift and strike" for Bosnia. He would lift the genocidal arms embargo that had been illegally imposed on the Bosnians, and then he would strike by air the Serbian Yugoslav artillery positions surrounding all the Bosnian cities and blowing the hell out of them, which you could watch live on CNN. So President Izetbegović accepted V-O on that assumption, that if it had been rejected by Milošević or Karadžić, that Clinton was going to go forward with his promise and lift and strike. So what happened was the President accepted V-O. I argued successfully to the World Court that V-O did not terminate our existence as a state but that the Republic would continue. Then Milošević did accept V-O and Karadžić rejected it. Everyone knows that Karadžić was a puppet for Milošević, so Milošević could have been using Karadžić as a cat's-paw here to say they were rejecting V-O. What Milošević really wanted was the agreement he had with Tudjman in 1991 to split Bosnia between the two of them. He wanted half of Bosnia. My guess is that Milošević was just using Karadžić as a cat's-paw. Rather than rejecting V-O himself, he had Karadžić reject it.

C: Do you think that at that point in time, the international negotiators were also convinced that territorial separation between the ethnic communities was necessary for peace in Bosnia?

FB: That is not the way Vance saw it, no.

[. . .]

The Europeans, like Owen and the rest of them, would have been happy to see Bosnia carved up, but I don't believe that that was the position of Vance because if you read the V-O plan, it cantonized Bosnia but it didn't carve us up.:

[. . .]

When it became clear that there would be no lift and strike, no enforcement of the World Court order, Vance resigned, turning the thing over to Owen because the next stage was to destroy the Republic of Bosnia-Herzegovina as a state. Vance knew it. He knew this was a real piece of dirty work and he didn't want his good name associated with that. I am not here to support Vance, I am just trying to give you my assessment of the situation. David Owen, or actually the entire European Union, came in, and took over the show. He recruited Stoltenberg from Norway because he knew the Nobel Peace Prize came out of Norway. So he figured that if he would have Stoltenberg on his team and he produced a deal, that would give him the inside track on the Nobel Peace Prize. I dealt personally with Owen and Stoltenberg and Stoltenberg was just a "yes"-man and a bootlicker. All the decisions were being made by David Owen.:

[. . .]

Europe just did not want a Muslim state in Europe. It was that simple. It went back to the Crusades.

[. . .]

This has to do with anti-Muslim prejudice in Europe going back to the Crusades, at least. At that time, before 9/11 2001, we really didn't have that in the United States. We didn't have experience with the Crusades and all the rest of that. But eventually, Clinton would go along with a carve-up too.

[. . .]

C: By the time the Owen-Stoltenberg proposal was on the table, did you think it was possible for the ethnic problems to be overcome by reconciliation or did you deem it necessary to separate the ethnic communities?

FB: I agreed fully with President Izetbegović. I was instructed and authorized to negotiate a Switzerland for Bosnia. [. . .] It works. It is a great success. What would have been wrong with a Switzerland for Bosnia? That was the impetus behind that Union of Republics, the idea to negotiate a Switzerland for Bosnia. I felt, certainly at the time, that if there had been good faith on the part of O and S, which there was not, we could have negotiated a Switzerland that would have preserved Bosnia as a state and protected the rights of all the ethnic groups in Bosnia, but it was not to be.

C: Why do you think that O and S were not susceptible to these ideas? Is there something in their background or in their way of thinking that disallowed them to think in these lines?

FB: Yeah, I dealt personally with David Owen. He is a typical British, imperialist, establishment, racist individual who believed Muslims were an inferior race of people. We were just supposed to do what he told us to do. I made it clear that that was not going to happen on my watch.

C: And there was consensus on that within their negotiation team?

FB: It was Owen running the show. Stoltenberg just sat there and didn't say anything and Szasz [their lawyer] carried out Owen's instructions. So he was running the show. That was the team: David Owen. He had full power from the members of the EU to do this, to get rid of Bosnia. That was the plan of the British Government at the time, under John Major and all the Tories. All except Margaret Thatcher, who supported us, but she was out of power.

C: So there wasn't a team of civil servants working with them? It was only the three of them?

FB: Well, Owen also had the entire British secret service up there in Geneva, following our every move and tapping our phone calls. But the key operatives are the people I told you Owen, Stoltenberg, and their lawyer Szasz. I dealt with all three of them. Owen, it was clear . . . You know, when he was in the negotiations, he didn't even pay attention to Stoltenberg. Stoltenberg was just there for the show because Owen was hoping, if he got the deal, that if Stoltenberg was there, he could get the Nobel Peace Prize. That's all Stoltenberg was there for. But technically, Stoltenberg was representing the UN. He should have stood up for all the member states and our existence, but he didn't. He went along with it.

C: You mentioned that your critique and the World Court orders did not really influence O and S, that they stuck with their plan and could not change it into a Swiss model like the one that you proposed . . .

FB: After the second World Court order [. . .] Owen had pretty much been discredited. That then is why President Clinton turned to [Dutch Foreign Minister] Kooijmans to spearhead the next "peace" plan, which was the Contact Group Plan, which was a reformulation of O-S.

C: Did you find support for your ideas or for your alternative among any international diplomats? Were people susceptible to look at these alternatives?

FB: The entire world was against us, including the U.S. Government. Warren Christopher called up the Turkish Ambassador and told him to tell President Izetbegović to sit on me. That's how spineless Warren Christopher was. Of course, the President wasn't going to do that, because he knew that I was helping to keep Bosnia alive. The whole world . . . Look, Bosnia was sent up to Geneva in late July–early August 1993 to be destroyed and everyone knew it. They all knew it. Everyone. The U.S. knew it; that's why the Foreign Service officers quit. The U.S. supported it, Europe supported it, the European Union supported it. I had a meeting with most of the Muslim ambassadors in Geneva and I briefed them on it. They knew it. One of them said to me, "What can we do about it?" We were abandoned and betrayed by all of Europe and the U.S. and in the Muslim world there wasn't much that they could do about it because we were there in the heart of Europe.

C: So as far as you know, no alternatives—not towards Bosnian unity but also not towards really splitting the country up with an international border—were discussed by these teams?

FB: We were given a diktat, just like Hitler, take it or leave it.

C: And amongst themselves, before presenting it to the Bosnians?

FB: I can't say amongst themselves. I wasn't part of their team. I can only say that . . . We did get a first O-S draft, which I didn't analyze, but the second draft – that was the operative document – was clearly genocidal.

C: Would you happen to still have that first version?

FB: I do, but these are all confidential documents. I really can't give them out.

C: Can you give me information on what the differences were between the first and the second draft?

FB: I never got to them, because in about twenty minutes they showed up saying, "There is a new document. Karadžić just showed up and this is the one that we are dealing with." It was by then 7 at night and I needed to have my analysis by 8 am the next morning. I spent the whole night analyzing the [. . .] second draft. I never looked at the first draft. I never had a chance.

[. . .]

C: Clearly, from day one the international community tried to split the state internally. Do you know if any other borders than ethnic borders were considered?

FB: That's what happened when we got to Dayton. The first draft of Dayton, by Richard Holbrooke, which I read, would have been a de jure carve-up of the Republic of Bosnia-Herzegovina into two states, two mini-states; the Federation of Bosnia-Herzegovina and the Republic of Srpska. I did point this out to President Izetbegović and to his credit, he insisted on the preservation of Bosnia and Herzegovina as a single state, so this became a de facto carve-up but not a de jure carve-up, which is what we have today.

[. . .]

It is kind of pathetic, isn't it? That the fate of an entire state and 4.5 million people are in the hands of four or five men, yet that is what happened.

C: And would you say, looking back, that the international negotiators saw ethnicity as an unchangeable human trait that was necessarily going to lead to conflict in the case of Bosnia?

FB: They just wanted to carve us up and get rid of us because we were an annoyance to the Europeans and the Americans. We were creating lot of problems for them. As Clinton said when he refused to lift and strike, he said, "I have bigger fish to fry with the Europeans." When you add in Europe the blatant anti-Muslim attitude that most Europeans had going back to the Crusades, that can probably account for it. Here in the U.S., certainly prior to September 11, 2001, there wasn't a great deal of anti-Muslims hysteria. Now there is, but back in those days, there wasn't. But you know, the Bosnians, we would stand up and fight for our existence. We would not give in. This was an irritant for them.

C: But if Bosnia was an annoyance, why would that make them want to carve it up?

FB: To get rid of us; to solve the problem. If you would get rid of Bosnia as a state . . . if it were carved up between Croatia and Serbia, there is no annoyance anymore except you accept the massacres. That was that.

Chapter 17

Stopping Genocide by the Government of Sri Lanka against the Tamils

I delivered this lecture before the Second International Conference on Tamil Nationhood and Genocide in Sri Lanka at Carleton University in Ottawa, Canada, on May 5, 2018:

> The Hindu-Christian Eelam Tamils living on the island known as "Sri Lanka" have been the victims of genocide as defined by the 1948 Convention on the Prevention and Punishment of the Crime of Genocide by the Sinhala-Buddhist Government of Sri Lanka (GOSL). I say that because of my practical experience: On April 8, 1993, and again on September 13, 1993, I won two World Court Orders on the basis of the 1948 Genocide Convention that were overwhelmingly in favor of the Republic of Bosnia and Herzegovina against Yugoslavia to cease and desist from committing all acts of genocide against the Bosnians in violation of the 1948 Genocide Convention—both directly and indirectly—for a sum total of six different provisional measures of protection. This was the first time ever that any government or lawyer had won two such Orders in one case since the World Court was founded in 1921. In addition, on August 5, 1993, I also won a so-called Article 74(4) World Court Order for Bosnia against Yugoslavia for genocide to the same effect. According to ICJ Statute Article 74(4), when the Full Court is not in session in The Hague, the President of the Court exercises the full powers of the Court and can issue an Order to the parties in a lawsuit that is legally binding upon them. The fact that the Hindu-Christian Eelam Tamils have been victims of genocide by the Sinhala-Buddhist GOSL only strengthens and reinforces their right to self-determination under international law, including establishing their own independent state of Tamil Eelam.

Article II of the Genocide Convention defines the international crime of genocide in relevant part as follows:

> In the present Convention, genocide means any of the following acts committed with intent to destroy, in whole or in part, a national, ethnical, racial or religious group, as such:
>
> (a) Killing members of the group
> (b) Causing serious bodily or mental harm to members of the group
> (c) Deliberately inflicting on the group conditions of life calculated to bring about its physical destruction in whole or in part
>
> . . .

Certainly the Sinhala-Buddhist GOSL and its legal predecessor Ceylon have committed genocide against the Hindu-Christian Eelam Tamils that actually started on or about 1948 and has continued apace until today in violation of Genocide Convention Articles II(a), II(b), and II(c).

For the past seven decades, the Sinhala-Buddhist Ceylon/Sri Lanka have implemented a systematic and comprehensive military, political, and economic campaign with the intent to destroy in substantial part the different national, ethnical, racial, and religious group constituting the Hindu-Christian Eelam Tamils. This Sinhala-Buddhist Ceylon/Sri Lanka campaign has consisted of killing members of the Hindu-Christian Eelam Tamils in violation of Genocide Convention Article II(a). This Sinhala-Buddhist Ceylon/Sri Lanka campaign has also caused serious bodily and mental harm to the Hindu-Christian Eelam Tamils in violation of Genocide Convention Article II(b). This Sinhala-Buddhist Ceylon/Sri Lanka campaign has also deliberately inflicted on the Hindu-Christian Eelam Tamils conditions of life calculated to bring about their physical destruction in substantial part in violation of Article II(c) of the Genocide Convention that still goes on today as we convene here now.

Since 1983 the Sinhala-Buddhist Ceylon/Sri Lanka has exterminated approximately 300,000 Hindu-Christian Eelam Tamils. Nevertheless, apologists for Sinhala-Buddhist Ceylon/Sri Lanka have argued that since these mass atrocities are not tantamount to the Nazi Holocaust against the Jews, therefore they do not qualify as "genocide." Previously, I had encountered and refuted this completely disingenuous, deceptive, and bogus argument against labeling "genocide" for what it truly is, when I was the Lawyer for the Republic of Bosnia and Herzegovina successfully arguing their case for genocide against Yugoslavia before the International Court of Justice. There the genocidal Yugoslavia was represented by Shabtai Rosenne from Israel as their lawyer against me. Rosenne proceeded to argue to the World Court that since he was an Israeli Jew, what Yugoslavia had done to the Bosnians was not the equivalent of the Nazi Holocaust against the Jews and therefore did not qualify as "genocide" within the meaning of the 1948 Genocide Convention.

I rebutted Rosenne by arguing to the World Court that you did not need an equivalent to the Nazi Holocaust against the Jews in order to find that wholesale atrocities constitute "genocide" in violation of the 1948 Genocide Convention. Indeed the entire purpose of the 1948 Genocide Convention was to prevent another Nazi Holocaust against the Jews. That is why Article I of the Genocide Convention clearly provided: "The Contracting Parties confirm that genocide, whether committed in time of peace or in time of war, is a crime under international law which they undertake *to prevent and to punish*" (emphasis supplied). You did not need six million dead human beings in order to constitute the international crime of "genocide."

Furthermore, in support of my 1993 genocide arguments to the World Court for Bosnia, I submitted that Article II of the 1948 Genocide Convention expressly provided: "In the present Convention, genocide means any of the following acts committed with the intent to destroy, *in whole or in part*, a national, ethical, racial or religious group, as such . . ." (emphasis supplied). In other words, that to be guilty of genocide a government did not have to intend to destroy the "whole" group as the Nazis intended to do with the Jews. Rather, a government can be guilty of genocide even if it intends to destroy a mere "part" of the group. Certainly Yugoslavia did indeed intend to exterminate all Bosnian Muslims if they could have gotten away with it, as proven by their subsequent mass extermination of at least 7,000+ Bosnian Muslim men and boys at Srebrenica in July of 1995. I would later become the Attorney-of-Record for the Mothers of Srebrenica and Podrinja as well as for the Women of Srebrenica at the International Criminal Tribunal for the Former Yugoslavia (ICTY). In that capacity, I convinced the ICTY Prosecutor Carla Del Ponte to indict Yugoslav President Slobodan Milošević for almost every crime in the ICTY Statute for the atrocities he inflicted upon the Bosnians, including two counts of genocide: one count of genocide for Bosnia in general, and the second count of genocide for Srebrenica in particular. Notice 7,000+ murdered human beings were enough to constitute genocide as far as the ICTY Prosecutor was concerned. Milošević died while on trial in The Hague after the ICTY itself denied his Motion to Dismiss these charges after the close of the Prosecution's case and sustained all of the charges against him including and especially the two counts of genocide: genocide in general in Bosnia, and genocide in particular against the 7,000+ Bosnian Muslim men and boys at Srebrenica.

But in 1993 it was not necessary for me to argue to the World Court that Yugoslavia intended to exterminate *all* the Bosnian Muslims. Rather, I argued to the World Court that at that point in time the best estimate was that Yugoslavia had exterminated about 250,000 Bosnians out of the population of about 4 million Bosnians, including therein about 2.5 million Bosnian Muslims. Therefore, I argued to the World Court that these exterminated Bosnian Muslim victims constituted a "substantial part" of the group and that the appropriate interpretation of the words "or in part" set forth in Article II of the Genocide Convention should mean a "substantial part."

The World Court emphatically agreed with me and rejected Rosenne's specious, reprehensible, and deplorable arguments. So on April 8, 1993, the International Court of Justice issued an Order for three provisional measures of protection on behalf of the Republic of Bosnia and Herzegovina against Yugoslavia that were overwhelmingly in favor of Bosnia to cease and desist from committing all acts of genocide against all the Bosnians, both directly and indirectly by means of their Serb surrogates. This World Court Order for the indication of provisional measures of protection was the international equivalent of a U.S. domestic Temporary Restraining Order and Injunction combined. The same was true for the Second World Court Order with three additional provisional measures of protection that I won overwhelmingly for the Republic of Bosnia and Herzegovina against Yugoslavia on September 13, 1993, on the basis of the 1948 Genocide Convention. You can read the oral and written submissions and the debates between Rosenne and me that I made in order to win these World Court Orders against genocide in my book *The Bosnian People Charge Genocide!* (Aletheia Press, 1996).

In its final Judgment on the merits in the *Bosnia* case that was issued on February 26, 2007, the World Court definitively agreed with me once and for all time that in order to constitute genocide, a state must only intend to destroy a "substantial part" of the group "as such":

In other words, in order to find the Sinhala-Buddhist GOSL guilty of genocide against the Hindu-Christian Eelam Tamils, it is not required to prove that the Sinhala-Buddhist GOSL has the intention to exterminate *all* Hindu-Christian Eelam Tamils. Rather, all that is necessary is to establish that the Sinhala-Buddhist GOSL intends to destroy a "substantial part" of the Hindu-Christian Eelam Tamils.

Furthermore, in paragraphs 293 and 294 of its February 26, 2007, *Bosnian* Judgment, the World Court found that you did not even need 250,000 exterminated Bosnians in order to constitute genocide, let alone six million exterminated Jews. Rather, even the 7000+ exterminated Bosnian Muslim men and boys at Srebrenica were enough to constitute genocide. According to the World Court, these victims constituted about one-fifth of the Srebrenica community. Certainly since the World Court ruled in its 2007 Judgment that the extermination of 7000+ Bosnians at Srebrenica constituted "genocide," then a fortiori and in spades the Sinhala-Buddhist GOSL extermination of about 140,000 Hindu-Christian Eelam Tamils in Vanni only two years later in 2009 also constituted genocide.

Historically the only way a people who have been subjected to genocide like the Hindu-Christian Eelam Tamils by the Sinhala-Buddhist GOSL have been able to protect themselves from further extermination and final annihilation has been the creation of an independent state of their own. Indeed the entire world witnessed during the first six months of 2009 the Sinhala-Buddhist GOSL wantonly, openly, shamelessly, and gratuitously exterminate about 140,000 Hindu-Christian Eelam Tamils in Vanni. Yet not one state in the entire world rose to protect them or to defend them or to help them in any way as required by Article I of the 1948 Genocide Convention as well as by the *jus cogens* (i.e., peremptory norm) customary international law obligation "to prevent" their genocide. The same was true for the entirety of the despicable United Nations Organization itself. So much for the world's mythical and hypocritical and meaningless and propagandistically bogus doctrine of "responsibility to protect" (R2P). The documentation for these assertions can be found in the Second Edition of my book *The Tamil Genocide by Sri Lanka* (Clarity Press, 2016).

Hence the need for the Hindu-Christian Eelam Tamils to create their own independent state in order to protect themselves from further extermination and total annihilation by the genocidal Sinhala-Buddhist GOSL that still transpires today. International law and practice prove that an independent state of their own is the only effective protection as well as the only appropriate reparation for a people who have been the victims of genocide. Bosnia's Statehood was the only thing that prevented the Bosnians from going the same way the Jews did in 1939. The creation of the independent state of Tamil Eelam will be the only thing preventing the Hindu-Christian Eelam Tamils from going the way of history. As we meet here today, the genocidal Sinhala-Buddhist GOSL is "deliberately inflicting on the [Hindu-Christian Eelam Tamils] conditions of life calculated to bring about [their] physical destruction in whole or in part" in gross and flagrant violation of Genocide Convention Article II(c) and the *jus cogens* customary international law obligation to the same effect, inter alia. Once a genocider, always a genocider!

In order to prevent yet another and predictable wholesale slaughter and acts of genocide by the already-proven genocidal Sinhala-Buddhist GOSL against the Hindu-Christian Eelam Tamils, Article I of the Genocide Convention requires: "The Contracting Parties confirm that genocide, whether committed in time of peace or in time of war, is a crime under international law which *they undertake to prevent and to punish*" (emphasis supplied). Pursuant to these twin obligations, I respectfully submit that this Conference must "undertake to prevent and to punish" the Sinhala-Buddhist GOSL for its still ongoing genocide against the Hindu-Christian Eelam Tamils by founding a Boycott, Divestment, and Sanctions (BDS) Campaign against the genocidal Sinhala-Buddhist GOSL.

So if you are asking me: "What can be done and how can we do it?" Go back and study what the entire world did to dismantle the racist genocidal/apartheid Afrikaner regime in South Africa and do the exact same thing to the racist genocidal/apartheid Sinhala-Buddhist GOSL and for the exact same reasons: a BDS Campaign! I was involved in large numbers of cases in this earlier campaign against the racist genocidal/apartheid South Africa defending anti-apartheid resisters. You can read about it in my book *Defending Civil Resistance under International Law* (Transnational Publishers Inc., 1987). This included obtaining the first acquittal ever of anti-apartheid protesters in Chicago at the South African Consulate, *Chicago v. Streeter* (1985). We even made the *New York Times* on that one. I know apartheid and genocide when I see them!

The racist genocidal/apartheid regime in South Africa that we were up against for all those years hired some of the top law firms and lobbying firms in the United States to oppose what we were doing. But eventually they lost and we won because we had Truth and Justice on our side! Today, there is no racist genocidal/apartheid regime in South Africa. Sure they have their problems—we have a lot of problems ourselves. But genocide and apartheid are not two of them.

So this is not a case of our reinventing the wheel here. We already have the wheel! Obviously, there is no way in this brief paper that I can deal comprehensively with all the legal reasons for and strategies behind dismantling the racist genocidal/apartheid regime in South Africa. Fortunately, I have analyzed those at great length in my book *Defending Civil Resistance Under International Law*. You can also obtain a *Special Paperback Edition* (1988) of this book expressly written *For Pro Se Protesters* at Amazon.com for $10. The extensive materials set forth in this book have already been successfully used all over the United States to help dismantle the racist genocidal/apartheid regime in South Africa. Almost identical legal arguments and strategies can be applied *ceteris paribus* to dismantle the racist genocidal/apartheid Sinhala-Buddhist GOSL regime.

To the same effect is the Palestinian Boycott, Divestment, and Sanctions (BDS) Campaign against the racist genocidal/apartheid Zionist regime in Israel. The historical origins behind and the legal arguments in support of the Palestinian BDS Campaign against the racist genocidal/apartheid Zionist regime in Israel can be found in my books *Palestine, Palestinians and International Law* (Clarity Press, 2003) and *Breaking All the Rules* (Clarity Press, 2008). Today the Palestinian BDS Campaign against the racist genocidal/apartheid Zionist regime in Israel has spread all over the world. It was recently nominated for the Nobel Peace Prize. Almost identical legal arguments and strategies can be applied *ceteris paribus* to dismantle the racist genocidal/apartheid Sinhala-Buddhist GOSL regime.

Go after the Sinhala-Buddhist money! People's precious money is something everyone in the world understands and appreciates. Going after their money was something the racist genocidal/apartheid Afrikaner regime in South Africa well understood. Because of that economic motivation in significant part, they ultimately released Nelson Mandela and commenced good faith negotiations with the African National Congress (ANC). The racist genocidal/apartheid Afrikaner regime in South Africa was dismantled. Their racist genocidal/apartheid Afrikaner Bantustans for the Black inhabitants of South Africa were terminated. Today the Black citizens in the apartheid-free Republic of South Africa are now able to determine their own future. The Tamils can do it too!

I cannot predict the future. But given the heavy dependence of the already-bankrupt racist genocidal/apartheid Sinhala-Buddhist GOSL economy on imports and exports such as tourism, textiles, tea, overseas remittances, etc., I think a worldwide BDS Campaign can reduce the racist genocidal/apartheid Sinhala-Buddhist GOSL to their knees within no more than a decade—maybe sooner. Then the Sinhala-Buddhists will have to deal with the Eelam Tamils!

The racist genocidal/apartheid Sinhala-Buddhist GOSL are not going to do this by themselves: Once a genocider, always a genocider! The United States government is not going to do it. The deplorable and atrocious United Nations Organization is not going to do it. It is up to you and me to do it! We must take the future of the Eelam Tamils and of Tamil Eelam into our own hands! Found the anti-GOSL BDS Campaign! Stop the ongoing GOSL genocide against the Eelam Tamils and Tamil Eelam! Start the Tamil BDS Campaign here and now! We will have Truth and Justice on our side! Thank you.

Chapter 18

The Native Hawaiian Independence Movement

This is my keynote address requested by the Office of Hawaiian Affairs before their Hawaiian Governance Symposium on Independence, Honolulu, November 1, 2014:

RESTORE THE KINGDOM OF HAWAII!

Thank you and Aloha. I am very happy to be here today speaking with you. I have one simple message that I want all the Kanaka Maoli to understand: There is a Convention coming up and I am asking all 135,000 Kanaka Maoli on the list to go to this Convention and vote to restore the Kingdom of Hawaii. It's so simple I want to repeat it: All 135,000 of you go to the Convention and vote to restore the Kingdom of Hawaii that was illegally stolen from you by the United States government in 1893. It's that simple.

You are the Kanaka Maoli. You are a people with the right of self-determination under international law and you are the only people in Hawaii with this right of self-determination. No one else has it, only you, the Kanaka Maoli. As a group of 135,000 people, you must go to this Convention and exercise your right of self-determination, to restore the Kingdom of Hawaii. This is your right of self-determination, go out and do it. This is what self-determination is all about. No one is going to give you your Kingdom back. You must do it yourself.

Now yesterday, Bumpy Kanahele[1] and I had a press conference in which Bumpy announced that he and his Ohana are going to the Convention and he, Bumpy, is going to make a motion to restore the Kingdom of Hawaii and to establish a provisional government of national unity for it. I want everyone to go to that Convention and vote to restore the Kingdom of Hawaii and to establish a provisional government of national unity.

We have the Kingdom. It was never lawfully terminated in the first place. The United States government illegally attacked and invaded the Kingdom of Hawaii in violation of several treaties that Hawaii had with the U.S. promising perpetual peace and amity—that meant forever—and those treaties were violated.

Despite what the previous speaker said, that this did not violate any intertemporal rule, the rule of international law at that time was: treaties must be obeyed! And they weren't. They were violated. Even the United States government's own Constitution expressly said in Article 6 that treaties are the supreme law of the land. In 1893 the United States government violated those treaties and violated its own Constitution. Nothing could be clearer. It also committed an act of war against the Kingdom of Hawaii in violation of its own Constitution.

Under the laws of war, the United States government is nothing more than the illegal belligerent occupant of the Kingdom of Hawaii, pure and simple. Nothing more than that. And the State of Hawaii is nothing more than the civilian arm of these military occupation forces. Under the laws of war at that time, the belligerent military occupation forces of the United States obtained no sovereignty over the Kingdom of Hawaii. Sovereignty always remained with the Kingdom of Hawaii. That's black-letter laws of war.

The Kingdom of Hawaii was and still is the displaced sovereign. It is still there. It has never been terminated. It still exists as a legal entity. But we must restore it. That can only be done by you, the Kanaka Maoli as a people with the right of self-determination going to this Convention and voting overwhelmingly, unanimously, all 135,000 of you, must go and vote to restore the Kingdom of Hawaii. When you do that, there is no way anyone in the world can deny your sovereign will!

Now, when you get there to this Convention, and you vote to restore the Kingdom of Hawaii, we have to have a government. A state must have a government to govern it, both internationally and domestically. And that is why I am recommending that the second act at this Convention would be to establish a provisional government of national unity for all Kanaka Maoli, all of you, even those who did not show up at the Convention. I understand that many of you have good-faith problems with going to this Convention. Fine. My advice is in this book, which was just published, *Restoring the Kingdom of Hawaii* (Clarity Press, 2015), explaining step-by-step why and how I think you can do it. I encourage you to read the book. But if you don't want to go, don't go. But I am encouraging all 134,000 of the rest of you to go and to vote. And don't go there to establish an Indian reservation. We don't want an Indian reservation! That's a one-way path to extermination. We want our Kingdom of Hawaii back, not an Indian reservation.

It's very clear if you read Act 195, the people who drafted it thought: "well, we're going to try to turn the Kanaka Maoli into an Indian tribe with an Indian reservation." But if you read 195, it says nothing about the ultimate outcome. It's clear, as I analyzed in my book, instead you can go there and vote to restore the Kingdom of Hawaii.

The hell with their Indian reservation! How dare they come in here and tell us Kanaka Maoli—and I was adopted into the Ohana Council by Bumpy years ago—how dare anyone tell us that we're going to become an Indian reservation, with all due respect to the Indians. They have a lot of problems of their own. But we, out here, are Kanaka Maoli! We have the Kingdom of Hawaii! It's still there as the displaced sovereign and we need to restore the Kingdom of Hawaii. But we have to have a government.

We have to have a government to run the Kingdom, to govern the Kingdom, for all Kanaka Maoli. Those at the Convention, those not at the Convention, those in the Diaspora. Set up a government and move forward from there. And in my book I trace out all the elements, the legal arguments for why you can do this.

I did work for President Vytautas Landsbergis on the restoration of the Republic of Lithuania. If the Lithuanians can do it, we can do it too. Why not? If the Estonians can do it, we can certainly do it. What's the difference between them and us? None that I'm aware of!

And also the work I did with the Palestinians. In 1987 I told the Palestinians: Set up your own state, declare independence, and move forward, to raise your diplomatic recognition and ultimately to membership in the United Nations Organization. I am telling you the same thing! Today the state of Palestine, this week was recognized de jure by Sweden, that's 135 states. It took 26 years, but we did it. And on November 29, 2012, the United Nations General Assembly recognized Palestine as an Observer State, just like Switzerland was before Switzerland became a full-fledged U.N. member state.

Well, we can do that too! But to do that we have to restore the Kingdom of Hawaii first. Then we have to set up a provisional government of national unity—exactly the way I set it up for the Palestinians where they too have a provisional government to govern their affairs internationally. That's exactly what we can do with the very successful precedents of both the Palestinians and the Lithuanians.

In our case we are going to have it easier than the Palestinians did, because they had to start out de novo from the beginning. They did not have a preceding state like we do, the Kingdom of Hawaii, and the legal continuity is still there for us. The Kingdom has just been displaced, not destroyed by the United States. It's called a displaced sovereign. The Kingdom is there. We have to work to restore the Kingdom of Hawaii, and only you, the Kanaka

Maoli, can do it, though of course with support from your colleagues and friends who are now not Kanaka Maoli.

Once this is done, you've restored the Kingdom of Hawaii, and then you have a provisional government of national unity for it, you must build up that state, the Kingdom of Hawaii, from the ground and the seas of Hawaii on up and out. You must provide for basic health care and education and food and housing and everything else for your people that the Kingdom of Hawaii and any other state must do. But you already have the basic infrastructure here to do that. Bumpy and I were talking about that yesterday. You have one trust for the education of Kanaka Maoli children. That's your Department of Education right there. They educate your children. You have another trust for land, Homestead Act, that provides for your homes. Health care, you have a hospital and a trust there.

So you go through all these trusts you already have out here for Kanaka Maoli and there the laws will work for the Kingdom to provide everything you need for your own people. Again, you build the state, the Kingdom, from the ground up. Exactly what Bumpy has been doing out there at his Village, building the Kingdom of Hawaii, from the ground up. We need to do that all over the islands, all over Hawaii, build the Kingdom from the ground up.

In addition, then, what you're also going to have to do, this provisional government of the restored Kingdom of Hawaii, at the same time is to work outward to get diplomatic recognition from other states. Again, this is exactly what the Palestinians have done. They have built up their state from the ground up in Palestine by providing food, health care, education, police services, administration, to their own people, but at the same time reaching out to other states to get diplomatic recognition.

And here, you're already ahead of the game. The Kingdom of Hawaii already had treaties and formal de jure diplomatic recognition with many other states of the international system at that time. Indeed, the Kingdom of Hawaii was part of the European System of Public International Law at that time. That was the Wisdom of your Kings and your Queens. They understood full well that they had to reach out to the entire world and have as many treaty relations as possible with other states, including embassies, consulates, and joining the Universal Postal Union. So what the Kingdom of Hawaii needs to do there, then, is to reach out first and foremost to all those states that the Kingdom had these relations with and the provisional government saying: "Hey, we're back. Here we are. We were just in a state of suspended animation for a period of time because of the illegal belligerent occupation by the United States. But we now want to resume diplomatic relations that we already had with you. We just want to resume them. And all you have to do is act in a manner to behave that the treaty we had with you still exists. It was never denounced. It's still there." And then the Kingdom of Hawaii provisional government could go to the Universal Postal Union and say: "Well, we're a party, we always have been a party, but due to the United States illegal attack and invasion in violation of international law at that time, we were not able to effectively exercise our membership. But now that is what we are going to do."

So the provisional government of national unity, in addition to taking care of your own people at home, has to go back around the world and resume all these relations and then reach out to other states that the Kingdom did not have diplomatic relations with at the time. As I said, the Palestinians, it took them 26 years, to go from zero to 135 states, Sweden, as of last week. 135 states out of 193, and soon all of Europe is going to fall in line as well. Someday, Palestine will have membership in the United Nations Organization. The only thing keeping them out has been the threat of the veto by the United States government and I have devised a means whereby at any time they intend to do so, they can overcome that threatened veto and join the United Nations as a full-fledged U.N. member state. It's really up to them to decide when to do this.

Well, that's the time frame we're looking at here. It took the Palestinians 25 years to do it. In my opinion, it will probably take the Kanaka Maoli 25 years. What's 25 years in the history of the Kanaka Maoli, going back forever. You people have been here since time in memoriam. 25 years is the bat of an eye. Hopefully I'll be here 25 years from now and I can celebrate your joining the United Nations Organization with you over in Iolani Palace. But we can't get there until you, the Kanaka Maoli go to this Convention, all 135,000 of you, vote to restore the Kingdom of Hawaii and then to set up a provisional government of national unity for it.

And all of that, I wrote this book expressly for that reason. The instructions are here, the details are here, it's written in plain English. Any Kanaka Maoli with an 8th-grade education can read this book and understand it. So it's there, you can read it and understand it.

So that's what we're talking about, 25 years. One-third of a lifetime. My Mom just turned 89, so I think I'll live as long as my Mom, and that means I'll be here in 25 years when you're admitted to the U.N. But you have to start the process now. You have to go to the Convention, vote to restore the Kingdom of Hawaii.

Finally, let me conclude with this process by the Department of the Interior and their proposed rules. These rules are mean, nasty, vicious, cruel, brutal, condescending, racist, and genocidal against the Kanaka Maoli. When has the United States government ever had the best interests of the Kanaka Maoli at heart? Never! Of course not! They want to turn you into an Indian tribe, with an Indian reservation, so they can better get rid of you just as they have done with large numbers of Indian tribes and Indian reservations over history. So we don't want federal recognition along those lines or the Department of the Interior. Last time I looked, Hawaii is not "interior" to the U.S. The U.S. is 2300 miles that way. They need a globe of the world to see we're not part of the U.S. out here in Hawaii. The Department of Interior, go home and stay home Yankee!

Finally, what type of federal recognition do we want? We want President Obama to recognize the Kingdom of Hawaii. That's what we want. We do not want recognition as an Indian tribe with an Indian reservation. The President of the United States of America has exclusive plenary power to recognize nation states. President Obama can do this all by himself without any approval or authorization by the U.S. Congress or by any court. He can recognize us as the Kingdom of Hawaii, and that's what we want.

President Obama owes this to the Kanaka Maoli and the Kingdom of Hawaii. He was born here. He was raised here. He was educated here. President Obama lived the formative years of his life here in Hawaii. And at a minimum, he owes the Kanaka Maoli to recognize the Kingdom of Hawaii. But again, none of this will happen unless you all 135,000 Kanaka Maoli on that list, go to the Convention, vote to restore the Kingdom of Hawaii, and set up a provisional government of national unity for it. Thank you.

TOWNHALL MEETING WITH THE NATION OF HAWAII AT WAIMANALO, OAHU

Saturday August 20, 2016

Bumpy [Kanahele] asked me to speak at the [Iolani] Palace tomorrow and I said I would, no problem there. But I said, how about if I come out a day early just to listen to what everyone has to say? Not me to talk, but me to listen to what you have to say because the last time I was here I didn't get a chance to listen to anyone. OHA set me up! Some of you were there in November 2014. OHA told me this was going to be a day-long session: The morning would be devoted to independence and then the afternoon session would be devoted to Federal recognition—turning the Kanaka Maoli into an Indian tribe. I said fine, as long as half the day is devoted to independence, that's okay with me.

I came out and got there at William McKinley High School, with a statue of William McKinley out there, and I thought: Well this is a pretty curious place for OHA to be having a seminar on independence. But I didn't say anything. So they had a coffee-and-donut session for all the speakers beforehand and I went back there. I don't mean any disrespect here to anyone who is an Indian. I work with Indians too. But everyone there was an Indian lawyer except me. So where were the speakers in favor of independence? I thought the whole morning was supposed to be about independence and restoring the Kingdom?

So I had to take a break from them. I just thought: Obviously I've been set up here. So I went out in the front yard and looked at William McKinley. And I thought, this is appropriate: OHA is having a forum, half of which is supposed to be devoted to independence, at the William McKinley high school right there with William McKinley standing and looking down upon us all.

I went back in and the first speaker was some idiot from Estonia. I have no idea where they lined this guy up, I had never heard of him. But he was there on Skype. And he said: "Well, the U.S. destroyed the Kingdom of Hawaii and that's that and there's nothing you can do about it." That was the first speaker, if you can believe it, on a half-day session devoted to independence. Of course that guy was an idiot because I have worked with Lithuanian President Vytautas Landsbergis on the restoration of their State after it had been occupied and annexed by Stalin and the Soviet Union. So in my comments, I said, well if the Estonians can do it then we Kanaka Maoli can do it! I'm part of Bumpy's Ohana here. We can do it! What's the difference?

I spoke for half an hour. Indeed, I was originally told it would be forty minutes and then when I got on the podium they said: "Well you get 30 minutes." I thought, okay, I'm a lawyer, so I stick to my timeframe. I came in at 29 minutes. Some of you were there. You can see the speech I gave on their OHA webpage [reprinted above]. But I was told 30 minutes, that's it. I was planning 40. Okay. So I made the speech in 30 minutes instead of 40.

Now I think OHA was really shaken up because as I said: "Well look all you Kanaka Maoli have to do—all 135,000 of you—is get together and restore the Kingdom of Hawaii. You have this Article 195 procedure. Go right ahead, get together and restore it. And no force on earth could possibly stop you!" And then the Nation's Chanter got up and said: "Well Professor Boyle, how about 40,000?" And I said: "Sure, 40,000 would do it as well!" I want to commend the Chanter and his Mother because his chant before I spoke gave me strength among the snakes there at OHA.

So then came on after me, instead of other independence advocates, were these two Indian lawyers. I thought, okay, I'll listen to what they have to say. It was clear OHA had paid them a large amount of money to do an official study for them on why the Kanaka Maoli should become an Indian tribe. Some of you were there. You heard these two lawyers—I'm not criticizing them one way or the other—but it's clear they were paid a large amount of money. Do you know how much OHA paid me to come out there? I got a $500 honorarium *less* my out-of-pocket expenses. And they bought me the worst possible seats on the airplane you could possibly imagine. They wouldn't even recline!

So I listened to the first speaker, and then I listened to the second speaker. I thought: "This is a setup. They're sandwiching me in between speakers designed to argue that you Kanaka Maoli should become Indians rather than restoring your Kingdom." So when the second speaker came out and he said: "Well you Kanaka Maoli can get your rights as indigenous peoples too." We know that's a crock! There are rights of indigenous peoples. It'll be a cold day in hell before you get any of those rights! We have a Kingdom, why should we revert to nothing more than rights of an indigenous people? So at that point I thought: "This thing is no more than a setup and I'm not going to have anything more to do with this. And I'm not going to be on a panel with these Indian lawyers arguing that the Kanaka Maoli should become Indians as opposed to restoring the Kingdom." So I walked out with Bumpy. We had a nice lunch and I went home. But regretfully I did not have a chance to talk to any of you and to hear your concerns.

When Bumpy asked me first to come out here in 1993, I said: "I'd be happy to speak, but I want you to take me out and meet all your people, to meet them and hear what they have to say." So Bumpy did. And I remember in 1993 out on the Big Island and there was a beach encampment, people living out there, and I was speaking on the beach in some type of shelter. And after I was done a very elderly Kupuna said to me: "Professor Boyle, why are you the first person to come out here and tell us what our rights are?" I didn't have an answer to her question, but I was glad I was the first one to go.

So that's why I'm here today. I am not here to give you a lecture. You heard my lecture there that I gave at OHA even though I was set up by those people, and it is on their webpage and it is reduced to 30 minutes and it's based on my book, which you can read if you want to. Bumpy has some copies here. [*Restoring the Kingdom of Hawaii* (Clarity Press, 2015)]. I'm just here to listen this time to what you people have to say—the Kanaka Maoli have to say and their supporters. I'm not here to lecture today. I want to hear what you have to say because in formulating my opinion, my advice to give to you and to Bumpy and to other leaders I deal with here who ask for my advice, I have to know what you're thinking.

Now, let me conclude with one point, which is that I think OHA was really shaken up by what I had to say: That 135,000 of you could go out and restore the Kingdom together, united, pursuant to your right of self-determination. Now if you want to hear a debate on this, it's with Poka [Laenui] and me, the night before on Kioni Dudley's TV program. It's on their website. It's a 3-hour debate I had with Poka. I'm not questioning Poka's good faith, but it was a very rough debate back and forth between the two of us arguing this out. And then someone from Keanu's [Sai] group came in too. And we all argued it out. So I was there and we argued it out—you can listen to the debate between Poka, disagreeing in good faith with me and my position. I know people out here have disagreements in good faith.

But I think OHA was shaken up, that they were worried that that's exactly what you're going to do. That 135,000 of you were going to get together and proclaim the Restoration of the Kingdom of Hawaii and that would be that. There would be nothing at that point anyone could do to stop you!

So they set up this fraudulent little Na'i Aupini process, OHA did, I think to head that off. I didn't say anything. I thought if OHA is going to do it, let's see what comes of it. But it seems to me OHA did that to head off 135,000 Kanaka Maoli coming together and restoring independence, the Kingdom. So they had preselected delegates that were acceptable to OHA, many of them, and it was not grassroots for all of you getting together. There were intermediates then, and OHA controlled the process and it seemed to me from a distance—now I was back in Champaign so I could only follow on the computer—that OHA was moving towards an Indian tribe.

Now, Bumpy went. Good! Good for Bump! Bumpy stayed for eight days and he tried to raise all these concerns and they shut him down. So finally Bumpy said "I had enough of this" and walked out. I put out a little *Statement* in support of Bumpy for walking out. It seems to me at this point I would hope Federal recognition is dead in the water. I guess in the lame-duck session of Congress after the elections, who knows what Obama and his people are going to do. That's a serious danger before Obama walks out of there. But my assessment is that that's where we are today. At this point I've come to listen to what you have to say. So those are my comments. I'm really here today to listen. That's it. Thanks.

SPEECHES AT IOLANI PALACE ON FAKE STATEHOOD DAY

Sunday August 21, 2016

Aloha. I'm very happy to be with you here today to talk about the fake state of Hawaii under international law. This is a fake and bogus state of the United States of America and everyone knows it. The United States of America is 2,000 miles that way. I just flew in over the Pacific Ocean the other night.

France tried to do the same thing with Algeria. They invaded Algeria. They annexed Algeria. And then they determined that Algeria was a department of France, like a state or province in France. No one believed that and certainly the Algerians didn't believe that—that's for sure! And today Algeria is a free and independent state and a member state of the United Nations Organization and most of the French have gone home. Some want to live there. That's fine.

Now I'm not going to review the entire history of the Kingdom of Hawaii and the Kanaka Maoli here. I've written a book which you're free to get. Bumpy has extra copies there, *Restoring the Kingdom of Hawaii*. And I have a beautiful picture on the back of Pele, drawn by a Kanaka Maoli artist who gave me the permission to put it on the book.

When the U.S. invaded the Kingdom of Hawaii in 1893 it was clearly an illegal invasion. There was a treaty that the U.S. had with the Kingdom of Hawaii guaranteeing peace and amity forever in perpetuity. They paid no attention at all to these solemn commitments, even under the terms of their own U.S. Constitution. Article 6 guaranteed that treaties are the supreme law of the land. They grossly violated this treaty and perpetrated an act of warfare on the Kingdom of Hawaii and even again in violation of another provision of their own Constitution. Article 1 section 8 says that only Congress can authorize and approve warfare. Congress never approved any warfare against the Kingdom of Hawaii and the Kanaka Maoli.

So nothing could be clearer that today the U.S. is the illegal occupant of the Kingdom of Hawaii and the Kanaka Maoli, and that the bogus State of Hawaii is nothing more than the agent, the instrument, of the illegal, belligerent occupant of the Kingdom of Hawaii known as the U.S. government. Now, when the U.S. invaded Hawaii in 1893, it became what is known under the international laws of war at that time as the belligerent occupant. The belligerent military occupant of Hawaii. What did that mean?

Number one, the U.S. never gained any sovereignty over Hawaii and the Kingdom of Hawaii. Belligerent occupation cannot transfer sovereignty and the U.S. never got sovereignty here in Hawaii. Second, under the laws of war, sovereignty resides in the hands of the displaced sovereign and in this case, the Kingdom of Hawaii and the Kanaka Maoli. Indeed, the Kanaka Maoli here in Hawaii have the right of self-determination under international law. Indeed, the Kanaka Maoli are the only people out here in Hawaii who have a right of self-determination under international law. It's that simple and that is what we are doing here today. We are exercising our right of self-determination and to denounce the bogus, fake state of Hawaii. And I say "we" because Bumpy Kanahele and the Ohana Council adopted me into the Ohana Council as far back as 1993. So yes, I'm Hanai, and I have a right here to speak on behalf of our Ohana.

So the U.S. and the fake State of Hawaii are nothing more than the belligerent occupation of the Kingdom of Hawaii. Now under the laws of war, if the U.S. wants to set up a puppet state and a puppet government to occupy Hawaii by means of belligerent occupation, it can. There's nothing illegal under the laws of war with setting up a puppet government and a puppet state. And that's what this fake State of Hawaii is all about. It's a puppet state and a puppet government of the U.S. acting here only pursuant to the laws of war. It's the civilian arm of the U.S. military occupation forces and that's the way you have to look at it.

The U.S. has paid absolutely no attention to the laws of war and belligerent occupation out here in Hawaii. They've tried to conquer, annex, dominate, exterminate you Kanaka Maoli, but you are still here. You are still in possession of your land and are a People with a right of self-determination exercising power over your own land. This is what sovereignty is all about and that's why we are here today. As an exercise of sovereignty and self-determination for the Kanaka Maoli and also the Kingdom of Hawaii. We're here in both causes together.

Now the normal rule when a treaty has been violated so grievously as the U.S. government did by waging illegal warfare against the Kingdom of Hawaii is what is called restitution. They must restore the situation to what it was before the violation. In the case of the Kingdom of Hawaii, as I explain in greater detail in my book, the U.S. government has the obligation to restore the Kingdom of Hawaii and evacuate Hawaii. Leave Hawaii! Lock, stock, and barrel! And allow the Kanaka Maoli to exercise their right of self-determination. Restore the Kingdom of Hawaii! Terminate this bogus, fake State of Hawaii and move on toward international recognition and membership in the United Nations Organization!

Now you might say: "Oh Professor Boyle, isn't that a pipe-dream?" Not at all! In 1987, I appeared at the United Nations as a guest of the Palestinians to talk about their future and at that time I said: "The time has now come for you Palestinians to unilaterally create your own state and then move for international recognition and membership in the United Nations Organization!" That's exactly what they did! On November 15, 1988, they adopted their Declaration of Independence and today, the State of Palestine has de jure diplomatic recognition from 136 states in the world. And Observer State Status at the United Nations Organization in 2012. That took 25 years of hard work and organization, but they did it—and living under a most brutal colonial genocidal military occupation where, today, Palestinians are being shot dead like dogs in the street. Yet they still resist on their own land! And I have devised the means whereby they can overcome the veto by the United States government [at the Security Council] to join the United Nations Organization as a full-fledged member state.

You Kanaka Maoli can and must do the same thing! Because the only protection the modern world has developed from genocide and extermination and assimilation and elimination is an independent state of your own: Restoring that Kingdom of Hawaii and then moving for international recognition of that Kingdom and eventually membership in the United Nations Organization. No

United Nations member state has ever been destroyed, and we must get to that point. It might take us 25 years like it did for the Palestinians. But if they can do it, we can do it too!

Now, as I said, then, this so-called "statehood" was bogus, completely. It was controlled, dominated, orchestrated by the U.S. government to set up a puppet state under the laws of war with a puppet government and we all know, they over there do whatever the Yankees tell them to do. So fine. But they're still a gang of puppets, and they have no validity at all under international law and they know it. They know that this is your land! They know that they stole it from you! They know that they destroyed the Kingdom of Hawaii! They know you Kanaka Maoli have the right of self-determination! They know they must restore the Kingdom of Hawaii to you as well as your lands and your oceans and your fish and your beaches and all your other natural resources!

But again, they are not going to do it voluntarily. It is up to you, the Kanaka Maoli, to demand it as you're doing here today. You are demanding your rights under international law. You are denouncing the fake State of Hawaii that has no legality or credibility at all. And you are demanding the Restoration of your Kingdom. Your Kingdom still exists as a legal entity. It is what we call a "displaced sovereign." It is up to you the Kanaka Maoli to bring it back to life. From the ground up, to build the Kingdom of Hawaii and to restore it. If the Palestinians can do it, you can certainly do it as well. There's no doubt in my mind that you can!

Now in addition, however, one of the requirements of an independent state under international law is a government. We have a State and by the way, that puts us ahead of the Palestinians. They did not have a state as of 1988. But now they do and it is recognized de jure by 136 states and the United Nations in 25 years. But we have a State, the Kingdom of Hawaii, it's just a displaced sovereign. So we just have to bring it back to life. That's what we have to do. That's what you have to do. That's why I flew all the way out from Chicago to Honolulu Friday night—just to help to restore this Kingdom of Hawaii back to life!

But to do this we're going to need a government and government structures to guide and direct the process. The Palestinians have their provisional government guiding their State's establishment until they can have democratic elections in a free unoccupied Palestine. So we need a provisional government out here and a provisional government of national unity.

Now, I've been coming out here to Hawaii since 1993. I've lectured all over the Islands. I've met many people and Kupunas and I know you all have good faith disagreements about how to proceed from here. In the comments I made yesterday, I didn't criticize any Kanaka Maoli leaders except OHA. They're clearly going for an Indian tribe. That's for sure, and we don't want to go in that direction. Look what the Americans did to the Indians! That's a one-way path to extermination! So OHA are Indian tribers, and in my opinion, we cannot rely upon them for any direction at all because they're moving towards this Indian tribe, this so-called Federal recognition as an Indian tribe. That will be the end of us for sure. And OHA knows it because I've told them so!

We need alternative leadership! A provisional government of national unity. Now, involving all of your Kupunas and your leaders, and to try to come together and put aside your good faith disagreements and to move forward, to restore the Kingdom of Hawaii, throw out the United States of America and its bogus, fake State of Hawaii. They have to go!

Now, we also have one other example from history of this being done, and that is Mahatma Gandhi in India. As we know, Gandhi applied his strategy and theory of *Satyagraha*, "truth-force," non-violent but truth-force. Forcing yourself upon the colonial occupying oppressor and demanding that they leave. Clearly Gandhi was a man of the East, not of the rotten, corrupt, decadent West. Gandhi had it all figured out from his own cultural and religious heritage. You can read it in his book *Satyagraha*. That's what we need here.

Satyagraha is consistent with your Spirit of Aloha. They're the exact same thing and that's what we need here. *Satyagraha* and the Spirit of Aloha together along with each and every one of you as self-determining Kanaka Maoli doing whatever you can to force the United States of America and this fake state of Hawaii out of here by means of Aloha and *Satyagraha*. I believe it can be done!

Gandhi threw the mighty British empire out of the entire Indian subcontinent with *Satyagraha*! Certainly I think the Kanaka Maoli using *Satyagraha* and your Spirit of Aloha can throw the mighty American empire out of the Kingdom of Hawaii and take its fake state with it along the way out the door and on the airplane home! But to do that, to move forward, we're going to need your leaders and your Kupunas to come together and try to set up this provisional government of national unity where you can all work together on this agenda. It can be done! It will be done! But it is up to you!

Finally, Bumpy asked this question about filing genocide charges against the United States for genocide against the Kanaka Maoli and the answer is yes! I was the Lawyer for the Republic of Bosnia and Herzegovina that filed genocide charges for them against Yugoslavia. I won two Orders of provisional measures of protection for the Bosnians against Yugoslavia to cease and desist from committing all acts of genocide against them. Now, that's the first time ever any lawyer had won two Orders in one case since the World Court was founded in 1921. So my opinion is: yes, we can, but not right away.

Now I had mentioned to you before the work I did with Palestinians starting from 1987 when I first said we should create our state until 2012 when we became an Observer State at the United Nations by vote of the UN General Assembly. So at that point I then advised the Palestinians that we are now in a position to sue Israel for genocide against the Palestinians at the International Court of Justice. This is a matter of public record. The Palestinian leadership—their Provisional Government for the State of Palestine—is considering it as we speak. If and when I get instructions, I'll file that lawsuit!

That being said, we're behind the Palestinians in terms of the establishment of our Statehood. We have to get to the point where they are, and then I could file genocide charges against the United States government. So what does that mean? It's up to all of you to get us to that point, to restore the Kingdom of Hawaii. To set up this provisional government of national unity like the Palestinians did so that I could act to file a genocide lawsuit against the United States.

As a matter of fact, I already argued genocide for the Kanaka Maoli in 1992 at the San Francisco Tribunal where my client and friend, the late Kekuni Blaisdell, showed up with his Ohana. I agreed to represent them and to argue their case before the San Francisco Tribunal, that the Kanaka Maoli were victims of genocide. And I explain this in my book here, if you want to read it, and chapter 1 is entitled "Kanaka Maoli Genocide." After my arguments for the Kanaka Maoli, my presentation of the case, the Tribunal of seven international human rights experts ruled as follows:

> The Tribunal further accepts a motion by the Prosecutor for the Native American Peoples to amend the face of the Indictment to include the following allegation which the Tribunal unanimously finds has been sufficiently proved by the evidence it has received.

Notice it says unanimous. Everyone agreed. The case was so clear-cut that the Kanaka Maoli were victims of genocide, as I argued to them. And what was their Ruling? This is their Ruling:

> The Federal Government of the United States of America has perpetrated crimes of genocide against the Kanaka Maoli (the Indigenous Hawaiian People) and has engaged in actions constituting gross violation of their human rights and their right to self-determination. All of which threaten to render the Kanaka Maoli extinct.

That was unanimous on two points: One, Kanaka Maoli have been a victim of genocide. Two, you have a right of self-determination, which I discussed in my first speech here today. It's up to you. It's in your hands. If you want to see any of this done, it's got to be done by you. We lawyers can't work miracles, I'll tell you that. It's up to your People to exercise self-determination to restore the Kingdom of Hawaii and toward that end to establish this provisional government of national unity. And then I can sue the United States government for genocide at the International Court of Justice. Thank you.

NOTE

1. Puuhonua Kanahele is the long-term leader of the Native Hawaiian Independence movement.

Chapter 19

Amnesty International Is a White Racist Western Colonial Imperialist Tool

When Israel invaded Lebanon in 1982 and murdered 20,000 Arabs/Muslims/Christians of Color with the full support of the United States, both Amnesty International (AI) headquartered in London and Amnesty International USA (AIUSA) headquartered in New York said and did nothing despite vigorous efforts by us, AIUSA Members, to get them both to say and to do something. When it became clear that AI and AIUSA were not going to say or do anything about Israel's wholesale slaughter of Arabs/Muslims/Christians of Color in Lebanon because of the marked Zionist bias by their staffs, boards, and funders, I called up the Irish Nobel Peace Prize Winner Sean MacBride at his home in Dublin and asked him to intervene with AI/London. What precious little AI/London said and did about 20,000 Arabs/Muslims/Christians of Color in Lebanon murdered by Israel with the full support of the United States was due to Sean MacBride, RIP.

MacBride then convinced the AI Secretary General in London to appoint me a Consultant to Amnesty International on the human rights situation in the Middle East. In that capacity, I attended the founding meeting of what would become the AIUSA Middle East Coordination Group. In other words, I was one of the founders of the AIUSA Mid-East Co-Group. At that founding meeting I said quite emphatically that Amnesty International and AIUSA would have absolutely no credibility whatsoever in the Middle East unless they dealt forthrightly and vigorously with violations of the human rights of Arabs and Muslims by Israel, and, in particular, Israeli atrocities against the Peoples of Lebanon and Palestine. Soon thereafter, I found out that the Members of the AIUSA Mid-East Co-Group had been instructed to have nothing more to do with me by a direct order coming from the Zionist AIUSA Board of Directors.

When Amnesty International USA refused to do anything about Israel murdering 20,000 Arabs/Muslims/Christians of Color in Lebanon, AIUSA members who knew of my efforts decided to nominate me and several others for the AIUSA Board of Directors by means of the AIUSA grassroots petition process—not their co-opted selection process. We were all knocked off the AIUSA Board ballot by the Zionist dominated and controlled AIUSA Board. Then my colleagues asked me to represent them as their Attorney against AIUSA. I threatened a lawsuit, sent a Demand Letter, and demanded, *inter alia*, that if we were not returned to the AIUSA Board ballot, I would invalidate their forthcoming elections. Not only did I have to threaten a lawsuit, but I actually had to fly out to New York in order to file the lawsuit against AIUSA at their headquarters on the very eve of them starting their Annual General Meeting (AGM) to conduct the elections. Only then did AIUSA settle on my terms on a late Sunday afternoon just before I was to file the lawsuit on Monday morning. That is what it took for me to get elected to the AIUSA Board of Directors in order to protect the basic human rights of Lebanese and Palestinians from being exterminated by Israel with the full support of the U.S. government.

To be fair about it, Amnesty was no worse than any of the other so-called human rights NGOs in the United States. None of them said or did anything at all about 20,000 Arabs/Muslims/Christians of Color being murdered by Israel in Lebanon with the full support of the U.S. government except for the American Friends Service Committee (AFSC). AFSC convened a working group on Lebanon and asked me to join. We put out a very courageous and hard-hitting report. We had to be sure the AFSC report was objective and thorough because they had people on the ground over there who were risking their lives working to obtain factual information for our information, evaluation, and reporting. I regret to report that over the years AFSC has become Zionized just like almost every other human rights NGO in the United States.

Since 1982 it is fair to say that Amnesty International subsequently released some desultory reports dealing with Israeli violations of human rights of the Palestinian People and the Lebanese People. But Israel had been consistently murdering, torturing, and destroying the Palestinians since at least the time when the Zionist war of invasion and occupation of Palestine began in 1948. Only since 1982 did Amnesty International get around to occasionally and half-heartedly condemning Israel for its massive human rights atrocities against the Palestinians. For example, while on the AIUSA Board, I tried to get AI/London and AIUSA to act on the basis of the infamous *Landau Report* whereby the Israeli Government officially sanctioned torture against Palestinians. I pointed out that at the time this made Israel the only state in the world to officially sanction torture. Nothing happened despite the fact that vigorous opposition to torture was supposed to be the very heart of the

Mandate for action by Amnesty International. It was nice to see that about a decade later Amnesty International finally agreed with me and said something about the matter. Better late than never.

Likewise, Israel had been rampaging around Lebanon with the full support of the United States to the grave detriment of the Lebanese People and Palestinians living there since at least the time when Israel invaded Lebanon in 1978. The primary reason why Amnesty International put out later reports that only occasionally and half-heartedly condemned Israeli human rights atrocities in Lebanon and against the Palestinians after decades of silence is because there are now some other human rights organizations that have acted against Israel when AI/London and AIUSA refused to act because of their innate Zionist tendencies. When it comes to protecting the human rights of Palestinians, Lebanese, and other Arabs/Muslims/Christians of Color from atrocities inflicted by Israel with the blank-check support of the United States, AI/London and AIUSA have always been too little and too late and on purpose.

While on the AIUSA Board I once saw the itinerary drawn up by AIUSA for the visit to the United States by the AI Secretary General coming from London. On the list was almost every major Zionist NGO in New York and Washington DC and about one Arab NGO. Given their standard operating procedures, I am confident these Zionist NGOs threatened the AI Secretary General that they would have their members withhold their contributions to AI and AIUSA if AI/London did not reign in its pathetic, pitiful, and meager criticisms of Israel. While I was on the AIUSA Board, AIUSA paid about 20 percent of the budget for AI/London. He who pays the piper calls the tune! In this regard, despite my best efforts to do so, the Secretary General of Amnesty International adamantly refused to establish an expedited procedure for the adoption of Israeli military refuseniks who courageously refused to inflict atrocities upon Palestinians and Lebanese at the cost of their own imprisonment as Amnesty International's much-touted "Prisoners-of-Conscience." He knew full well that would spell the end of his job.

Amnesty International is primarily motivated not by human rights but by politics. Second comes publicity. Third comes money. Fourth comes getting more members. Fifth, internal turf battles. And only then, finally, come genuine human rights concerns. To be sure, if you are dealing with a human rights situation in a country that is an officially or unofficially designated enemy of the United States or Britain or Israel, it gets massive amounts of attention, resources, people, and publicity. AI can throw as much as they want against that officially or unofficially designated enemy state. But if AI is dealing with violations of human rights by the United States, Britain, Israel, then it's like pulling teeth to get them to really do something effective on the situation. AI might, very reluctantly, and after an enormous amount of fighting and battles and pressures, half-heartedly and occasionally act somewhat to ameliorate the situation—if at all.

Even far worse yet, let us consider Amnesty International's Kuwaiti Dead Babies Report and Campaign that both Amnesty International and AIUSA maliciously used for the express purpose of mongering for war against Iraq. The Kuwaiti Dead Babies Report was a shoddy Amnesty International document in support of an infamous hoax that catalyzed American public support for Operation Desert Storm, the launch of the First Gulf War by U.S. president George Bush Senior in January of 1991. At an October 1990 U.S. congressional hearing, a young woman claimed to have seen Iraqi soldiers take premature infants from incubators and leave them on the floor of a hospital in Iraqi-occupied Kuwait. The witness was later identified as the daughter of the Kuwaiti ambassador to Washington, who had not been anywhere near the Persian Gulf and was prepped for this disinformation stunt by CIA-linked lobbyists from the Hill and Knowlton public relations firm.

As a member of the AIUSA Board, I received a pre-publication copy of their Kuwaiti Dead Babies Report, which I studied quite carefully. I could not tell if any of these explosive charges were true based upon what I was reading. But first and foremost: That Amnesty International report contained several technical errors that should have precluded its publication. Second, even if all these sensational allegations had been true, it was clear to me that the publication of the report at that critical moment in December of 1990 would be used by the United States and Britain for war-mongering against Iraq. I expressed these objections in the strongest terms possible to AIUSA and for their official conveyance to AI/London. I stated quite forcefully that this report should not be published because it was inaccurate. Or alternatively, that if for some reason it were to be published, it must be accompanied by an *errata* sheet, which I calculated would significantly undercut its impact. It was clear to me that this report was a rush-job for political reasons that obviously did not meet the normal standards of quality control for Amnesty International reports. It was an AI setup for war.

Notwithstanding my best efforts, Amnesty International published its Kuwaiti Dead Babies Report despite my vigorous objections, and then AI and AIUSA launched their war-mongering disinformation campaign against Iraq. From that episode, the obvious conclusions were that AI/London deliberately intended the Kuwaiti Dead-Babies Report and Campaign to tip the balance of public opinion in favor of war against Iraq, and that AIUSA knowingly and maliciously went along with it. In January of 1991 the U.S. Senate voted in favor of war against Iraq by a thin margin of only a handful of votes. Several Senators publicly stated that the Amnesty International report had influenced their votes in favor of war against Iraq. That genocidal war waged by the United States, Britain, France, and their lackey states led to the deaths of about 200,000 Iraqis, half of whom were civilians, and paved the way for their second and even deadlier invasion of Iraq in March of 2003 under U.S. president George Bush Junior and U.K. prime minister Tony Blair. Amnesty International shall always have the blood of the Iraqi people on their hands!

Once it became clear that there never were any dead babies in Kuwait as alleged, AI/London proceeded to engage in a massive cover-up. Soon after the launch of the U.S.-led attack upon Iraq, it came out publicly that the dead-baby claim was a Kuwaiti propaganda stunt. I demanded an investigation in the strongest terms possible!

Nothing happened. There was never an investigation, only stonewalling from AI London, which refused to admit their wrongdoing. To the best of my knowledge, there has since never been an investigation and explanation of what happened. The entire episode of faked infant deaths went down the "memory hole" as in George Orwell's *1984*. When this episode was all over, my final conclusion was that the high-level official of Amnesty International in London who was in charge of producing the report was a British intelligence agent. My friend the Chair of the AIUSA Board of Directors reached the exact same conclusion independently of me.

For all I know, some of the same people at AI/London who waged this war-mongering Kuwaiti Dead-Babies Disinformation Campaign against Iraq are still at AI/London Headquarters generating more disinformation against Arab/Muslim States and Peoples in order to further the political and economic interests of the United States, Britain, and Israel at the behest of MI5 and MI6. And AIUSA is a wholly owned and closely held subsidiary of U.S. Zionists. Because of their war-mongering Kuwaiti Dead-Babies Disinformation Campaign against Iraq and its ensuing cover-up, Amnesty International and AIUSA will never have any credibility in the Middle East!

During the next decade, about 1.5 million people in Iraq died as a direct result of genocidal sanctions maliciously imposed upon them primarily at the behest of the United States and Britain. Included in that death toll were about 500,000 dead Iraqi children murdered by the deliberate shortages of infant formula, medicines, food, and the prevalence of their concomitant diseases that finished them off. While on the AIUSA Board of Directors, I tried to get them and AI/London to do something about these genocidal sanctions against the people of Iraq. Both AI/London and AIUSA obstinately refused to act despite the grievous harm that their war-mongering Kuwaiti Dead-Babies Disinformation Campaign had already inflicted upon the people of Iraq, including their helpless children.

Instead of action, AI members were conveniently told that the Amnesty International Mandate precluded action against such genocidal economic sanctions. This claim was utter nonsense! While I served on the AIUSA Board, our Chairperson put me in charge of handling Mandate "reform" for the Board and AIUSA. I know all about the AI Mandate because it was my responsibility as an expert on both international law and human rights. Generally put, when AI/London and AIUSA want to take action on a matter because it will bring them publicity, money, members, and political "influence," they pay no attention whatsoever to their so-called Mandate. Conversely, when AI/London and AIUSA decide for political and/or economic reasons that they will not work on human rights problems, they trot out their so-called Mandate to justify non-action.

Thus same type of bogus Mandate argument was used by the White racist AI/London Headquarters and AIUSA to prevent their organizations and their memberships from taking effective action against the racist criminal apartheid regime in South Africa that had been oppressing tens of millions of Black People for decades. To the best of my knowledge, Amnesty International and AIUSA were the only human rights NGOs in the entire world to have refused to condemn apartheid in South Africa. The spurious argument made here was that the Amnesty International Mandate precluded AI from taking a position on a type of government. My response to that disingenuous dodge was that according to the 1973 Apartheid Convention, apartheid is a "Crime against Humanity." To no avail! Despite my best efforts, Amnesty International and AIUSA obstinately refused to take a stand against a Crime against Humanity perpetrated by a gang of White genocidal racists against tens of millions of Black human beings.

The truth of the matter was that Amnesty International was and still is headquartered in London, and AIUSA was and still is headquartered in New York and Washington. The biggest political supporters of the racist criminal South African apartheid regime were the governments of Britain, the United States, and Israel. Likewise, the biggest sources of economic investments in the racist criminal apartheid regime in South Africa came from Britain and the United States.

Once again, he who pays the piper calls the tune at Amnesty International and indeed for all the Western NGOs on human rights. This sacrosanct Piper Principle operating behind all Western NGOs includes the much-vaunted International Committee of the Red Cross (ICRC), who arrogantly portray themselves as some sort of High Priesthood for so-called "international humanitarian law." All these Western NGOs are shot through with Western and/or Zionist intelligence assets and agents.

There was no way the White racist AI/London and AIUSA were ever going to work effectively against the political and economic interests of Britain, the United States, and Israel operating together in support of the racist genocidal apartheid regime in South Africa in order to help tens of millions of Black human beings. So AI/London and AIUSA concocted this spurious rationale for non-action. Likewise, the same was done by AI/London and AIUSA to justify their non-action against the genocidal economic sanctions imposed primarily by the United States and Britain against Arabs/Muslims/Christians of Color in Iraq. There is no way AI/London and AIUSA will act immediately and effectively against the political and economic interests of the United States, Britain, and Israel.

Notice how these specious justifications for AI non-action fit in quite neatly with the strategic objectives of the United States, Britain, and Israel around the world. By their deliberate non-action AI/London and AIUSA were indirectly supporting the aggressive and genocidal and racist policies of the United States, Britain, and Israel against Peoples of Color in Third World countries. If you want to do effective human rights work in opposition to the imperial, colonial, racist, genocidal, and aggressive policies of the United States, Britain, and Israel, there is no point working with Amnesty International. You will simply be wasting your time, your efforts, your resources, and your enthusiasm. Even worse yet, you will unwittingly become a cog in the White racist Amnesty International Imperial Machine against Third World countries and Peoples of Color. And even against a First World developed state like Russia (and its legal predecessor, the Soviet Union) that the United States and Britain have slated for subjugation and conquest. Basically, Amnesty International is there to drain away and keep preoccupied on meaningless tasks those people of good faith and good will who really want to do effective and meaningful human rights work around the world: "Let's go write a letter to the Prime Minister of Israel on behalf of some poor Palestinian political prisoner whom the Zionists are torturing to death!" Not even worth expending the electrons to send it by email.

Permit me to further substantiate this assertion that Amnesty International and AIUSA are Western colonial imperialist tools by reference to other areas of the world. It is well known that AI/London has done little effective work to help Irish Catholics in Northern Ireland. As Sean MacBride once said: Amnesty International will never treat Irish Catholics fairly so long as it is headquartered in London. Indeed Sean once told me that AI will have no real independence from the British government unless and until its Headquarters are moved out of London and into some Third World and Non-Aligned country.

The long and sordid history of AI/London non-action in the face of genocidal violations of the most fundamental human rights of Irish Catholics living in Northern Ireland by Britain is well known among Irish Americans and Irish People living in Ireland, Northern Ireland, and around the world in the Irish Diaspora. For example, a gratuitous letter by a former AI Secretary General maliciously sabotaged public support for the defense of IRA Volunteer Joe Doherty here in the United States from being returned to face British persecution by Maggy Thatcher herself. Later, it required a massive internet campaign organized by me to force AI/London to do anything at all to save the lives of the Irish baby Loinnir McAliskey and her Irish single young mother Roisin McAliskey from British persecution after the Deputy Director of Amnesty International in London told me to take a hike when acting on their behalf.

Let me now move from the British colony in Northern Ireland to the American colony in Puerto Rico. While I was still on the AIUSA Board, a fellow Board Member asked me to draft two resolutions for adoption by the Annual General Meeting (AGM) of AIUSA calling for a comprehensive AI Study on human rights violations by the United States in Puerto Rico and on behalf of Puerto Rican political prisoners held in U.S. jails. These resolutions passed the AIUSA/AGM overwhelmingly, and without any dissent that I could detect. I was then invited by the Amnesty International Chapter in Puerto Rico to give the Keynote Address at their Annual General Meeting in San Juan on the subject of the right of the Puerto Rican political prisoners in American jails to be treated as prisoners of war in accordance with the requirements of the Geneva Conventions and Protocols. Immediately thereafter, AI/London and AIUSA applied massive pressure on AI/Puerto Rico in order to sabotage and prevent my speech. To their great credit, little AI/Puerto Rico refused to cave in to these Big Bullies at AI/London and AIUSA.

I went down to Puerto Rico to attend their AGM, gave the Keynote Address, and also investigated U.S. human rights violations against the Puerto Ricans, including torture, summary executions, and disappearances—all of which atrocities incontestably fall within the Amnesty International Mandate for action. Upon my return home, AIUSA attempted to stiff me out of my expenses despite the fact that I was attending the AI/Puerto Rico AGM in my official capacity as an invited AIUSA Board Member. Perhaps I missed it due to the press of other duties at the time, but I am not aware of any comprehensive Amnesty International Study and Campaign against U.S. human rights abuses in Puerto Rico and on behalf of Puerto Rican political prisoners in U.S. jails.

Finally, let me say a few words about the deliberate non-action by AI/London and AIUSA against Indigenous Peoples living in the United States and in its racist, colonial, imperial, and genocidal ally Canada. Back when I was on the AIUSA Board, AI/London decided to launch an international campaign on behalf of Indigenous Peoples around the world. As usual, I received a pre-publication copy of the campaign material. On reading it, I immediately noticed that almost nothing was to be said or done to help the Indigenous Peoples living under genocidal conditions in the United States and Canada. I protested this to AI/London and to AIUSA, and demanded that the Indigenous Peoples living in the United States and Canada be added as an integral component of this campaign. To the best of my knowledge, this was not done. I leave it to the Indigenous Peoples still living in the United States and Canada under genocidal conditions to decide for themselves how helpful Amnesty International has been to them over the years.

I will not belabor the obvious here any longer in this brief chapter. But based upon my over two decades of experience having dealt with AI/London and AIUSA at the highest levels, it is clear to me that both organizations manifest a consistent pattern and practice of following the lines of the racist, imperial, colonial, genocidal, and aggressive foreign policies of the United States, Britain, and Israel. You can certainly see this in AI's work and non-work with respect to the Middle East, Northern Ireland, Puerto Rico, South Africa, Russia/Soviet Union, Indigenous Peoples in North America, and so on. Effectively, Amnesty International and AIUSA function as tools for promoting the White racist, imperialist, colonial, genocidal, and aggressive policies by the United States, Britain, and Israel around the world.

There are many people of good faith and goodwill working at the grassroots level of Amnesty International and AIUSA who genuinely believe that they are doing meaningful and effective work to protect human rights around the world. But at the top of these two organizations you will find self-perpetuating cliques of co-opted Imperial Elites who deliberately shape and direct the work of AI and AIUSA so as to either affirmatively support, or else not seriously undercut, the racist, imperial, colonial, genocidal, and aggressive policies of the United States, Britain, and Israel. The Imperial Leadership Elites of AI/London and AIUSA have always considered themselves to be the self-styled "loyal opposition" to the White racist, imperial, colonial, genocidal, and aggressive policies of the United States, Britain, and Israel. I would ask the good people working at the grassroots level of Amnesty International and AIUSA whether they want to continue being part of the "loyal opposition" to White Western racism, imperialism, colonialism, genocide, and aggression perpetrated by the United States, Britain, and Israel, and especially against States and Peoples of Color, particularly in the Arab and Muslim worlds.

It is not for me to tell those people of good faith and goodwill currently working with AI/London and AIUSA and Amnesty International around the world what to do. But I stopped paying my membership dues to Amnesty International several years ago. I could no longer in good faith and conscience aid and abet AI's White racist Western colonial, imperial, genocidal, and aggressive agenda. What you do with your conscience and with your money is up to you. All I can do is write this chapter for your respectful consideration.

Conclusion

Implications of the Worldwide COVID-19 Pandemic for World Politics, Human Rights, and International Law

On Friday, January 24, 2020, I was contacted by a journalist working for the publication *Geopolitics and Empire* in order to give them a video-recorded interview about the outbreak of the coronavirus pandemic in Wuhan, China, that was then rapidly emerging into the widespread attention of all international news media sources. From a previous interview I had given this reporter on biological weapons, he knew that I had personally called for and drafted the U.S. domestic implementing legislation for the 1972 Biological Weapons Convention that was named the Biological Weapons Anti-terrorism Act of 1989 (BWATA), which was passed unanimously by both Houses of the U.S. Congress and signed into law by President George Bush Senior. My BWATA was prompted by and specifically intended to deal in material, but not exclusive, part with criminalizing the abuse of DNA genetic engineering by the neoconservative Reagan administration to research, develop, test, and stockpile biological weapons in violation of the Biological Weapons Convention. My 1989 BWATA provided for up to life imprisonment for violators and is still in the U.S. Criminal Code as amended today.[1]

I adamantly resisted pressure from the U.S. Department of Justice to provide for the death penalty for BWATA violators because of my near lifelong opposition to capital punishment. These matters have already been discussed and analyzed in detail above in Chapter 13 of this book as well as in my books *The Future of International Law and American Foreign Policy* 277-316 (Transnational Publishers Inc.: 1989) and *Biowarfare and Terrorism* (Clarity Press: 2005). So I will not recapitulate any of this history and these arguments and the evidence and the authorities in support of them here going back to 1985.

During the course of that January 24, 2020, interview I stated quite emphatically that the Wuhan coronavirus was an offensive biological warfare weapon involving DNA genetic-engineering that included gain of function properties to make it more lethal and more infectious, and which had leaked out of the Biosafety Level 4 Laboratory (BSL4) located in the city of Wuhan, China. I then proceeded to explain in detail the reasons for my conclusions. I also stated that every BSL4 and BSL3 in the world must be immediately shut down because they all presented existential threats to the entire human race. This is an injunction I had publicly issued in the award-winning documentary *Anthrax War* (2009) by Coen and Nadler in which I appeared and served as a consultant. I also repeated this injunction in that October 2015 interview published above in Chapter 13 of this book: "This is a biocatastrophe waiting to happen here in the United States." My long-standing prediction finally came true with the outbreak of the worldwide COVID-19 pandemic at the Wuhan BSL4 in November of 2019.

That interview I gave to *Geopolitics and Empire* was then distributed by them, including onto the internet, by the middle of the very next week, and quickly went viral all over the world. After giving that interview I was inundated by requests from news media sources all over the world to explain the reasons for my conclusions and my recommendations for dealing with the worldwide COVID-19 pandemic. This deluge of interviews continued relentlessly until about June 1, 2020, when they gradually and mercifully began to taper off. By then everyone in the world knew exactly where I stood on the origins of the COVID-19 pandemic from the Wuhan BSL4 and what must be done about it.

In order to give that plethora of interviews, I had to work full-time researching and reading and analyzing all of the information that emerged into the public record about the Wuhan coronavirus and the Wuhan BSL4 and the worldwide COVID-19 pandemic. In the process of doing that, I also had to read, analyze, and refute my numerous critics who arose to object to my conclusions and recommendations by regurgitating the simplistic propaganda originally generated by the Chinese government as a cover-up that the worldwide COVID-19 pandemic had somehow magically "jumped" from animals to human beings at the so-called wet-market located in Wuhan, China, despite substantial documented evidence to the contrary. It turns out that my critics were directly and personally involved in the U.S. offensive biological warfare industry discussed above in Chapter 13 of this book. These death scientists had vested economic, professional, organizational, and personal interests in attacking my conclusions and in particular my clarion call for shutting down every BSL4 and BSL3 in the world for creating existential threats to all humanity like COVID-19 has already done. They would all be out of a job! In addition, some of them who are American citizens could also be prosecuted for violating my Biological Weapons Anti-Terrorism Act of 1989 and subjected to life imprisonment. It was pretty easy for me to discredit my critics and their attacks upon me and my conclusions and recommendations by performing simple due diligence research on their professional backgrounds—as the reader can easily do so as well if you want to by means of an internet search. I am not going to review or summarize or list all of my many news media interviews here since the reader can easily find them and either read them or watch them or both by doing a Google search under my name after January 24, 2020, if you so desire. But the most recent and succinct account of my position can be found online in a June 26, 2020, lecture on *The Covid-19 Pandemic* that I delivered before a scholarly conference on the "Eradication of Biological and Chemical Weapons" that was convened by the Maharashtra Institute of Technology (MIT) School of Government at the World Peace University in Pune, India, over that weekend.[2]

In the meantime, at the end of April 2020, I was contacted by an Israeli law firm that had sued China over the COVID-19 pandemic in the Israeli court system.[3] They requested me to intervene in their lawsuit on their behalf and that of their clients and to provide them with a *Declaration* of my already publicly expressed Expert Opinion on COVID-19 being an offensive biological warfare weapon that had leaked out of the Wuhan BSL4 to be used in their ongoing Israeli litigation against China. Because of the monumental importance of this litigation for *World Politics, Human Rights, and International Law,* I agreed to do so. On August 22, 2020, this Israeli law firm informed me that the Israeli Foreign Ministry had officially served my *Declaration* upon the Government of China as part of these Israeli legal proceedings against it. My *Declaration* is now a matter of public record. I have published it here below for the first time anywhere so that the reader can understand and evaluate the bases for my conclusion that COVID-19 is an offensive biological warfare weapon that leaked out of that BSL4 located in Wuhan, China. My *Declaration* was signed and dated June 6, 2020. Everything that has emerged into the public record since then and since my MIT School of Government Lecture in Pune, India, on June 26, 2020, further supports and strengthens my arguments that COVID-19 is an offensive biological warfare weapon that leaked out of that Wuhan BSL4.[4]

As this book goes into print, all humanity is facing an existential crisis presented by the worldwide COVID-19 pandemic. Today the human race is now fighting World War III against the offensive biological warfare weapon known as COVID-19. At this preliminary stage of the worldwide COVID-19 pandemic, I cannot predict what the consequences of COVID-19 will be for *World Politics, Human Rights, and International Law*. But as of now they are shaping up to be existentially catastrophic. We human beings are now in the fight of our lives against the worldwide COVID-19 pandemic. COVID-19 could prove to be almost as exterminationist for the human race as was the Spanish flu virus of 1918.

In the meantime, while we are fighting World War III against the worldwide COVID-19 pandemic, the rules of international law and the principles of international human rights law will provide us guidance and direction about how to conduct this battle. I cannot at this time anticipate all the circumstances that will arise during this mortal struggle for the future of humanity. However, our foremost lodestars of international law and international human rights law for dealing with all the problems, crises, and dilemmas that will face us in our war against the worldwide COVID-19 pandemic are the United Nations Charter of 1945, the International Covenant on Civil and Political Rights of 1966, and the Biological Weapons Convention of 1972, inter alia. It is my professional opinion and firm personal belief that unless and until the leaders of the world come clean, level with, and publicly admit and explain to their respective peoples that COVID-19 is an offensive biological warfare weapon that must be dealt with accordingly, they will not be able to effectively combat it—let alone to defeat it! Toward those ends, this Conclusion has been written and my June 6, 2020, Israeli court *Declaration* is published here below:

DECLARATION OF PROFESSOR FRANCIS A. BOYLE

Pursuant to 28 USC 1746, Francis A. Boyle makes the following Declaration under penalty of perjury:

1. My name is Francis A. Boyle.
2. I am legally able to make this Declaration because I am over the age of 18 years old and legally competent in every way to swear to these facts.
3. I make this Declaration from within the territory of the United States of America.
4. I am a former advisory board member for the Council for Responsible Genetics and a professor of international law at the University of Illinois College of Law.
5. My educational background includes an undergraduate degree from the University of Chicago, a juris doctor (lawyer) magna cum laude degree from Harvard University Law School in 1976, a Master's Degree in 1978 from Harvard University and a Ph.D. in 1983 from Harvard University in political science specializing in international relations and international politics, from the Harvard Graduate School of Arts and Sciences Department of Government. I went through the exact same Ph.D. Program at Harvard that graduated Henry Kissinger before me and

was also an Associate at the Harvard University Center for International Affairs for two years. I was a Teaching Fellow for Harvard Undergraduates for two years in courses on International Organizations, International Law, and International Human Rights Law before becoming an Assistant Professor of Law at the University of Illinois College of Law in 1978.

6. I am the author of *Defending Civil Resistance Under International Law, The Future of International Law and American Foreign Policy, World Politics and International Law*, and other books, as well as major articles on a range of related international law and human rights issues.
7. My professional memberships include the American Society of International Law, the American Bar Association, the American Political Science Association, and the Lieber Group on the Laws of War.
8. I have been a consultant to Amnesty International and the American Friends Service Committee.
9. I had represented Bosnia-Herzegovina in the International Court of Justice. http://www.un.org/Overview/Organs/icj.html
10. For decades, I have advocated against the development and use of bioweapons. This experience is relevant here because my experience causes me to believe that the *SARS*-CoV-2 virus or COVID-19 disease is a bioweapon.
11. I drafted the United States domestic implementing legislation for the Biological Weapons Convention known as the Biological Weapons Anti-terrorism Act of 1989 that was passed unanimously by both Houses of the United States Congress and signed into law by President George H.W. Bush Sr, which still remains on the U.S. Statute books today as amended. My BWATA was also specifically intended to prevent the use of DNA Genetic Engineering in order to research, develop, test, and manufacture biological weapons. The story is told in my book *Biowarfare and Terrorism* (Clarity Press: 2005), with a *Foreword* by MIT Professor Jonathan King, a Co-Founder of the Council for Responsible Genetics.
12. I won the University of Chicago's Sigma Xi certificate of merit and prize in biology for my graduating year in 1971. They gave out one per year and it went to seniors, but in my case, they had to make a special exception because I was a graduating junior.
13. Based on my knowledge, experience, and expertise, the origins of the novel coronavirus, SARS-CoV-2 is a Biological Warfare Weapon.
14. The term "novel coronavirus" means it is a new virus not previously known to previously infect humans.
15. The currently held conventional view is that SARS-CoV-2 was transmitted through animals (zoonotic transmission), specifically bats.
16. I dismiss this notion categorically.

17. This is indeed a bioengineered synthetic virus that was not transmitted from animals to humans without human intervention.
18. For starters, a *Lancet* paper published on February 15, 2020, by physicians who treated some of the first COVID-19 patients in China showed that patient zero, the one believed to have started the transmission, was nowhere near the Wuhan seafood market.
19. What's more, there were no bats of the type in question sold in or even close to the market.
20. At least one-third of the patients reviewed at the start of the outbreak also had no exposure or links to that market.
21. This data supports my counterargument that SARS-CoV-2 was not zoonotically transmitted but is in fact a bioengineered virus.
22. U.S. and foreign politicians and intelligence agencies are starting to say they believe the virus leaked from the Wuhan BSL4 (biosafety level 4) lab, which is China's equivalent to the United States' Fort Detrick, where they research, develop and test biological weapons.
23. The novel coronavirus is SARS, which is a weaponized version of the coronavirus to begin with, to which was added gain-of-function capabilities that increases its virulence, which makes it more infectious and more lethal. Covid-19 also appears to have been aerosolized by means of nanotechnology at the Wuhan BSL4, which is China's Fort Detrick that has done the same with biowarfare agents.
24. A scientific article reveals that the Australian Health Board was working with the Wuhan BSL4 "genetically engineered HIV into SARS." So, that is all verified in scientific papers. In addition, it seems to me that they took that all back to the Wuhan BSL4 and applied nanotechnology to it. Covid-19 appears to have been aerosolized by means of nanotechnology at the Wuhan BSL4, which is China's Fort Detrick that has done the same with biowarfare agents for aerial delivery. Aerosolization is a hallmark of a biological weapon so that human beings might breathe it. This is something you need to do in a BSL4 Biological weapons lab. Applying nanotechnology is so dangerous that people working with it have to wear a moon suit with a portable air supply to breathe.
25. We also know that one of the cooperating institutions to Wuhan BSL4 was my triple alma mater Harvard, and that the chairman of the Harvard chemistry department, Dr. Charles Lieber, a specialist in nanotechnology, set up an entire laboratory in Wuhan where according to reports he specialized in applying nanotechnology to chemistry and biology. Harvard is also listed as a co-operative research institution at the Wuhan BSL4—China's Fort Detrick.
26. My evaluation is, based on what I've read in the literature, that they tried to weaponize all that together. And that is SARS-CoV-2 that we are dealing with now.

27. So, SARS-CoV-2 is SARS, which is a biowarfare agent to begin with.
28. Second, SARS-CoV-2 has gain-of-function properties, which makes it more lethal and more infectious.
29. It has HIV that was DNA genetically engineered into there. That was *also* confirmed by the Indian scientists. And the French Nobel Prize Winner in Medicine who won it for discovering that HIV causes AIDS has also stated that HIV has been genetically engineered into Covid-19.
30. It looks like nanotechnology has been applied to aerosolize and weaponize Covid-19. An MIT scientist who did a study found that SARS-CoV-2 traveled 27 feet through the air. And that, I guess, was in laboratory conditions. That, I think, is why it's so infectious, and that is what I believe we are dealing with here.
31. This is also why the 6-foot social distancing recommended by the CDC is preposterous, even doubling that might do you no good. If there is nanotechnology involved, it floats above the air, on the air, in the air, and with the air.
32. I am not saying that China deliberately released this, shooting itself in the foot. But it was clear they were developing an existentially dangerous biological weapon that had never been seen before to humanity, and it leaked out of the lab.
33. And as you see in the *Washington Post,* U.S. State Department officials reported back to Washington that there were inadequate safety precautions and procedures in that lab to begin with. We also know that SARS has leaked out of other Chinese biological warfare labs. So right now, I believe that is what happened here.
34. I personally believe that until our political leaders come clean with the American people, both at the White House and in Congress and our state governments, and publicly admit that this is an existentially dangerous offensive biological warfare weapon that we are dealing with, I do not see that we will be able to confront it. The same is true for Israel.

    The Origin of SARS-CoV-2.

35. One of the primary investigators on the 2015 paper from the University of North Carolina—"A SARS-like Cluster of Circulating Bat Coronaviruses Shows Potential for Human Emergence"—was Dr. Shi Zhengli, a virologist who in 2010 had published a paper discussing the weaponization of the SARS virus.
36. Normally, while the coronavirus found in bats may be SARS, it typically does not infect humans as it does not target the ACE-2 receptor.
37. The infectious agent causing the current pandemic is called SARS-CoV-2—SARS standing for "serious acute respiratory infection" and CoV-2 indicating that it's a second type of SARS coronavirus known to infect humans.

38. SARS-CoV-2, of course, contains the genetic modification to attach to ACE2 receptors in human cells, which allows it to infect them. Zhengli's publications show that she engineered this bat coronavirus into one which crosses species and infects humans. She has in fact been working on this for more than 10 years.

> "That is why I said SARS was a bioengineered warfare weapon to begin with," Boyle says. "And that is what the University of North Carolina and the Australian lab were trying to make even more dangerous with the gain-of-function and the HIV. So ... SARS was a biological warfare agent to begin with, it leaked, and that is the origin of the COVID-19 epidemic."

39. In addition, an Indian paper that ended up being withdrawn due to intense political pressure, shows a specific envelope protein from the HIV virus called GP41 was integrated in the RNA sequences of SARS-CoV-2.
40. In other words, the implication is that the HIV virus was genetically engineered into SARS.
41. So, in summary, SARS-CoV-2 appears to be a bioengineered bat coronavirus—which was initially benign and non-transmittable to humans without human intervention.
42. Zhengli then genetically modified the virus to integrate spike proteins that allows the virus to enter human cells by attaching to ACE-2 receptors. That was the first modification.
43. The second modification was to integrate an envelope protein from HIV called GP141, which tends to impair the immune system. A third modification appears to involve nanotechnology to make the virus light enough to remain airborne for a long time, apparently giving it a range of up to 27 feet. And then of course it was given Gain of Function Properties at the University of North Carolina BSL3.

    Nanotech Expert with Wuhan Connection Arrested
44. While the BSL4 lab in Wuhan may have leaked the virus, its creation does not appear to be limited to the Chinese. The chairman of the Harvard Department of Chemistry and nanoscience expert Dr. Charles Lieber, was arrested earlier this year by federal agencies, suspected of illegal dealings with China. Lieber has denied the allegations.
45. The Wuhan University of Technology (WUT) allegedly paid Lieber $50,000 a month from 2012 to 2017 to help establish and oversee the WUT-Harvard Joint Nano Key Laboratory. Lieber also received another $150,000 a month in living expenses from China's Thousand Talents program. Given the facts that I spent seven years as a student at Harvard, I have 3 degrees from Harvard, and I spent two years teaching at Harvard, I am confident that Harvard knew what the Chair of their Chemistry Department was doing in Wuhan. It has also been reported that Professor

Lieber worked for Fort Detrick—undoubtedly to aerosolize biological warfare weapons for them.

Researchers Working on Gain-of-Function to Spanish Flu

46. If you think SARS-CoV-2 is bad, be glad it's not the weaponized version of Spanish flu, which has also been in the works. As I wrote elsewhere:

> "The University of North Carolina's work was existentially dangerous and they knew it at the time. If you read the UNC scientific article co-written by the Wuhan BSL4 scientist Shi Zhengli … it says, 'Experiments with the full-length and chimeric SHC014 recombinant viruses were initiated and performed before the GOF research funding pause and have since been reviewed and approved for continued study by the NIH.'
>
> It says recombinant … So, they admit it was gain-of-function research. The research was paused by the National Institutes of Health. Why was it paused by NIH? Because there was a letter put out by large numbers of life scientists at the time saying this type of gain-of-function work … could be existentially dangerous if it got out in the public. Therefore, it had to be terminated … But the NIH was funding this in the beginning …
>
> A footnote here: I read the NIH's pause letter to the University of North Carolina, and UNC was doing two gain-of-function research projects. The other one was with Dr. Yoshihiro Kawaoka from the University of Wisconsin, who had resurrected the Spanish flu virus for the Pentagon.
>
> According to the pause letter, they were also doing gain-of-function work on the flu virus—one could only conclude it was the Spanish flu virus. It did not say the Spanish flu, but they also put a gain-of-function pause on that type of deadly research …
>
> I mean, the Spanish flu, we all know what that is, so imagine giving the Spanish flu gain-of-function properties, making it even more lethal and more infectious. That's exactly what was going on there at that UNC lab …"
>
> Disturbingly, while the NIH halted funding of this kind of gain-of-function research on lethal pathogens in 2014, it reauthorized it in December 2017, and I suspect Kawaoka's work may have been restarted as well, although I have not found proof of it yet.
>
> "So, this was existentially dangerous work that was going on at that UNC lab. Everyone knew it, NIH funded it, NIAID under Dr. Fauci funded it as

well. They knew exactly how dangerous this was. They paused it and then they resumed it," Boyle says.

47. At the first convention of synthetic biologists, in their final report, one of their key recommendations was the repeal of my Biological Weapons Anti-Terrorism Act, because they fully intended to use synthetic biology to manufacture biological weapons, to which my BWATA applied by name.
48. My BWATA law still applies. It provides for life imprisonment for everyone who has done this: all the scientists involved at the University of North Carolina and everyone who funded this project, knowing that it was existentially dangerous—and that includes Fauci and people at the NIH, UNC, Food and Drug Administration, the Dana Farber Cancer Institute at Harvard, inter alia.
49. So, just how would we get that process of justice going?
50. One of the variants of criminal intent is the demonstration of grave indifference to human life. And that is the criminal intent necessary for homicide.
51. So in my opinion, and my advice would be, if we can't get attorney general William Pelham Barr to sign off on prosecuting these people, then the district attorney, state's attorney, attorney general out there in North Carolina, institute an investigation and indict everyone involved in this North Carolina work for homicide.
52. And that could include up to and including murder, malice aforethought. Again, one of the elements can be manifestation of grave indifference to human life. And it's clear from the 2015 UNC paper, they knew it was gain-of-function, they paused it because it was existentially dangerous, it was then reapproved and they continued it.
53. All BSL3 and BSL4 laboratories must be closed down and all biowarfare work with lethal pathogens ceased. They are all existentially dangerous. This is a catastrophe waiting to happen. And it is now happened. Here we are. It's staring us in the face.
54. Certainly, COVID-19 is nowhere near as devastating as the Black Death or the Spanish flu of 1918, both of which exacted a shocking death toll, all without the aid of synthetic molecules and nanotechnology.
55. The very idea that any of these horrific illnesses might be brought back in turbo-charged form should be terrifying enough for the world to unite in saying "No thanks; we don't want or need that kind of research going on." What value have these dangerous laboratories provided to date compared to the risk they are exposing all of us to?
56. I believe COVID-19 has the ability to become a serious pandemic killer.

57. Based on my expertise and analysis, I conclude that the known characteristics of SARS-CoV-2 are consistent with a bioengineered virus taking a pre-existing natural virus and adjusting or modifying the SARS virus with parts of other viruses.
58. This lawsuit in Israel is of utmost and critical importance for bringing Justice to the Victims of Covid-19 all over the world.

I declare under penalty of perjury that the foregoing is true and correct to the best of my knowledge and belief.

Professor Francis Anthony Boyle
University of Illinois at Urbana Champaign
College of Law
204 Law Building
504 East Pennsylvania Avenue
Champaign, IL 61820 USA
voice: 217/333-7954
fax: 217/244-1478
E-mail fboyle@illinois.edu
June 6, 2020

NOTES

1. *Biological Weapons Anti-Terrorism Act of 1989*, 18 U.S.C.§175 (2002).
2. Francis A. Boyle, *The Covid-19 Pandemic*, "Valedictory – Legal Framework for Implementing CWC & BWC," *YouTube: Vishwanath Karad*, June 26, 2020, https://youtu.be/AKmDPXzBDWs (analysis from 1:08:00 to 1:30:41).
3. Adam Eliyahu Berkowitz, "Israelis, Americans Join Cause to Sue China over Coronavirus," *Israel365 News*, August 28, 2020, 6:13 PM), https://www.israel365news.com/148034/israelis-americans-team-up-to-sue-china-over-coronavirus/.
4. Joseph Mercola, *More Experts Point to SARS-CoV-2 Being Created in a Lab*, Doctor Mercola Newsletter (Sep. 04, 2020), https://articles.mercola.com/sites/articles/archive/2020/09/04/coronavirus-chimera.aspx.

Appendix

Around the World with the Institute for Public Accuracy

During the past two decades, it has been my great pleasure to work with the Institute for Public Accuracy in Washington, DC in order to produce a large number of press releases for their distribution to thousands of news media sources all over the world on urgent and cutting-edge issues related to *World Politics, Human Rights, and International Law* contemporaneously as they occurred. These IPA press releases then served as the prompts and the bases for me to give interviews off of them to interested news media sources that contacted me because of them. I want to express my sincere gratitude to my friend Sam Husseini for preparing and producing these concerned press releases that are partially excerpted below. Their original texts with comments by other experts together with the accompanying hypertext links can be found on the IPA website at accuracy.org. Nevertheless, I alone am responsible for my comments reprinted below:

From: Institute for Public Accuracy
To: Boyle, Francis A
Subject:

For more information, contact at the Institute for Public Accuracy:
Sam Husseini, (202) 347-0020
Institute for Public Accuracy
980 National Press Building, Washington, D.C. 20045
(202) 347-0020 * accuracy.org * ips@accuracy.org

AFGHANISTAN

Another Gulf of Tonkin Resolution?
September 13, 2001
Francis Boyle

Professor of international law at the University of Illinois College of Law, Boyle said today: "According to the facts in the public record so far, this was not an act of war and NATO Article 5 does not apply. President Bush has automatically escalated this national tragedy into something it is not in order to justify a massive military attack abroad and an apparent crackdown on civil liberties at home. We see shades of the Tonkin Gulf Resolution, which the Johnson administration used to provide dubious legal cover for massive escalation of the Vietnam War."

Critical Voices
September 21, 2001
Francis Boyle

Professor of international law at the University of Illinois College of Law, Boyle said today: "The United States is under an absolute obligation to resolve this dispute with Afghanistan in a peaceful manner as required by UN Charter Article 2(3) and Article 33 . . . Accordingly, this dispute must be resolved by invoking the 1971 Montreal Sabotage Convention and the 1997 U.N. International Convention for the Suppression of Terrorist Bombings. Furthermore, the United States should offer to submit this entire dispute with Afghanistan to the International Court of Justice in The Hague (the so-called World Court)."

ASSANGE

Contrary to Reports, the U.S. Gov. Can Add Charges After Assange Extradition
April 12, 2019
In "Julian Assange Arrested in London as U.S. Unseals Hacking Conspiracy Indictment," Charlie Savage, Adam Goldman and Eileen Sullivan of the *New York Times* state: "If Mr. [Julian] Assange is convicted on the conspiracy to hack offense alone, he could face up to five years in prison. The government could later seek to charge him with additional offenses, but because of extradition practices, any such superseding

indictment would most likely need to come soon, before Britain formally decides whether to transfer custody of him."

Francis Boyle, fboyle@illinois.edu

Boyle is professor of international law at the University of Illinois College of Law. His books include *Foundations of World Order* (Duke University Press).

He said today: "The *New York Times* report is wrong and understates the dangers to Assange. What it states is normally the case in extradition treaties, but it's not the case in the relevant U.S.-British extradition treaty.

"Once the U.S. government has Assange over here, they can concoct whatever charges they want to against him for anything and then ask the British to waive what's called the Rule of Specialty. That could add up to much more than the current five years Assange is facing. The British government will almost certainly consent, unless Jeremy Corbyn becomes prime minister.

"I'd expect that Assange's lawyers will try to use the European Court of Human Rights to stop the extradition and in any event, they would need to ensure that the British government receives assurance from the U.S. government that the death penalty will not be sought."

. . .

BIOLOGICAL WARFARE

Making Harvey Worse? * Ecology * Biolab

August 28, 2017

Texas Tribune published an in-depth investigation about Houston's vulnerabilities in 2016 titled "Boomtown, Flood Town," which notes: "Climate change will bring more frequent and fierce rainstorms to cities like Houston. But unchecked development remains a priority in the famously un-zoned city, creating short-term economic gains for some while increasing flood risks for everyone." The reporting offers analysis as well as graphs and maps showing how building in Houston has aggravated problems and threats.

Francis Boyle, fboyle at illinois.edu

Professor at the University of Illinois College of Law, Boyle's books include *Biowarfare and Terrorism.* He notes a lack of government assurance and media inquiry regarding the state of the BSL-4 biolab at hard-hit Galveston. ABC News reported in 2013: "Texas Biolab Loses Deadly Guanarito Virus."

Ebola: Are U.S. Bioweapons Labs the Solution, or the Problem?

October 21, 2014

On Friday, the *New York Times* published the article "White House to Cut Funding for Risky Biological Study," which states: "Prompted by controversy over dangerous research and recent laboratory accidents, the White House announced Friday that it would temporarily halt all new funding for experiments that seek to study certain infectious agents by making them more dangerous." The piece quotes Richard H. Ebright, "a molecular biologist and bioweapons expert at Rutgers University, [who has] argued that the long history of accidental releases of infectious agents from research labs made such work extremely risky and unwise to perform in the first place. Dr. Ebright called Friday's announcement 'an important, albeit overdue, step.'" See *USA Today* from Aug. 17: "Hundreds of Bioterror Lab Mishaps Cloaked in Secrecy."

Francis Boyle, fboyle at illinois.edu

Professor at the University of Illinois College of Law, Boyle drafted the U.S. Biological Weapons Anti-Terrorism Act of 1989, which is the U.S. domestic implementing legislation for the Biological Weapons Convention. His books include *Biowarfare and Terrorism.*

He said today: "If, as some in the Liberian press are claiming, this outbreak of Ebola is from one of the labs in west Africa run by the CDC and Tulane University, it could be an unprecedented human disaster. That could mean it was GMOed into a 'Fluebola.' Recall that the 2001 weaponized anthrax attacks were traced to a U.S. government lab. It's incredibly odd that this outbreak occurred 1,000 miles from past outbreaks and it is clearly more easily transmissible.

"Scientists like Yoshihiro Kawaoka at the University of Wisconsin have been 'researching' Ebola for years. Since the anthrax attacks, some $79 billion has been spent. But we still don't have a vaccine ready to protect us. These labs have actually spent government money, including from the National Institutes of Health, to make viruses more deadly. The work done at these labs shouldn't be curtailed or temporarily suspended as the administration seems to be talking about but stopped. This work is criminal. It violates the Biological Weapons Anti-Terrorism Act of 1989, which I wrote. It was passed unanimously by both Houses of Congress and states:

"'Whoever knowingly develops, produces, stockpiles, transfers, acquires, retains, or possesses any biological agent, toxin, or delivery system for use as a weapon, or knowingly assists a foreign state or any organization to do so, shall be fined under this title or imprisoned for life or any term of years, or both. There is extraterritorial Federal jurisdiction over an offense under this section committed by or against a national of the United States.'

"After the law was passed, the government has claimed that it's not violating it because it is creating these more deadly viruses to help protect against them should they develop elsewhere. It's a ridiculous argument to get around the blanket prohibition in the law. This policy has been a catastrophe waiting to happen—a statistical certainty."

Ebola: Are We Being Told the Truth?

October 8, 2014

CNN reports: "Thomas Eric Duncan, a man with Ebola who traveled to the United States from Liberia, died Wednesday morning at Texas Health Presbyterian Hospital in Dallas, the hospital said." Reuters reports at least 3,439 people have died in the current outbreak.

Francis Boyle, fboyle at illinois.edu

Professor at the University of Illinois College of Law, Boyle drafted the U.S. Biological Weapons Anti-Terrorism Act of 1989, which is the U.S. domestic implementing legislation for the Biological Weapons Convention. His books include *Biowarfare and Terrorism.*

He said today: "Different United States government agencies have a long history of doing allegedly defensive biological warfare research at labs in Liberia and Sierra Leone. This includes the CDC, which is now the point agency for managing the Ebola spill-over into the United States. Why is the Obama administration dispatching the elite 101st Airborne Division to Liberia when they have no medical training to provide medical treatment to dying Africans? How did Zaire/Ebola get to West Africa from about 3,500 kilometers away from where it was first identified in 1976?

"Why is the CDC not better prepared for this emergency after the United States government has spent somewhere in the area of $70 billion dollars after the October 2001 anthrax attacks to prepare for this exact contingency? It is clear that those anthrax attacks originated from United States government sources."

CHINA

Tension with China: Interviews Available

April 3, 2001

In the aftermath of a U.S. spy plane landing in China, the following analysts are available for interviews:

Francis Boyle

Professor of international law at the University of Illinois College of Law, Boyle said today: "This is very provocative action by the U.S. off the coast of China. The argument that this plane is U.S. sovereign territory is without merit. It would normally have immunity, but that is compromised when you're spying, like the Gary Powers case, though that went directly over the USSR. The U.S. would never tolerate similar behavior by China; we maintain a 200-mile Air Defense Intercept Zone. Just because we say that this is international airspace doesn't mean that the Chinese accept it; this area in the South China Sea is highly disputed."

GEORGIA

Bush Policy on Russia and Georgia

August 13, 2008

The *New York Times* reports today: "The United States took a series of steps that emboldened Georgia: sending advisers to build up the Georgian military, including an exercise last month with more than 1,000 American troops; pressing hard to bring Georgia into the NATO orbit. . ." Neither President Bush this morning nor Secretary of State Rice yesterday took questions following their comments.

Francis Boyle

Professor of international law at the University of Illinois, Boyle is author of *Breaking All The Rules* and *Destroying World Order*. He said today: "It is curious but not surprising how the Bush administration and its allies have now found renewed respect for international law in the Caucasus, but not when it comes to (1) the United States invading Afghanistan and Iraq, while threatening to attack Iran; (2) Israel invading Lebanon and Palestine, attacking Syria, and threatening to attack Iran; (3) Ethiopia invading Somalia; (4) Colombia attacking Ecuador, etc. From an international law perspective, the real issue here is whether during her trip to Tbilisi a month ago, U.S. Secretary of State Rice gave the proverbial green light to Georgia to attack South Ossetia and thus deliberately provoke an overreaction by Russia. And how does this fit in with the U.S./U.K. naval armada currently steaming for the Persian Gulf and possible military confrontation with Iran over its right to engage in nuclear enrichment under the Nuclear Non-Proliferation Treaty?"

GITMO KANGAROO COURTS

* Military Tribunals * Ashcroft's "Voluntary" Interviews

March 21, 2002

Francis Boyle

Professor of international law at the University of Illinois College of Law, Boyle commented today on the military tribunals: "These are still kangaroo courts that violate the terms of the Third Geneva Convention and the U.S. [War Crimes] Act."

HAITI

Haiti: * Canceling Debt * Adoptions * Just Back

February 4, 2010

Francis Boyle

Boyle, a professor of international law at the University of Illinois in Champaign, said today: "Various countries are right to say that the U.S. is occupying Haiti. As such, under the Fourth Geneva Convention the United States cannot be deporting or transferring Haitian children out of Haiti unless for emergency, life-saving medical treatment only available in the United States and not in Haiti."

HUMAN RIGHTS

If Catholic Anti-Nuclear Weapons Activists in North Korea or Iran Were Jailed

July 3, 2018

On Monday, attorneys filed motions to dismiss all criminal charges against the Kings Bay Plowshares in Federal court in Brunswick, Georgia. The seven Catholic defendants are "charged with three Federal felonies and one misdemeanor for their actions in going onto the Naval Base at Kings Bay Georgia and symbolically disarming the massive amount of nuclear weapons at that base." The group states that their actions are "to make real the prophet Isaiah's command to 'beat swords into plowshares.'" The seven are: Mark Colville, Clare Grady, Martha Hennessy, Jesuit Fr. Stephen Kelly, Patrick O'Neill, Carmen Trotta and Elizabeth McAlister (the widow of Philip Berrigan). See legal update on the case: *KingsBayPlowshares7.org/impact*

The request to dismiss ends the supporting memorandum with the following paragraph: "If the defendants took their actions in North Korea or Iran, the U.S. government would hail their actions. The same U.S. government cannot be allowed to criminally prosecute them at home. The charges should be dismissed." . . .

The group states: "The Motion to Dismiss is supplemented by four important declarations. . .

"Professor Francis Boyle, a renowned Harvard Law graduate and professor of law at the Illinois College of Law, advised the court that nuclear weapons are flatly illegal and the actions of defendants are in full compliance with the law.

"Catholic Bishop Thomas Gumbleton declared that the actions of the Kings Bay Plowshares are totally consistent with and supported by Catholic social teaching that any use or threat of use of nuclear weapons is totally immoral.

"Jeffery Carter, Executive Director of Physicians for Social Responsibility, explained to the court the fact that his organization and the American Medical Association condemn any use of nuclear weapons because of the horrific impact upon millions, perhaps even billions, of people.

"The Kings Bay Naval Station is home to at least six nuclear ballistic missile submarines. Each submarine carries 20 Trident II D 5 MIRV thermonuclear weapons. Each of these individual Trident thermonuclear weapons contains four or more individual nuclear weapons ranging in destructive power from a 100 kilotons to 475 kilotons. To understand the massive destructive power of these weapons remember that the nuclear bomb dropped on Hiroshima was a 15 kiloton bomb."

For interviews and more information, see KingsBayPlowshares7.org and contact:

Jessica Stewart, (207) 266-0919, Paul Magno, kingsbayplowshares at gmail.com

Also, see coverage of Plowshares movement in the *National Catholic Reporter.*

Pope's Blind Spots: * Militarism * Child Sex Abuse

September 24, 2015

Francis Boyle, fboyle at illinois.edu

Boyle is professor of international law at the University of Illinois College of Law. He was the lawyer for the Republic of Bosnia and Herzegovina before the World Court charging Yugoslavia with genocide for raping 40,000 Bosnian women. He said today: "Pope Francis' remarks yesterday that the Church had shown '*courage*' regarding their child sexual abuse scandal is itself scandalous. The Catholic Church hierarchy are accessories to crimes against humanity as defined by the Rome Statute for the International Criminal Court." Boyle wrote the piece "*The Pope, Cardinals And Bishops Should Be Prosecuted For The Sexual Abuse Of Children*," Countercurrents .org, Feb. 13, 2013.

Critics Question Human Rights Standards

July 1, 1998

WASHINGTON—While many applaud statements by President Clinton in China specifically citing the Universal Declaration of Human Rights, analysts associated with the Institute for Public Accuracy are raising questions about selective adherence to the Declaration's provisions.

Among those available for comment are:

Francis Boyle

A professor of International Law at the University of Illinois College of Law who has worked extensively on human rights cases in the U.S.,

Boyle said: "Clinton has urged China to sign the international covenants on Economic, Social and Cultural Rights, and on Civil and Political Rights. The U.S. signed the ESC but did not ratify it. As for the Civil and Political Covenant, the U.S. Senate attached many conditions to our ratification for the express purpose of rendering that ratification meaningless."

IRAN

Iran Attack? * Pretext for War * Impeaching Bolton

June 20, 2019

The U.S. and Iranian governments are giving contradictory accounts surrounding the downing of a large U.S. drone over the Strait of Hormuz. A major issue revolves around whether the downed drone was in international waters; see below. The Trump administration is meeting this afternoon with members of Congress, some of whom have argued that the administration already has authorization to attack Iran.

See accuracy.org news release from last week: "Persian Gulf of Tonkin?"—a reference to the U.S. government deceiving its way to the massive escalation of the Vietnam War in 1964. Also last week, the *New York Times* reported: "One of the tankers that were attacked in the Gulf of Oman was struck by a flying object, the ship's Japanese operator said on Friday, disputing at least part of the account of United States officials who had blamed Iran for the attack."

While many pointed out Bush administration falsehoods after the 2003 invasion of Iraq, accuracy.org produced some of the most hard-hitting scrutiny prior to the invasion, including: "U.S. Credibility Problems" and "White House Claims: A Pattern of Deceit." See from 2013: "Legacy of Iraq War Myths Ten Years Later." Also. see accuracy.org news release from last month: "Postol: Newly Revealed Documents Show Syrian Chemical 'Attacks Were Staged'" regarding the pretext for U.S. attacks on Syria in April of 2018.

Francis Boyle, fboyle at illinois.edu

Professor of international law at the University of Illinois, Boyle's books include *Destroying World Order*. He said today: "Iran has not committed an 'armed attack' upon the United States that would trigger the right of self-defense set forth in UN Charter Article 51. So under the current circumstances as they stand now, a U.S. military attack upon Iran would constitute a violation of international and domestic law. The 2001 AUMF most certainly does not authorize force in this case as some have claimed.

"Given the manner in which National Security Advisor John Bolton is pressing for war, a member of the House should put in a Bill of Impeachment against him immediately. It may be the best way to avoid a catastrophic war." Boyle was a lead author of the bill of impeachment put forward by Rep. Henry Gonzalez in 1991 against George H.W. Bush, who later wrote that fear of impeachment prevented him from a full invasion of Iraq.

Regarding the Strait of Hormuz, Boyle said: "This is not an international strait or waterway as defined by the International Court of Justice in the *Corfu Channel Case*. So U.S. warships and planes and drones need the permission of the territorial sovereign (Oman or Iran) to pass through there including their respective airspaces." See below for more details.

. . .

Regarding the U.S. claim that the drone was in international waters, the U.S. Energy Information Administration states that: "At its narrowest point, the Strait [of Hormuz] is 21 miles wide." Countries are entitled to a belt of coastal waters extending 12 nautical miles.

United Nations Convention for the Law of the Sea maybe relevant, except for the fact that UNCLOSdebate.org notes: "Iran signed the 1982 Convention in [the] same year, but it has not ratified it, primarily due to their opposition to the 'innocent passage' provisions of UNCLOS that allow U.S. warships freedom of navigation." Will Rogers, writing for the Center for a New American Security, has advocated the U.S. ratify the treaty—as a way to gain leverage over Iran: "Ratification will also help the United States deflate Iran's recent challenges to U.S. freedom of navigation through the Strait of Hormuz."

Persian Gulf of Tonkin?

June 14, 2019

During what the *Nikkei Asian Review* is reporting was the first visit to Tehran by a Japanese leader since the 1979 revolution, there was an attack on two Japan-bound tankers, near the Straits of Hormuz Thursday.

Iranian Foreign Minister Javad Zarif tweeted: "Reported attacks on Japan-related tankers occurred while [Prime Minister Abe] @AbeShinzo was meeting with [Iranian Supreme Leader Ali Khamenei] @khamenei_ir for extensive and friendly talks. Suspicious doesn't begin to describe what likely transpired this morning. Iran's proposed Regional Dialogue Forum is imperative."

U.S. Secretary of State Mike Pompeo—who made a statement at the State Department and refused to take questions—tweeted: "It is the assessment of the U.S. government that Iran is responsible for today's attacks in the Gulf of Oman."

Journalist Rania Khalek, warned that national security adviser John Bolton and Secretary of State Mike Pompeo "are trying to create a Gulf of Tonkin incident with Iran," referring to a falsified incident that the Johnson administration used in 1964 to dramatically escalate the Vietnam War.

. . .

Francis Boyle, fboyle@illinois.edu

Professor of international law at the University of Illinois, Boyle's books include *Destroying World Order*. He said today: "Some are claiming that the 2001 Authorization for Military Force would authorize attacking Iran. This is totally false. The AUMF is currently being stretched in a highly dubious manner and should be rescinded. To apply it to Iran would be totally absurd.

"Given the manner Bolton is pressing for war, a member of the House should put in a Bill of Impeachment against him immediately.

"It's certainly possible that some Iranian faction, like the Revolutionary Guard, which the U.S. government designated as terrorists earlier this year (see accuracy.org news release), could have done this, but Pompeo provided no serious evidence. His basic reasoning, that Iran is likely guilty largely because it had the capacity to conduct such attacks, could just as easily be applied to the U.S., Saudi, or Israeli governments or possibly groups they support.

"And it's the U.S. government that has the most dramatic history of violence in this respect. The civilian Iran Air Flight 655 was downed by the USS Vincennes over the Persian Gulf in 1988. And Iran brought a suit against the U.S. at the International Court of Justice in the *Oil Platforms Case*. The court eventually ruled that 'the actions of the U.S. against Iranian oil platforms . . . cannot be justified as measures necessary to protect the essential security interests of the U.S., though the court rejected the call for reparations by Iran."

. . .

How the Iran Deal "Snap Back" Could be Manipulated

July 20, 2015

Francis Boyle, fboyle at illinois.edu

Boyle is a professor at the University of Illinois College of Law. His books on international law include *Destroying Libya and World Order*.

He said today: "President Obama and others have stated that if Iran violates the agreement, the sanctions on Iran will 'snap back' into place. That's true, but what's menacing about this is what they don't highlight: the sanctions could quite conceivably 'snap back' based on some bogus pretext after Iran has dismantled the guts of its nuclear industry that is lawful under the Nuclear Non-Proliferation Treaty. Everyone knows that Iran does not have nuclear weapons to begin with.

"Under the agreement, this current or some future U.S. administration would only need the votes of the European powers to enact such a scenario since decisions will be made by the majority of a group that includes not only Iran, China, Russia, France and the UK, but also Germany and the EU. They have in effect set up a mechanism that gets around the possibility of a Russian and/or Chinese veto.

"The UN Security Council resolution passed today states that disputes arising from the agreement will be dealt with by this panel and that 'If the Security Council does not adopt a resolution' then the sanctions Iran has been under 'shall apply in the same manner as they applied before the adoption of this resolution.' So if the U.S. vetoes action by the Security Council, the sanctions come back.

"There has been misreporting on this issue, for example rightwing outlets like CNN falsely claiming: 'Iran Deal Includes Loophole in Sanctions "Snapback" Mechanism.' Meanwhile, most mainstream or liberal reporting or commentary about this has been laudatory about the way the 'snap back' mechanism works: 'How the Iran Deal's 'Snap Back' Mechanism Will Keep Tehran Compliant.'

"This ignores the record of the U.S. government on these issues. In the recent case of Libya, Muammar Gaddafi eliminated his nuclear equipment and then was literally stabbed in the back—NATO bombed the country, he was murdered, and there's a failed state there now, leading to untold human suffering. At a minimum, the United States government will use the 'snapback' mechanism as a cudgel to beat the Islamic Republic of Iran into 'regime change,' which has been its objective all along."

IRAQ

Is Obama Falsifying Legacy and Legality of Iraq War—and Crimea?

March 27, 2014

Activists and legal experts are criticizing President Obama's remarks in Brussels on Wednesday on war and international law. Among other things, Obama claimed: "But even in Iraq, America sought to work within the international system. We did not claim or annex Iraq's territory. We did not grab its resources for our own gain. Instead, we ended our war and left Iraq to its people in a fully sovereign Iraqi state that can make decisions about its own future."

Francis Boyle, fboyle at illinois.edu

Boyle is a professor at the University of Illinois College of Law. His books include *Foundations of World Order* (Duke University Press: 1999). He said today: "In March 2003 the United States launched an illegal and criminal war of aggression against Iraq based on false pretexts, a Nuremberg Crime against Peace. The United States destroyed Iraq as a functioning state and effectively carved-up Iraq de facto into three mini-statelets that are at war with each other today, killing an estimated 1.4 million Iraqis in the process. Suicide bombings in Iraq continue to be a fact of everyday life. By comparison, the Russian annexation of Crimea was almost bloodless."

* Mideast: Bush and Presidential Race * Rallying against Iran * Elliott Abrams

January 9, 2008

Francis Boyle

Professor of international law at the University of Illinois, Boyle is author of the just-released *Breaking All the Rules: Palestine, Iraq, Iran and the Case for Impeachment*. He said today: "The real purpose of this trip is to line up support from Arab 'leaders' throughout the Middle East for a U.S./Israeli bombing campaign against Iran—despite the clear and convincing evidence that Iran does not have a nuclear weapons program."

A Move to Impeach Bush

June 10, 2008

The Politico reports: "Rep. Dennis Kucinich (D-Ohio) introduced 35 articles of impeachment against President Bush on Monday night, reading the resolution into the Congressional Record . . . Kucinich has introduced a similar impeachment resolution against Vice President Cheney. That resolution was referred to the House Judiciary Committee, which has taken no action on the measure. Speaker Nancy Pelosi (D-Calif.) and other top House Democratic leaders have stated that there will be no consideration of impeachment proceedings against Bush, calling the idea 'off the table.'"

Francis Boyle law at the University of Illinois, Boyle urged impeaching Bush as early as October 2002, during the buildup to the Iraq invasion. His books include *Destroying World Order: A Guide to Impeaching President George W. Bush*.

Who Was Right About Iraqi WMDs? Why? What Now?

March 31, 2005

Francis Boyle

Professor of international law at the University of Illinois, in October of 2002 Boyle launched a campaign to impeach Bush. He said today: "The Bush administration was lying about WMD in Iraq right from the get-go, and those of us in the American peace movement were saying so at the time, beginning as of late August in 2002 when Vice President Cheney went public with these absurd charges for the express purpose of mongering for war with the American people and the U.S. Congress . . . Bush, Cheney, Rumsfeld and Rice are now desperately trying to have U.S. intelligence agencies take the fall. . ."

"Tough Questions for Bush on Iraq Tonight," March 6, 2003

"Considering that the U.S. government has based its case for war against Iraq on a non-existent IAEA report, a plagiarized dossier, non-existent Iraq-Al'Qaida link, and twisting of the words of Saddam's late son-in-law Hussein Kamel (see the March 3 [2003] *Newsweek* for background information), what evidence can you offer to support your claim that Iraq represents a threat to the world today?"

Bush Rebuffed Plan for Other Nations' Troops in Iraq; U.S. Setting Stage for Rigged Iraqi Elections?

October 20, 2004

Newsday has reported that "President George W. Bush rebuffed a plan last month for a Muslim peacekeeping force that would have helped the United Nations organize elections in Iraq, according to Saudi and Iraqi officials."

The paper reported: "As a result, the UN continues to have a skeletal presence in Iraq, with only four staff members working full time on preparing for elections set for the end of January. UN Secretary-General Kofi Annan has refused to establish a new UN headquarters in Baghdad unless countries commit troops for a special force to protect it . . . Diplomats said Annan accepted the plan. But the Bush administration objected because the special force would have been controlled by the UN instead of by U.S. military officers who run the Multi-National Force in Iraq."

According to the Associated Press, White House spokesman Scott McClellan "said the interim Iraqi government in Baghdad had 'some real concerns' about having troops from a neighboring country inside Iraq."

But the *Newsday* report, which was published on Oct. 18, stated that "Iraqi officials already had worked out a deal with the Saudis ruling out the involvement of any country that borders Iraq." The report stated that, according Saudi sources, "Pakistan, Bangladesh, Malaysia, Algeria and Morocco were 'seriously interested'" in contributing troops to fulfill the plan.

Francis Boyle

Professor of international law at the University of Illinois and author of the new book *Destroying World Order*, Boyle said today: "The only way to have a free, fair and democratic election would be for the United States and the United Kingdom to terminate their role as the Belligerent Occupants of Iraq, withdraw, and then permit the United Nations to organize elections. It recently did this in East Timor."

With Bush at U.N.: Iraq War Illegal?

September 21, 2004

Heads of state, including George W. Bush, address the U.N. General Assembly today. U.N. Secretary General Kofi Annan recently stated the invasion of Iraq "was not in conformity with the U.N. Charter from our point of view, from the Charter point of view, it was illegal."

Here are some relevant excerpts from the U.N. Charter:

"All Members shall settle their international disputes by peaceful means in such a manner that international peace and security, and justice, are not endangered. All Members shall refrain in their international relations from the threat or use of force against the territorial integrity or political independence of any state, or in any other manner inconsistent with the Purposes of the United Nations. . .

"The parties to any dispute, the continuance of which is likely to endanger the maintenance of international peace and security, shall, first of all, seek a solution by negotiation, enquiry, mediation, conciliation, arbitration, judicial settlement, resort to regional agencies or arrangements, or other peaceful means of their own choice. . .

"The Security Council shall determine the existence of any threat to the peace, breach of the peace, or act of aggression and shall make recommendations, or decide what measures shall be taken . . . to maintain or restore international peace and security."

U.N. Charter (Chapter I, Article 2; Chapter VI, Article 33; Chapter VII, Article 39)

Francis Boyle

Boyle is professor of international law at the University of Illinois and author of the new book *Destroying World Order*. He said today: "The entire legal argument for the invasion of Iraq was a fraud and that was clear before the invasion took place. The U.S. government drove towards war, it did not attempt to avoid it as the Charter calls for. Kofi Annan should have clearly said that it was illegal at that time. But stating it now does pull the legal rug out from under continued U.S. military occupation of Iraq. The United Nations must ensure the immediate departure of all foreign military forces from Iraq, and the exercise of their sovereign right to self-determination by the Iraqi people freed from the current U.S.-imposed puppet government."

[See Boyle's quote on the IPA news release of Nov. 1, 2002, "Interviews on Iraq: U.N. Endgame,"]

* Bush: A Call for Censure * Prosecuting Protestors

February 10, 2004

Francis Boyle

Boyle is author of the book *Destroying World Order: U.S. Imperialism in the Middle East Before and After September 11th*, which includes a "Guide to Impeaching President George W. Bush."

Captive Saddam: Looking Deeper

December 16, 2003

Francis Boyle

Boyle is professor of International Law at the University of Illinois and author of *Destroying World Order: U.S. Imperialism in the Middle East Before and After September 11*. He said today: "This is the 21st century equivalent of the Roman Emperor parading the defeated barbarian king before the assembled masses so that they might all shout in unison: Hail Caesar!"

Interviews Available: Bush at the UN
September 23, 2003
Francis Boyle
Professor of international law at the University of Illinois and author of the forthcoming *Destroying World Order*, Boyle said today: "A real and independent UN Peacekeeping Force should be deployed to Iraq under the auspices of the UN General Assembly (not the U.S. co-opted UN Security Council), pursuant to its powers under the Uniting for Peace Resolution (1950) . . . This is exactly what happened in the 1956 Middle East 'war' when the UN General Assembly deployed the UN Emergency Force to the Sinai in order to facilitate the withdrawal of aggressor military forces by the U.K., France and Israel. . ."

* Mideast 'Honest Broker'? * Iraq Turmoil * Iran
June 17, 2003
Francis Boyle
Professor of international law at the University of Illinois College of Law and author of *Foundations of World Order*, Boyle set up a campaign in October 2002 advocating impeachment proceedings against President George W. Bush—a possibility that others, such as former Counsel to the President of the United States, John W. Dean, are now raising. Boyle cited a pattern of deceit in the build-up to the invasion of Iraq while Bush was rallying Congress and the American public.

Interviews Available: Ending Iraq Sanctions
May 22, 2003
Francis Boyle
Professor of international law at the University of Illinois and author of *Foundations of World Order*, Boyle said today: "Bush is basically getting the Security Council to reverse the long-standing Stimson Doctrine: That the world will not recognize the fruits of an aggressive war. But that is exactly what the Security Council has just done."

Interviews Available: Lifting Sanctions; Controlling Oil; A New Mideast
May 9, 2003

Today's lead story in the *Washington Post* about the U.S. proposal to lift the economic sanctions on Iraq—headlined "U.S. to Propose Broad Control of Iraqi Oil, Funds"—notes that "the proposal would give the United States far greater authority over Iraq's lucrative oil industry than administration officials have previously acknowledged." Also today, President Bush is giving a speech on his administration's vision for a new Mideast. The following are available for comment:

Francis Boyle

Professor of law at the University of Illinois and author of *Foundations of World Order*, Boyle said today: "The U.S. draft resolution at the U.N. outlines the piracy not just of Iraq's oil, but also Iraq's assets around the world . . . The question of sanctions on Iraq ignores the broader questions of the legal basis for sanctions in general. After Iraq illegally invaded Kuwait in 1990, the U.N. Security Council applied economic sanctions to force Iraq's withdrawal. The U.N., following the same principle, should clearly do the same to the U.S. now and impose sanctions on it. . ."

Will the Oil of Iraq Belong to the Iraqi People?

April 28, 2003

On Friday (April 25) the *Wall Street Journal* reported on U.S. government plans to restructure Iraq's oil industry. These plans, which would replace the oil ministry with a U.S. corporate model, are expected to be announced this week. The *Journal* reports that the Iraqi oil industry will be overseen by an "advisory board." The board is slated to be headed by Philip Carroll, an American who is a former chief executive of Shell Oil, the U.S. arm of Royal Dutch/Shell Group.

Francis Boyle

Professor of law at the University of Illinois and author of *Foundations of World Order*, Boyle said today: "The United Nations Security Council must continue to control Iraq's oil and convert the proceeds into a trust fund that it will administer for the benefit of the Iraqi people in accordance with the international laws of belligerent occupation. Otherwise, the Bush administration and its private sector cronies will loot Iraq's oil fields, exploit the Iraqi people, and mortgage their future by setting up a puppet government. . ."

Iraq: Oil-For-Food; War No Matter What?

November 25, 2002

Francis Boyle

Boyle is professor of international law at the University of Illinois College of Law and is available for interviews regarding the recent UN Security Council resolution, particularly the argument advanced by the Bush administration that Iraqi firings in the "no-fly zones" constitute a violation of the recent resolution.

An Analysis of the United Nations Security Council Resolution 1441

November 13, 2002 By journalist

as Adopted on November 8, 2002

The Security Council, Recalling all its previous relevant resolutions, in particular its resolutions 661 (1990) of 6 August 1990, 678 (1990) of 29 November 1990, 686 (1991) of 2 March 1991, 687 (1991) of 3 April 1991, 688 (1991) of 5 April 1991, 707 (1991) of 15 August 1991, 715 (1991) of 11 October 1991, 986 (1995) of 14 April 1995, and 1284 (1999) of 17 December 1999, and all the relevant statements of its President,

. . .

Francis Boyle, professor of international law at the University of Illinois College of Law: "In 1990, France, the Soviet Union, and China all sold Iraq out at the Security Council . . . Russia can be bought by getting admitted to the WTO and being given a free hand on Georgia and Chechnya, as well as having its oil interests guaranteed in Iraq. China wants an end to proposed high-tech U.S. weapons sales to Taiwan. France wants its oil interests in Iraq protected, as well as its sphere of influence in Francophone Africa respected. The serious bargaining has yet to begin. Meanwhile, Kofi Annan plays the role of Pontius Pilate. Remember that under the UN Charter, the UN Secretary-general is not supposed to be an errand boy for the Permanent 5. And yet he is. The bottom line here is that the Bush Junior administration originally sought and has now failed to obtain the same language from the UN Security Council that the Bush Senior administration obtained in resolution 679 (1990), authorizing UN Member States 'to use all necessary means' to expel Iraq from Kuwait. So a unilateral attack by the United States and the United Kingdom against Iraq without further authorization from the Security Council would still remain illegal and therefore constitute aggression. In recognition of this fact, British government officials are already reportedly fearful of prosecution by the International Criminal Court. And the Bush Junior administration is doing everything humanly possible to sabotage the ICC in order to avoid any prospect of ICC prosecution of high-level U.S. government officials over a war against Iraq. Lawyers call this 'consciousness of guilt.'"

Interviews on Iraq: UN Endgame

November 1, 2002

"All Members shall settle their international disputes by peaceful means in such a manner that international peace and security, and justice, are not endangered. All Members shall refrain in their international relations from the threat or use of force against the territorial integrity or political independence of any state, or in any other manner inconsistent with the Purposes of the United Nations."—UN Charter (Chapter I, Article 2) [See: www.un.org/aboutun/charter]

Francis Boyle

Professor of international law at the University of Illinois College of Law, Boyle said today: "If the UN Security Council gives the Bush administration this legal fig-leaf for its pre-planned aggression against Iraq, the Security Council shall prove its own legal and moral bankruptcy."

U.S. Demanding an "Occupation Arrangement"?

October 2, 2002

Francis Boyle

Professor of international law at the University of Illinois College of Law, Boyle said today: "The resolution is just a pretext for war. No way Iraq, or any other state, could accept such a resolution . . . The U.S. government is [currently] violating the U.N. Charter . . . by using military force to allegedly 'police' the illegal 'no-fly' zones. . ."

The United States, the World and War

September 10, 2002

Francis Boyle

Professor of international law at the University of Illinois College of Law and author of *The Criminality of Nuclear Deterrence: Could the U.S. War on Terrorism Go Nuclear?*, Boyle said today: "President Bush is exploiting the terrible human and national tragedy of September 11 in order to monger for war against Iraq at the United Nations."

Iraq and Impeachment: Interviews Available

December 16, 1998

Francis Boyle

Professor of International Law at the University of Illinois College of Law in Champaign, Illinois, Boyle said: "The incentive is to start bombing and continue until January 6th, when the new Congress convenes and the resolution of the House Judiciary Committee dies. The new Congress would have to start impeachment proceedings all over again . . . The War Powers clause of the United States Constitution, Article I, Section 8, expressly requires authorization by Congress before the President can engage in acts of war, unless there is a direct attack upon the United States. Clinton has also violated the War Powers Resolution of 1973 that was enacted by Congress over President Nixon's veto in order to prevent a repetition of the Vietnam War scenario, where Americans were misled by repeated presidential lies, misrepresentations, deceits and falsehoods at every step of the way."

IRELAND

St. Patrick's Day and the Irish Famine

March 16, 2011

Francis Boyle

Professor of international law at the University of Illinois College of Law in Champaign, Boyle is author of *United Ireland, Human Rights and International Law.*

He said today: "Some controversy has surrounded the use of the word 'genocide' with regard to the Great Irish Famine. But this controversy has its source in an apparent misunderstanding of the meaning of genocide. No, the British government did not inflict on the Irish the abject horrors of the Nazi Holocaust. But the definition of 'genocide' reaches beyond such ghastly behavior to encompass other reprehensible acts designed to destroy a people." Boyle wrote "*The Irish Famine Was Genocide*," History News Network, March 18, 2010.

Background: "The Famine Year" by Speranza, the mother of Oscar Wilde

Judicial Nominations

KAVANAUGH

Is Kavanaugh a War Criminal?

September 25, 2018

Amnesty International USA just issued a "*Rare Call for a Halt on Kavanaugh Nomination.*"

The group states: "Amnesty International believes that the vetting of Brett Kavanaugh's record on human rights has been insufficient and calls for the vote on his nomination for Supreme Court of the United States to be further postponed unless and until any information relevant to Kavanaugh's possible involvement in human rights violations—including in relation to the U.S. government's use of torture and other forms of ill-treatment, such as during the CIA detention program—is declassified and made public."

Margaret Huang, executive director of Amnesty International USA said: "Amnesty International takes no position on the appointment of particular individuals to government positions, unless they are reasonably suspected of crimes under international law and could use their appointment to the position in question to either prevent accountability for these crimes or to continue perpetration."

See report from earlier this month on "*Confidential Emails Reveal Kavanaugh Wanted to Make Author of Bush-era Torture Memo a Judge*" about just some of Kavanaugh's documents highlighted by Sen. Cory Booker.

Francis Boyle, fboyle at illinois.edu
Boyle is professor of international law at the University of Illinois College of Law. He was an elected member of the Board of Directors of Amnesty International USA from 1988 to 1992.

He said today: "Contrary to the mantra that the Democrats on the Senate Judiciary Committee have it in for Kavanaugh, they've largely let him off the hook on a number of critical issues, instead favoring theatrics.

"While there's substantial attention being paid to the serious charges of sexual assault by Kavanaugh, there's been very little note that he is a putative war criminal. Specifically, recently released documents show that while Kavanaugh worked for the George W. Bush administration, one of the people he attempted to put on the judiciary was John Yoo, who authored many of the justifications for torture that came out of the Bush administration.

"I've had very serious problems with others placed on the Supreme Court, but I've never thought of them as putative war criminals. And while other parts of Kavanaugh's professional record are unseemly, including his lying under oath, his work for Ken Starr and for Bush's election during the Florida standoff in 2000, this stands out even in such a record.

"And while some of the current members of the Supreme Court have been members of the Federalist Society, none have been of this ilk of members like John Yoo and Bush Attorney General/White House Counsel Alberto Gonzalez—as Kavanaugh, who worked for Gonzalez at the White House. The U.S. Senate must not place a putative war criminal on the U.S. Supreme Court." See Boyle's analysis in *The Guardian,* "The Stakes Are Astronomical: Supreme Court Hearing Will Be a Battle," Sept. 3, 2018.

The following exchange is from a debate between Yoo and Doug Cassel, director of Notre Dame Law School's Center for Civil and Human Rights held on Dec. 1, 2005:

Cassel: "If the president deems that he's got to torture somebody, including by crushing the testicles of the person's child, there is no law that can stop him?"
Yoo: "No treaty."
Cassel: "Also no law by Congress—that is what you wrote in the August 2002 memo."
Yoo: "I think it depends on why the president thinks he needs to do that."

Listen to audio here.

Will Kavanaugh Take a Lie Detector Test?
September 17, 2018

The *Washington Post* reports: "An attorney for Christine Blasey Ford, the woman who alleged Judge Brett M. Kavanaugh assaulted her when the two were in high school, said Monday that Ford is willing to testify about the allegations before the Senate Judiciary Committee." The *Post* also reports "On the advice of [attorney Debra] Katz, who said she believed Ford would be attacked as a liar if she came forward, Ford took a polygraph test administered by a former FBI agent in early August."

Time magazine just published the piece "Brett Kavanaugh Can't Be Trusted. We Know Because We Worked as Counsel to Senators When He Was in the Bush White House."

Francis Boyle, fboyle at illinois.edu

Boyle is professor of international law at the University of Illinois College of Law and has taught criminal law. He said today: "Kavanaugh clearly has little compulsion against lying under oath. Prof. Christine Blasey Ford has taken and passed a lie detector test. So the question becomes: Will Kavanaugh take a lie detector test?" See Boyle's analysis in *The Guardian* and the IPA news release "Kavanaugh and the Federalist Society" and "Will a Member of Congress Move to Impeach Kavanaugh?"

See recent piece from The Daily Beast: "Newly Released Emails Show Brett Kavanaugh May Have Perjured Himself at Least Four Times."

Also, see from FAIR: "Establishment Media Shy Away From Claims of Perjury by Kavanaugh."

Will a Member of Congress Move to Impeach Kavanaugh?

September 10, 2018

Francis Boyle, fboyle at illinois.edu

Boyle is professor of international law at the University of Illinois College of Law. He said today: "What's needed is a brave member of the House to introduce a Bill of Impeachment against Kavanaugh immediately for perjury to force this issue. That's what we need. Machinations from the Democratic Party leadership are more Kabuki theater." See recent comments from Boyle on The Real News, Sept. 6, 2018, in *The Guardian* and the IPA news release "Kavanaugh and the Federalist Society."

Boyle was was legal adviser to Rep. Henry B. González when he released classified material on the House floor in 1992 in an attempt to impeach George H. W. Bush following the Gulf War. Bush would later write in his memoirs that if the Gulf War "drags out, not only will I take the blame, but I will probably have impeachment proceedings filed against me."

See recent piece from The Daily Beast: "Newly Released Emails Show Brett Kavanaugh May Have Perjured Himself at Least Four Times," which notes the documentation of Kavanaugh's past falsehoods is only due to recently released emails, but that "only 7 percent of Kavanaugh's White House records have been released to the public. . .

"The clearest contradiction between Judge Kavanaugh's sworn testimony and the formerly confidential email record concerns the nomination of Judge

William Pryor, a conservative firebrand. In 2006, Kavanaugh was asked, by the late Sen. Ted Kennedy, whether Pryor's extreme statements disturbed him. Kavanaugh replied that he was not involved in the selection or vetting of Judge Pryor."

The Daily Beast notes that last week, Sen. Patrick Leahy entered "a formerly-confidential email into the record that states clearly that Kavanaugh actually did interview Pryor. 'How did the Pryor interview go?' he was asked in December, 2002. 'Call me,' he replied."

The just-disclosed emails also show a leading voice defending Kavanaugh knew he was actually involved in the Pryor nomination. Benjamin Wittes, senior fellow at the Brookings Institution and editor-in-chief of *Lawfare* blog was himself communicating with Kavanaugh about the Pryor nomination at the time, writing to Kavanagh: "I take it back. I will write something about the decision to nominate Pryor promptly . . . You should send over any exculpatory information you might have quickly."

Wittes just responded to this revelation by writing: "I'm off Twitter until further notice."

Will the Public See Incriminating Kavanaugh Documents?

September 6, 2018

Sen. Cory Booker (D-NJ): "I stand by the public's right to have access to this document and know this nominee's views on issues [that are] are profoundly important—like race and the law, torture and other issues."

Francis Boyle, fboyle at illinois.edu

Boyle was legal adviser to Rep. Henry B. González when he released classified material on the House floor in 1992 in an attempt to impeach George H. W. Bush following the Gulf War. See *New York Times* piece at the time: "C.I.A. Chief Says Legislator Disclosed Secrets."

Boyle, who is professor of international law at the University of Illinois College of Law, said today: "If Booker and the other Democratic senators are serious here, they should all start sequentially releasing all prejudicial and incriminating documents against [Supreme Court nominee Brett] Kavanaugh now during the course of the hearings when they will be protected by the Speech or Debate Clause [of the Constitution]. This would include documents relating to torture and war crimes."

Boyle was featured in a recent *Guardian* overview piece on the Kavanaugh nomination. Also, see his comments on an IPA news release: "Kavanaugh and the Federalist Society."

Kavanaugh: "Stakes are Astronomical"

September 4, 2018

Boyle is professor of international law at the University of Illinois College of Law. He is quoted in a *Guardian* overview "'*The Stakes are Astronomical':*

Brett Kavanaugh Confirmation Hearing Will be a Battle Royale," Sept. 3, 2018, which states: "'The only hope the country has is that Democrats will treat Kavanaugh like a hostile witness on the witness stand under cross-examination, throw him off script and break him down,' said Francis Boyle, a law professor at the University of Illinois. 'You do not need a gentleman or gentlewoman to deal with Kavanaugh. You need a district attorney. Some Democrats are going to have to go for the jugular.'"

"But Kavanaugh, 53, is no Daniel in the lions' den. He is the ultimate Washington insider, steeped in the city's political and legal establishments. His father spent more than two decades in the city as a lobbyist for the cosmetics industry . . . The groups Women's March and Center for Popular Democracy Action are planning a day of action in Washington on Tuesday."

"Boyle . . . shares these concerns. 'I think Kavanaugh was put on there to ensure *Roe* is overturned,' he said. 'He has used the Roberts dodge of saying it is settled law. So what? The Supreme Court can unsettle it tomorrow. He did not say it was decided correctly.'

"Critics note that Trump has relied heavily on the rightwing Heritage Foundation and Federalist Society to develop his shortlist for Supreme Court nominations. Boyle said: 'Kavanaugh is an extreme ideologue and a legal hatchet man for the Federalist Society. He was their spear carrier for years. He is being put on there by Trump to do their business and make the court as far right as he can under the circumstances. It's going to be bad for a lot of people: for Gays, for African Americans, for labour, for women.'"

Kavanaugh and the Federalist Society

July 10, 2018

Supreme Court nominee Brett Kavanaugh claimed Monday night: "No president has ever consulted more widely or talked to more people from more backgrounds to seek input for a Supreme Court nomination."

Francis Boyle, fboyle at illinois.edu

Boyle is professor of international law at the University of Illinois College of Law. He is a longtime critic of the Federalist Society. See this in-depth piece on the group in *Emerge* magazine, "Hijacking Justice," October 1999.

He said today: "Brett Kavanaugh was chosen off a list of possibilities put to Trump by Leonard Leo, who is 'on leave' as executive vice president of the Federalist Society.

"Kavanaugh drafted portions of the Starr report, a political hit job. Perhaps more importantly, he drafted parts of the Ken Starr 'referral' to the U.S. Congress recommending that Bill Clinton be impeached for a blowjob and lying about a blowjob.

"Kavanaugh worked for then-Republican nominee George W. Bush in *Bush v. Gore*, which effectively robbed the American people of the presidency.

"Kavanaugh amusingly invoked the name of Elena Kagan in his remarks last night, as if her hiring him at Harvard made him some kind of moderate. But it was Kagan who said 'I love the Federalist Society.'

"The fact that if Kavanaugh gets through, the entire Supreme Court will have gone to Harvard or Yale is terrible for the country. And I say that as having graduated magna cum laude from Harvard Law.

"Trump acknowledged Edwin Meese last night, which is fitting because in addition to being Ronald Reagan's Attorney General, he was a leading founder of the Federalist Society. The Independent Counsel in the Iran-Contra Scandal Judge Lawrence Walsh found that Meese was the architect of its cover-up by the Reagan administration.

"Almost all of the Bush administration lawyers responsible for its war and torture memos are members of the Federalist Society. Many members of the Federalist Society say that *Brown v. Board of Education* [which struck down 'separate but equal'] was decided wrongly and practice to overturn it at the United States Supreme Court."

Boyle said in a recent interview with The Real News "*Justice Anthony Kennedy's Retirement: End of Roe v. Wade?,*" June 28, 2018, that since the Robert Bork nomination "all these nominees have learned that lesson, and they will present their narrative, their script, and they will stick to it to the end . . . And the Democrats aren't going to call them. They didn't really call Gorsuch on anything. So this is all about raw power politics."

Boyle added: "I first received the ire of the Federalist Society when they had a meeting about how to stop me from helping expose them, when I passed around a quote from Lawrence Walsh about the group. He, a lifelong Republican, wrote: 'I was concerned about the continuing political allegiance of Republican judges as manifested in the Federalist Society. Although the organization was not openly partisan, its dogma was political. It reminded me of the communist front groups of the 1940s and 1950s, whose members were committed to the communist cause and subject to communist direction but were not card-carrying members of the Communist Party. In calling for the narrow construction of constitutional grants of government power, the Federalist Society seemed to speak for right-wing Republicans. I was especially troubled that one of White House Counsel Boyden Gray's assistants had openly declared that no one who was not a member of the Federalist Society had received a judicial appointment from President Bush.'"

BARRON

Rand Paul to Filibuster Pro-Drone Lawyer's Judgeship
May 21, 2014

The *Los Angeles Times* is reporting: "President Obama's Justice Department will release a long-sought secret document laying out the legal basis for using drones to kill Americans suspected of terrorist activities abroad, administration officials confirmed Tuesday.

"Rather than appeal a court order that the so-called 'drone memo' be released under the Freedom of Information Act, Atty. Gen. Eric H. Holder Jr. concurred with the decision of Solicitor Gen. Donald Verrilli not to pursue the appeal and agreed to release a redacted version of the document, the officials said . . .

"The news leaked a day before the Senate was scheduled to hold a procedural vote to advance the judicial nomination of the writer of the memo, David Barron, a former Justice Department official nominated to serve on the U.S. 1st Circuit Court of Appeals in Boston.

"The promise of disclosure did not appear to derail a promised filibuster of the nomination by Republican Sen. Rand Paul of Kentucky. Paul said last week that he had read the memo and wasn't satisfied.

"And in an advance excerpt from his prepared remarks, released Tuesday, Paul said he would oppose the nomination of 'anyone who would argue that the president has the power to kill American citizens not involved in combat.'"

Rand Paul tweeted this morning: "Why don't we wait on the memos to be released before voting on Barron's nomination? #StandWithRand."

Francis Boyle, fboyle at illinois.edu

Boyle is a professor at the University of Illinois College of Law and author of *Tackling America's Toughest Questions*. While the administration now states it will release the memos Barron wrote only after the Senate votes on his judgeship, an associated white paper has been made public.

Boyle said of the white paper: "It's not a serious piece of legal scholarship or analysis. Rather, the entire purpose is to provide legal cover to Obama, [CIA Director John] Brennan, the CIA and JSOC [Joint Special Operations Command] for the drone murders, including of U.S. citizens."

Boyle added: "Barron co-authored the infamous Justice department opinion authorizing Obama's murder of U.S. citizens. This is a total disgrace. If approved, we will have a murderer and a war criminal sitting on the U.S. First Circuit . . . So here Barron and [his coauthor in the legal opinion Martin] Lederman deliberately and maliciously write a get-out-of-jail-free card for Obama so that he can murder U.S. citizens, which he does . . . Barron is neither fit nor qualified to serve as a judge on the First Circuit—a post which would make him a prime candidate for a U.S. Supreme Court seat . . . This is exactly how Bush paid back Jay Bybee [author of legal memos on torture] when he put him on the Ninth Circuit. Obama is worse than Bush in that Obama is a lawyer and knows better."

Left and Right Unite Against Pro-Drone Lawyer's Judgeship

May 6, 2014

The Guardian reports: "Senator Rand Paul and the American Civil Liberties Union are threatening to derail the confirmation of one of President Barack Obama's nominees to the Federal judiciary until the Obama administration releases secret legal opinions the nominee wrote blessing the killing of US citizens without trial in extreme circumstances.

"David Barron, formerly of the Justice Department's office of legal counsel, is set to receive a Senate floor vote as early as this week to sit on the United States court of appeals for the first circuit . . .

"But both Paul and the ACLU, which on Monday sent a letter to senators about Barron's nomination, are using what leverage they possess to highlight a lack of disclosure around the drone strike memos Barron penned."

Francis Boyle, fboyle at illinois.edu

Boyle is a professor at the University of Illinois College of Law and author of *Tackling America's Toughest Questions*. He said today: "Barron co-authored the infamous Justice department opinion authorizing Obama's murder of U.S. citizens. This is a total disgrace. If approved, we will have a murderer and a war criminal sitting on the U.S. First Circuit . . . So here Barron and [his coauthor in the legal opinion Martin] Lederman deliberately and maliciously write a get-out-of-jail free card for Obama so that he can murder U.S. citizens, which he does . . . Barron is neither fit nor qualified to serve as a judge on the First Circuit—a post which would make him a prime candidate for a U.S. Supreme Court seat . . . This is exactly how Bush paid back Jay Bybee [author of legal memos on torture] when he put him on the Ninth Circuit. Obama is worse than Bush in that Obama is a lawyer and knows better."

Pro-Drone Lawyer Up for Judgeship while Drone Protesters Face Prison

January 23, 2014

While 29 of President Obama's judicial nominees were voted out of committee last week, one is coming under criticism from both the left and right. *Legal Times* reports that Sen. Chuck Grassley (R-Iowa) "voiced numerous concerns about [David] Barron for the First Circuit, saying he has advocated for positions 'far outside the mainstream.' Barron, Grassley said, quoting from a *New York Times* article, participated in crafting the Justice Department legal memo authorizing the use of drones to kill U.S. citizens in other countries. The committee voted 10-8 to approve Barron's nomination."

Just after his November nomination, the *New York Times* noted that Barron "signed memorandums declaring that it would be lawful for the United States to kill Anwar al-Awlaki, a United States citizen suspected of plotting terrorist attacks, if it were not feasible to capture him."

Francis Boyle, fboyle at illinois.edu

Boyle is a professor at the University of Illinois College of Law and author of *Tackling America's Toughest Questions*. He said today: "Barron co-authored the infamous Justice department opinion authorizing Obama's murder of U.S. citizens. This is a total disgrace. If approved, we will have a murderer and a war criminal sitting on the U.S. First Circuit . . . So here Barron and [his coauthor in the legal opinion Martin] Lederman deliberately and maliciously write a get-out-of-jail-free card for Obama so that he can murder U.S. citizens, which he does . . . Barron is neither fit nor qualified to serve as a Judge on the First Circuit—a post which would make him a prime candidate for a U.S. Supreme Court seat . . . This is exactly how Bush paid back Jay Bybee [author of legal memos on torture] when he put him on the Ninth Circuit. Obama is worse than Bush in that Obama is a lawyer and knows better."

Meanwhile, the trial of the "Hancock 17" peace activists is taking place. The defendants and their allies released a statement: 'After awaiting trial for 15 months, the defense case of the Hancock 17 will begin at 5 p.m., Thursday, Jan. 23, continuing on Friday, Jan. 24, in De Witt Town Court, near Syracuse. On Oct. 25, 2012, 17 people were arrested for symbolically blocking the three gates at Hancock National Air Guard Base which is a site where MQ 9 Reaper drones are piloted over Afghanistan . . . They stood in front of the gates with banners and and signs calling for an end to drone warfare and read a citizen's War Crimes Indictment to the base personnel at the gates. They called for an end of attacks on civilians that are illegal under international law.'

"After almost three hours outside the gates, the protesters were arrested and arraigned on charges of Trespass and Disorderly Conduct . . . The protesters were also issued Orders of Protection for Col. Earl Evans which require them to stay away from the base. Violating the Order carries potential misdemeanor or even felony charges . . .

"The defendants' case is supported by former Attorney General Ramsey Clark, Law Professor Francis Boyle, Urbana Champaign, University of Illinois, expert on drones and international law."

KAGAN

Byrd, Kagan Hearings and the Constitution

July 1, 2010

CBS News reports: "The Senate Judiciary Committee will suspend Solicitor General Elena Kagan's Supreme Court confirmation hearing from 10 a.m. to 4 p.m. on Thursday while the late-Sen. Robert Byrd lies in state at the Capitol."

Byrd famously made a habit of carrying a copy of the U.S. Constitution in his shirt pocket. In 2004, he succeeded in passing legislation that deemed September 17 "Constitution Day."

Byrd is prominently featured in the 2007 film "Body of War" by Phil Donahue.

During the Kagan hearings, several Republicans urged Kagan to be a "strict constructionist" (Sen. Tom Coburn, R-Okla.). Meanwhile, many Democrats argued she would "uphold the Constitution" (Sen. Dick Durbin, D-Ill.). Several legal analysts however warn that both Democratic and Republican administrations have been violating basic Constitutional rights.

Available for interviews:

Francis Boyle

Professor of law at the University of Illinois, Boyle is author of *Tackling America's Toughest Questions*. He said today: "After 9/11 Sen. Byrd made repeated appearances in the Senate condemning violations of the Constitution, the war against Iraq, and the Bush police state tactics. During the same period, Kagan was remarkably silent and has supported most of those Bush policies in her capacity as U.S. Solicitor General. As Dean of Harvard Law, she hired Jack Goldsmith who wrote torture memos for Bush and is testifying on Kagan's behalf."

Kagan "Similar to Bush on Executive Power"

June 28, 2010

Francis Boyle

Professor of law at the University of Illinois, Boyle is author of *Tackling America's Toughest Questions*. The *Los Angles Times* on Sunday wrote that Supreme Court nominee Elena Kagan's "most audacious move [while Dean at Harvard Law School] was to recruit Jack Goldsmith, a lawyer who had served in the George W. Bush Justice Department and helped craft anti-terrorism policy.

"Kagan backed the hire against criticism from some liberal faculty and alumni. 'I think it was a disgrace,' said Francis Boyle, a Harvard Law graduate and a professor at the University of Illinois."

Goldsmith is on the witness list in favor of Kagan. Boyle said today: "Goldsmith is regarded by myself and many others in the field as a war criminal. He wrote some of the memos that attempted to make violations of the Geneva Conventions appear legal. Kagan actually bragged about 'how proud' she was to have hired Goldsmith after one of his criminal Department of Justice memoranda was written up in the *Washington Post*." See *Washington Post*: "Memo Lets CIA Take Detainees Out of Iraq: Practice Is Called Serious Breach of Geneva Conventions."

Also see IPA news release with Boyle: "Supreme Court Pick: Kagan 'Loves' the Federalist Society."

Kagan: * Goldman Sachs * Shifting Court to Right?
May 10, 2010
The *Wall Street Journal* reports: "The White House said Friday that Elena Kagan's membership on an advisory panel for the securities firm Goldman Sachs Group Inc. wouldn't disqualify her for a position on the Supreme Court . . . From 2005 to 2008, Ms. Kagan was a paid member of the Research Advisory Council of Goldman Sachs Global Markets Institute, according to financial disclosure reports she filed after being appointed to her current job. The form shows she was paid $10,000 in 2008, when she was dean of Harvard Law School."

On April 9, Obama said he would nominate "someone who, like Justice Stevens, knows that in a democracy, powerful interests must not be allowed to drown out the voices of ordinary citizens."

Professor of law at the University of Illinois, Boyle is author of *Tackling America's Toughest Questions*. He was recently quoted on an Institute for Public Accuracy news release titled "Supreme Court Pick: Kagan 'Loves' the Federalist Society," in which Boyle stated: "Five currently on the U.S. Supreme Court were or are members of the Federalist Society: Harvard Law graduate Roberts; Harvard Law graduate Scalia; Harvard Law graduate Kennedy; Yale Law graduate Thomas; and Yale Law graduate Alito. A narrow elite is imposing itself through the legal system, and ordinary Americans need to start asserting themselves."

Supreme Court Pick: Kagan "Loves" the Federalist Society
April 13, 2010
Solicitor General Elena Kagan is widely reported to be a leading contender for the Supreme Court position being vacated by John Paul Stevens.
Francis Boyle
Professor of law at the University of Illinois, Boyle is author of *Tackling America's Toughest Questions*. He said today: "As dean of the Harvard Law School, Kagan hired Bush's outgoing director of the Office of Legal Counsel, Jack Goldsmith, as a law professor. Goldsmith is regarded by myself and many others in the field as a war criminal. He wrote some of the memos that attempted to make violations of the Geneva Conventions appear legal. Kagan actually bragged about 'how proud' she was to have hired Goldsmith after one of his criminal Department of Justice memoranda was written up in the *Washington Post*.

"During the course of her Senate confirmation hearings as Solicitor General, Kagan explicitly endorsed the Bush administration's bogus category of 'enemy combatant,' whose implementation has been a war crime in its own right. Now in her current job as U.S. Solicitor General, Kagan is quarterbacking the continuation of the Bush administration's illegal and unconstitutional positions in U.S. Federal court litigation around the country, including in the U.S. Supreme Court. For example, early this month, the Obama administration lost an illegal wiretapping case. One of the lawyers in the case who won, Jon Eisenberg, said the Obama administration is as bad or worse than the Bush administration when it comes to issues like state secrets and wiretapping.

"Kagan is apparently being backed by several people who are indebted to her from her time at Harvard. [Professors Laurence] Tribe, [Charles] Ogletree and [Alan] Dershowitz all had plagiarism scandals while Kagan headed up the law school—and she in effect bailed them all out. Tribe and Ogletree were teachers/mentors to Obama and still advise him today, Tribe recently taking a job in the Department of Justice along with Kagan. She was named dean at Harvard by Larry Summers, who helped deregulate much of Wall Street in the Clinton administration and organize much of its bailout under Obama.

"Kagan has said 'I love the Federalist Society.' This is a right-wing group; almost all of the Bush administration lawyers responsible for its war and torture memos are members of the Federalist Society. Many members of the Federalist Society say that *Brown v. Board of Education* [which struck down 'separate but equal'] was decided wrongly.

"Five currently on the U.S. Supreme Court were or are members of the Federalist Society: Harvard Law graduate Roberts; Harvard Law graduate Scalia; Harvard Law graduate Kennedy; Yale Law graduate Thomas; and Yale Law graduate Alito. A narrow elite is imposing itself through the legal system, and ordinary Americans need to start asserting themselves."

Boyle is a former chair of the Harvard Law School Fund Campaign for Greater Illinois and a magna cum laude graduate of Harvard Law School.

Background:

Glenn Greenwald on Tuesday wrote in "The Case Against Elena Kagan": "The prospect that Stevens will be replaced by Elena Kagan has led to the growing perception that Barack Obama will actually take a Supreme Court dominated by Justices Scalia (Reagan), Thomas (Bush 41), Roberts (Bush 43), Alito (Bush 43) and Kennedy (Reagan) and move it further to the Right. Joe Lieberman went on Fox News this weekend to celebrate the prospect that 'President Obama may nominate someone in fact who makes the Court slightly less liberal.'"

The *New York Times* reported on Friday: "In an interview last week, [Stevens] said that every one of the dozen justices appointed to the court since 1971, including himself, was more conservative than his or her predecessor. 'We'll wait and see to see if the most recent change fits that,' he said of Justice Sonia Sotomayor, who joined the court last year. 'But prior to Sonia's joining the court that was true with the possible exception of Ruth Ginsburg.'"

The Murdoch-owned *Wall Street Journal* reported Monday: "As dean of Harvard, Ms. Kagan cultivated good relations with conservatives, hiring several professors with right-leaning views and reaching out to the Federalist Society, a training ground for lawyers who often go on to populate Republican administrations."

Jeff Cohen wrote last year: "Will Obama Move Supreme Court Rightward?"

The Obama White House responded to these criticisms in Michael Kranish, "As Potential Pick for Court, Kagan Gets Fire From Left," Boston Globe, April 15, 2010.

Kagan on the Supreme Court?

May 1, 2009

Solicitor General Elena Kagan is widely reported to be a leading contender for the Supreme Court position being vacated by David Souter.

Francis Boyle

Professor of law at the University of Illinois, Boyle is author of *Tackling America's Toughest Questions*. He said today: "As dean of the Harvard Law School, Kagan hired Bush's outgoing director of the Office of Legal Counsel, Jack Goldsmith, as a law professor. Goldsmith is regarded by myself and many others in the field as a war criminal. He wrote some of the memos that attempted to make violations of the Geneva Conventions appear legal. Kagan actually bragged about 'how proud' she was to have hired Goldsmith after one of his criminal Department of Justice memoranda was written up in the *Washington Post*.

"Then, during the course of her Senate confirmation hearings as Solicitor General, Kagan explicitly endorsed the Bush administration's bogus category of 'enemy combatant,' whose implementation has been a war crime in its own right. Now in her new job as U.S. Solicitor General, Kagan is quarterbacking the continuation of the Bush administration's illegal and unconstitutional positions in U.S. Federal court litigation around the country, including in the U.S. Supreme Court."

Boyle is a former chair of the Harvard Law School Fund Campaign for Greater Illinois and a magna cum laude graduate of Harvard Law School.

For background, see *Washington Post*: "Memo Lets CIA Take Detainees Out of Iraq: Practice Is Called Serious Breach of Geneva Conventions."

Solicitor General Nominee Hired Torture Memo Writer

February 9, 2009

Harvard Law School Dean Elena Kagan is scheduled to have a hearing before the Senate Judiciary Committee on Tuesday for the position of solicitor general. She has frequently been mentioned as a possible nominee to fill Ruth Bader Ginsburg's seat on the Supreme Court.

Francis Boyle

Professor of law at the University of Illinois, Boyle is author of *Breaking All the Rules*. He said today: "As dean of the Harvard Law School, Kagan hired Bush's outgoing director of the Office of Legal Counsel, Jack Goldsmith, as a law professor. Goldsmith is regarded by myself and many others in the field as a war criminal. He wrote some of the memos that attempted to make violations of the Geneva Conventions appear legal. Kagan actually bragged about 'how proud' she was to have hired Goldsmith after one of his criminal Department of Justice memoranda was written up in the *Washington Post*.

"Kagan is neither fit nor qualified to become Solicitor General for the U.S. Department of Justice—the proverbial 'Tenth Justice' of the U.S. Supreme Court—and thus become a leading contender to replace the anti-totalitarian but now cancer-stricken Justice Ginsburg."

Boyle is a former chair of the Harvard Law School Fund Campaign for Greater Illinois and a magna cum laude graduate of Harvard Law School.

For background, see *Washington Post*: "Memo Lets CIA Take Detainees Out of Iraq: Practice Is Called Serious Breach of Geneva Conventions."

ALITO

The Filibuster Option

January 25, 2006

Francis Boyle

Professor of law at the University of Illinois, Boyle said today: "Alito is an extremist. Any judge who refuses to declare that an innocent person has a constitutional right to be free from execution is by definition an extremist . . . If confirmed by the Senate, Alito will join Scalia, Thomas, and Roberts to form a solid block of four Federalist Society justices . . . We need only one U.S. Senator with courage, integrity, principles, and a safe seat in order to start the filibuster."

Presidential Powers

January 10, 2006

Francis Boyle

Boyle is professor of law at the University of Illinois. Today Sen. Patrick Leahy asked Judge Samuel Alito: "If the Congress passed a law prohibiting torture," could the president "immunize people from prosecution if they violated our laws on torture?" Said Boyle: "Instead of just saying 'no' to Leahy's question, Alito is prepared to quibble about the president's 'right' to torture, and leave that 'right' open, depending upon the circumstances."

Fitzgerald · Alito

November 1, 2005

Francis Boyle

Boyle is professor of law at the University of Illinois. The *Washington Post* noted today that "Alito has been a member of the Federalist Society." Boyle commented: "The Federalist Society and its members such as Judge Alito stand for the general proposition that the United States Supreme Court should return to what they believe to be the 'good old days' of the Herbert Hoover administration and its Supreme Court."

More Information

Background: People for the American Way

"In one case that came before Alito, an African American had been convicted of felony murder and sentenced to death by an all-white jury from which black jurors had been impermissibly struck. Alito cast the deciding vote and wrote the majority opinion in a 2-1 ruling rejecting the defendant's claims. The full Third Circuit reversed Alito's ruling, and the majority specifically criticized him for having compared statistical evidence about the prosecution's exclusion of Blacks from juries in capital cases to an explanation of why a disproportionate number of recent U.S. presidents have been left-handed. According to the majority, '[t]o suggest any comparability to the striking of jurors based on their race is to minimize the history of discrimination against prospective Black jurors and Black defendants.'"

ROBERTS

As the UN Meets: Interviews Available on International Law · Roberts · Chavez · Sharon

September 14, 2005

Francis Boyle

Professor of international law at the University of Illinois, Boyle said today: "As Roberts made clear in Tuesday's hearings during his interchange with Senator Leahy, he is a partisan of the Imperial Presidency. For example, Roberts refused to repudiate and condemn the infamous *Korematsu* decision which authorized the president to intern U.S. citizens of Japanese descent during World War II. In his own recent *Hamdan* decision, Roberts gave President Bush a blank-check to wage his 'war on terrorism' in violation of the Geneva Conventions. . ." Boyle is author of the book *Destroying World Order: A Guide to Impeaching President George W. Bush.* [Boyle can also address the subject of Roberts and membership in the Federalist Society.]

Law Professors Scrutinize Roberts * Quid Pro Quo? * Guantánamo Ruling * Federalist Society

August 18, 2005

Francis Boyle

Professor of international law at the University of Illinois, Boyle said today: "In his answers to the Senate Judiciary Committee, John Roberts stated that he had 'no recollection' of his membership in the Federalist Society and being on its Steering Committee for Washington, D.C. Nevertheless, a high-level official in the Federalist Society has confirmed Roberts' membership, and it has also been confirmed that all Federalist Society members pay dues. In other words, Roberts lied to Congress, which is a crime in its own right. For that reason alone, Roberts is disqualified to be confirmed by the U.S. Senate as an Associate Justice of the U.S. Supreme Court . . . The Senate Judiciary Committee must grill Roberts on all the positions and activities of the Federalist Society and its prominent members before rejecting him, thus exposing before a national audience the pernicious and insidious role that the Federalist Society has played in the American legal profession for the past two decades."

FEDERALIST SOCIETY

Judicial Nominees: Implications as Federalist Society Supplants ABA

May 9, 2001

As President Bush makes appointments to federal courts, the following analysts are available for interviews:

Francis Boyle

Law professor at the University of Illinois, Boyle said today: "The Federalist Society lawyers want to go beyond getting rid of affirmative action. They want to go back to *Brown vs. Board of Education*. We have Justice Antonin Scalia (who advised the Federalist Society at its inception and later hired two of its three founders as his law clerks); a few years ago he gave a public lecture at Columbia Law School where he stated that if *Brown vs. Board of Education* was to be presented to him today, he would rule against the plaintiffs . . . What we are seeing under the Federalist Society is the judiciary, law schools, and legal education being used to promote a right-wing, reactionary political agenda to the detriment of people of color and the poor of our society."

Francis A. Boyle
Law Building
504 E. Pennsylvania Ave.
Champaign, Illinois 61820

Phone: 217-333-7954
Fax: 217-244-1478
fboyle@law.uiuc.edu
9 September 1997
Memorandum

To: Robert H. Bork
Federalist Society

Dear Bob:

Concerning your fund-raising letter of 28 August that just came to my attention, I want to thank you from the bottom of my heart for publicly associating me with a Lawyer and a Judge who has the principles, courage, and integrity of Lawrence Walsh.

For your information, that message and others like out were sent out all over the internet, not just to 30 professors, together with the full text of Judge Walsh's attack on the Federalist Society. Out of respect for Judge Walsh, I certainly do hope that my professorial colleagues will pay the most serious attention to what he had to say about the Federalist Society. After all, Judge Walsh is a pillar of the American Legal Establishment and of the Republican Party. As for myself, I have always been a political independent and resent your implication that I am a member of the Democrat Party.

Be that as it may, it seems to me that you have only (once again!) made a fool of yourself by publicly attacking a Lawyer and a Judge with the courage, integrity, and principles of Judge Walsh—characteristics that you yourself were not noted for as Solicitor General (when you fired Archie Cox, the first Special Prosecutor), during your tenure on the bench, or during your Supreme Court nomination hearings. Rather than publicly attacking Judge Walsh, I suggest that you personally as well as the Federalist Society institutionally should be giving the most serious consideration to what he had to say.

Yours very truly,

Francis A. Boyle
Professor of Law

cc: Judge Lawrence Walsh

KOREA

Trump's Korea Threat
April 26, 2017

The *New York Times* is reporting: "Fearing Korean Nuclear War, Women of 40 Nations Urge Trump to Seek Peace."

Francis Boyle, fboyle [at] illinois.edu

Boyle is professor of international law at the University of Illinois College of Law. He said today: "This is a dangerous situation because what Trump could be doing here is to lay some bogus Constitutional predicate for war against DPRK [North Korea], claiming that he's consulting Congress. In fact, Trump has no authorization for war against DPRK. There was never a Declaration of War by Congress against DPRK. He is currently in violation of the War Powers Resolution Section 2(c) since he is putting U.S. armed forces 'into situations where imminent involvement in hostilities is clearly indicated by the circumstances.' He would also be violating the United Nations Charter because the Security Council has not authorized the use of military force to deal with the current situation."

* Korea Armistice "Dead" * Why Military Exercises?

March 13, 2013

Francis Boyle, [email]

Boyle is a professor at the University of Illinois College of Law and author of *Tackling America's Toughest Questions*. The *New York Times* wrote on Friday "The North said this week that it considered the 1953 armistice agreement that halted the Korean War to be null and void as of Monday because of the joint military exercises. The North has threatened to terminate that agreement before, but American and South Korean military officials pointed out that legally, no party armistice can unilaterally terminate or alter its terms."

Boyle said today: "Nonsense. An armistice agreement is governed by the laws of war and the state of war still remains in effect despite the armistice agreement, even if the armistice text itself says additions have to be mutually agreed upon by the parties. Termination is not an addition. Under the U.S. Army Field Manual 27-10 and the Hague Regulations, the only requirement for termination of the Korean War Armistice Agreement is suitable notice so as to avoid the charge of 'perfidy.' North Korea has given that notice. The armistice is dead." See Army Field Manual: "In case it [the armistice] is indefinite, a belligerent may resume operations at any time after notice."

LEBANON

Lebanon and the Law

July 25, 2006

On July 23, the United Nations Emergency Relief coordinator, Jan Egeland, visited Beirut. The BBC reported: "[Egeland] said the 'disproportionate response' by Israel was a 'violation of international humanitarian law.'"

BBC

The United Nations' top human rights official, Louise Arbour, warned on July 19: "International law demands accountability. The scale of the killings in the region, and their predictability, could engage the personal criminal responsibility of those involved, particularly those in a position of command and control."

Francis Boyle

Professor of international law at the University of Illinois, Boyle said today: "Although Lebanon is not a party to the Statute of the International Criminal Court, nevertheless Lebanon can and should file a declaration . . . [and] ask the ICC prosecutor to initiate an investigation into war crimes and crimes against humanity committed by Israel in Lebanon." Boyle is author of the books *Biowarfare and Terrorism* and *Destroying World Order.*

LIBYA

Hollande and Obama: Doubling Down on "Imperialism"?

November 23, 2015

French president François Hollande will be visiting President Barack Obama at the White House Tuesday. He will visit Russian President Vladimir Putin in Moscow on Thursday. For upcoming events, see *accuracy.org/calendar.*

Brussels, with 170,000 residents—and seat of the headquarters of NATO and the EU—is under lockdown.

Francis Boyle, fboyle at illinois.edu

Boyle is professor at the University of Illinois College of Law. In his book on *Destroying Libya and World Order*, Boyle predicted the outcome of the Libya intervention would be a collapsed state and increased jihadi elements in nearby countries including Mali and Algeria. The *New York Times* reports now: "Mali Hotel Attackers Are Tied to an Algerian Qaeda Leader."

He said today: "The UN Security Council resolution passed over the weekend was not a Chapter 7 resolution, so legally it doesn't authorize the use of force, but the U.S. and France will use it to give legal cover for their illegal bombing of Syria, which has gone on for more than a year now. It appears that British Prime Minister Cameron will now be doing the same. The Russian bombing of Syria is technically legal because they have the explicit permission of the Syrian government, but of course Putin will ultimately act in accord with his interests, not what is best for the Syrian people." Boyle's other books include *Tackling America's Toughest Questions* and *Biowarfare and Terrorism.*

Libya War Illegal?

June 15, 2011

CNN reports: "A bipartisan group of House members [lead by Reps. Dennis Kucinich (D-Ohio) and Walter Jones (R-NC)] will file a lawsuit Wednesday challenging U.S. participation in the Libya military mission. Meanwhile, President Barack Obama is set to defend U.S. military involvement in Libya to Congress, according to the White House . . . House Speaker John Boehner, R-Ohio, said in a letter to Obama on Tuesday that the administration could be in violation of the War Powers Resolution if it fails to get congressional authorization by Sunday, which he notes will be the 90th day since the mission began."

Francis Boyle, fboyle at law.uiuc.edu

Professor of international law at the University of Illinois College of Law in Champaign and author of *Tackling America's Toughest Questions*, said today: "After 60 days Congress must expressly authorize ongoing military operations, unless Obama asks for another 30 days, which he has not done. And Obama's Libya War was unconstitutional to begin with."

Referring to the court case brought by members of Congress today, Boyle added: "This lawsuit is a cop-out of their Constitutional responsibilities on the part of Congress. These issues have already been argued and lost before in *Campbell v. Clinton*, 203 F.3d 19 (D.C.Cir. 2000), where the court ruled that members of Congress did not have standing to sue. The real remedy here is a bill of impeachment against President Obama. The courts are not going to pull Congress's chestnuts out of this Constitutional fire for them."

Background: Boehner's letter

Kucinich's news release

From FAIR: "Libya and the Law: Media Show Slight Interest in War Powers, Geneva"

Debate on Libya and Intervention

March 8, 2011

Francis Boyle

Professor of international law at the University of Illinois College of Law in Champaign, Boyle said today: "Without authorization by the United Nations Security Council and express authorization from the U.S. Congress pursuant to the terms of the War Powers Resolution, for President Obama to establish any type of so-called 'no-fly zone' over Libya would be illegal and unconstitutional." While serving as the lawyer for the Republic of Bosnia and Herzegovina in 1993, Boyle procured the NATO no-fly zone over Bosnia. He is author of *The Bosnian People Charge Genocide!*

PALESTINE AND THE PALESTINIANS

UN Vote on Jerusalem: U.S. as "Capo dei Capi"

December 21, 2017

C-SPAN has been covering the UN General Assembly debate on a resolution demanding that countries abide by Security Council resolutions on Jerusalem. The representative of Venezuela spoke on behalf of the Non-Aligned Movement, which was backed by the South African delegation and other speakers. The final vote was 128-9-35, achieving the two-thirds required under the "Uniting for Peace" procedure.

Francis Boyle, fboyle at illinois.edu

Boyle, professor of international law at the University of Illinois College of Law, served as legal adviser to the PLO. His books include *The Palestinian Right of Return under International Law*. He recently wrote the piece "Trump's National Security Strategy: More unlimited imperialism," Intrepid Report, Dec. 21, 2017.

He noted that the General Assembly resolution being voted on today at the United Nations is under a special "Uniting for Peace" procedure, giving it greater legal force. He advocates greater use of Uniting for Peace by UN member states (including admission of Palestine to the United Nations) and said today: "In its *Certain Expenses Advisory Opinion* (1962) the International Court of Justice upheld the legality of the Uniting for Peace Resolution. As a matter of fact, it was originally introduced and first used by the United States government in order to overcome the veto by the former Soviet Union at the United Nations Security Council. Sauce for the goose is sauce for the gander."

"Recognition of Israel's annexation of Jerusalem violates the U.S. government's own longstanding Stimson Doctrine (1932), which forbids recognition of any legal consequences as a result of the use of force."

* Jerusalem * Can the Palestinians Launch a "Legal Intifadah"?

December 6, 2017

Francis Boyle, fboyle at illinois.edu

Boyle, professor of international law at the University of Illinois College of Law, served as legal adviser to the PLO. His books include *The Palestinian Right of Return under International Law*.

He said today: "Trump's move is a symbolic but still critical step in Israeli designs to control not just Jerusalem, but all of historic Palestine. The Palestinian leadership needs to deal with this threat by all available legal means, including what I call a legal intifadah. The U.S. has prevented full Palestinian membership at the United Nations. The PLO could remedy this by using the Uniting for Peace mechanism, which would mean a vote on the issue in the General Assembly and not the Security Council where the U.S. government has a veto.

"No member state of the United Nations organization has ever been destroyed or eliminated. Some of them have broken off into constituent units but they have never been extinguished. Israel would like all of Palestine, the West Bank, East Jerusalem—without the Palestinians. A legal strategy dealing with this threat is needed."

See an interview with Boyle elaborating on legal strategies, *Counterpunch*, Dec. 4, 2012.

Does Netanyahu's Victory Open Door for One State? Bigger BDS?
March 18, 2015
Francis Boyle, fboyle at illinois.edu
Boyle, professor of international law at the University of Illinois College of Law, served as legal adviser to the PLO. His books include *The Palestinian Right of Return under International Law*. He just wrote the piece "Netanyahu Victory Opens Door for One-State Solution." He said today: "Many have argued that the two-state solution has failed and therefore the Palestinian leadership should go back to pursuing a one-state solution, akin to how the South African conflict was resolved, giving one-person-one-vote to everyone regardless of their religious, ethnic or language group. Indeed, the Palestinian leadership has indicated it would embrace it if the two-state solution proved a dead end. For example, almost exactly three years ago, Hanan Ashrawi, a member of the Palestine Liberation Organization's executive committee, was asked: 'Do you think that after one, two, or three years the PLO would say that it is time to pursue a one-state option?' She responded: 'It probably might be even sooner than one, two, or three years, because at the pace that is being pursued by this Israeli government, they really are making sure that the two-state solution is dead.'"

Netanyahu Victory Opens Door for One-State Solution
March 18, 2015 By journalist
Netanyahu Victory Opens Door for One-State Solution
by Francis Boyle

Just before the election, Israel Prime Minister Netanyahu ruled out the creation of a Palestinian State, which means that he repudiated the two-state solution to the dispute between the Israelis and the Palestinians.

This has been the pronounced objective of American foreign policy since the Madrid Conference and the Middle East Peace Negotiations in 1991 held under the auspices of the United States government and with the full support of the international community.

If implemented, Netanyahu's decision will leave the Palestinians no alternative but to pursue the creation of one-state of Palestine that will include what is known today as Palestine, Israel and Jerusalem and where a majority of its citizens will be Palestinians.

Before the Palestinian Declaration of Independence of 15 November 1988, the position of the Palestine National Council and the Palestine Liberation Organization was that there should be only one, democratic, and secular state for the entire mandate for Palestine, which would include Israel within it.

It was PLO Chairman Yasser Arafat himself who encouraged the Palestine National Council to accept the two-state solution in the Palestinian Declaration of Independence of 15 November 1988. After 27 years of fruitlessly trying to pursue a two-state solution, it is now time for the Palestine National Council and the PLO to reconsider their options.

Professor Francis A. Boyle, University of Illinois College of Law, served as Legal Adviser to the PLO and Chairman Yasser Arafat on the 15 November 1988 Palestinian Declaration of Independence and as legal adviser to the Palestinian delegation to the Middle East peace negotiations and its chair Dr. Haidar Abdul Shaffi from 1991 to 1993. His books include Palestine, Palestinians, and International Law (2003) and The Palestinian Right of Return under International Law (2011).

ICC and Israel: Claims of Genocide and the Means to Stop It

August 7, 2014

Francis Boyle, fboyle at illinois.edu

Boyle is a professor at the University of Illinois College of Law and author of *Palestine, Palestinians, and International Law* and *The Tamil Genocide by Sri Lanka*. He said today: "The ICC has shown that the hope that many of us had for it was not deserved, it's been a tool of the pro-Israeli Western powers. Under no circumstances must the Palestinians accede to the Rome Statute for the International Criminal Court. ICC prosecutor Fatou Bensouda is 'Black Skin, White Masks' a la Frantz Fanon. She will decapitate the entire Palestinian political leadership. The Palestinians will be back to where they were before the founding of the PLO in 1964."

Instead, Boyle recommends that nations that are signatory to the Genocide Convention invoke it against Israel at the World Court. Numerous world leaders, including the presidents of Bolivia, Venezuela, Nicaragua, Pakistan and Iran have referred to Israel's actions as genocidal.

Says Boyle: "An appropriate legal remedy is to apply the 1948 Convention on the Prevention and Punishment of the Crime of Genocide against Israel at the World Court. Palestinians have been victims of genocide by that treaty's definition. In 1993 I won two World Court Orders on the basis of the 1948 Genocide Convention that were overwhelmingly in favor of the Republic of

Bosnia and Herzegovina against Yugoslavia to cease and desist from committing all acts of genocide against the Bosnians in violation of the 1948 Genocide Convention. I won the first emergency order in three weeks. See *The Bosnian People Charge Genocide!* (1996).

"In the event the United States were to exercise a veto at the Security Council against the enforcement of this World Court Cease-and-Desist Order against Israel, you can then invoke the General Assembly's Uniting for Peace Resolution of 1950 in order to have the World Court Order turned over to the United Nations General Assembly for enforcement measures against Israel." Boyle was legal advisor to Dr. Haidar Abdul Shaffi, chair of the Palestinian delegation to the Middle East peace negotiations from 1991-1993.

See: "If It's a Genocide in Gaza, then Invoke the Convention to Stop it" by Sam Husseini.

War Crimes in Gaza? Genocide?

July 24, 2014

BBC is reporting today: "At least 15 people have been killed and more than 200 injured when a UN-run school used as a shelter in Gaza was shelled, the Gaza health ministry says . . . In the past 16 days of fighting, more than 750 Palestinians and 32 Israelis have been killed, officials say."

Time magazine reports: "The UN Human Rights Council voted Wednesday to launch an inquiry into potential violations of human rights by Israel in its conflict with Hamas in the Gaza Strip . . . The council's inquiry would investigate 'all violations of international human rights law and international humanitarian law' in Palestinian areas. The resolution was drafted by Palestine, and supported by 29 of the 46-member council. The U.S. voted against the resolution, while European countries abstained."

Francis Boyle, fboyle at illinois.edu

Boyle is a professor at the University of Illinois College of Law and author of *Palestine, Palestinians, and International Law* and *The Tamil Genocide by Sri Lanka*. He said today: "I read the entire Navi Pillay Letter to the Human Rights Council. She said that war crimes and crimes against humanity have been committed and need to be investigated. So what? That's exactly what [Richard] Goldstone did after Operation Cast Lead [in 2008-9] and nothing came of it.

"An appropriate legal remedy is to apply the 1948 Convention on the Prevention and Punishment of the Crime of Genocide. Palestinians have been victims of genocide by that treaty's definition. In 1993 I won two World Court Orders on the basis of the 1948 Genocide Convention that were overwhelmingly in favor of the Republic of Bosnia and Herzegovina against Yugoslavia to cease and desist from committing all acts of genocide against the Bosnians in violation of the 1948 Genocide Convention. See *The Bosnian People Charge Genocide!* (1996).

"You did not need an equivalent to the Nazi Holocaust against the Jews in order to find that wholesale atrocities against a civilian population constitute 'genocide' in violation of the 1948 Genocide Convention. Indeed the entire purpose of the 1948 Genocide Convention was to *prevent* another Nazi Holocaust against the Jews. You did not need six million dead human beings in order to constitute 'genocide.'"

See: "Israel's Incremental Genocide in the Gaza Ghetto" by the Israeli historian Ilan Pappe.

Could Israel be Brought Before the International Criminal Court?
November 29, 2012

Reuters reports: "The U.N. General Assembly is set to implicitly recognize a sovereign state of Palestine on Thursday despite threats by the United States and Israel to punish the Palestinian Authority by withholding much-needed funds for the West Bank government."

AFP reports: "Britain threatened Wednesday to abstain from a vote for enhanced Palestinian status at the United Nations . . . British Foreign Secretary William Hague . . . said to win Britain's vote, the Palestinians would also have to pledge not to sue Israel for war crimes through the International Criminal Court . . . If the request is approved, it will give the Palestinians access to a range of UN agencies and also potentially to the ICC, where they could accuse Israel of war crimes."

Legal analysts note that if the Palestinian Authority has the political will it could do a wide range of things.

Francis Boyle, [email] Professor of international law at the University of Illinois College of Law and author of *Palestine, Palestinians, and International Law*, Boyle said today: "This can be the start of a 'Legal Intifadah' by Palestine against Israel:

1. "Palestine can join the Rome Statute for the International Criminal Court and file a Complaint with the ICC against the illegal settlements and settlers, who are committing war crimes;
2. "Palestine can join the Statute for the International Court of Justice, sue Israel at the World Court, and break the illegal siege of Gaza;
3. "Palestine can join the Law of the Sea Convention and get its fair share of the enormous gas fields lying off the coast of Gaza, thus becoming economically self-sufficient;
4. "Palestine can become a High Contracting Party to the Four Geneva Conventions [this deals with the laws of war];
5. "Palestine can join the International Civil Aviation Organization and gain sovereign, legal control over its own airspace;

6. "Palestine can join the International Telecommunications Union and gain sovereign legal control over its own airwaves, phone lines, bandwidths."

Boyle was also legal advisor to the Palestine Liberation Organization and Chairman Yasser Arafat on the Palestinian Declaration of Independence of Nov. 15, 1988, as well as to the Palestinian delegation to the Middle East peace negotiations and its chair, Dr. Haidar Abdul Shaffi, from 1991 to 1993.

See Amnesty International UK's statement: "William Hague Should Stop Using ICC as 'Political Football' in Palestinian UN Status Vote."

* Netanyahu "Distracting Attention" with Iran * Does Abbas Really Want Full U.N. Membership?

September 28, 2012

Francis Boyle

Professor of international law at the University of Illinois College of Law in Champaign, Boyle served as legal advisor to the Palestine Liberation Organization and Yasser Arafat on the 1988 Palestinian Declaration of Independence, as well as to the Palestinian delegation to the Middle East peace negotiations from 1991 to 1993, where he drafted the Palestinian counter-offer to the now defunct Oslo Agreement. His books include *Palestine, Palestinians, and International Law* and the recently-released *The Palestinian Right of Return under International Law.*

He said today: "Palestine effectively has observer state status with the United Nations and basically all the rights of a U.N. member state except the right to vote. Palestine has de facto U.N. membership. The only thing keeping Palestine from de jure U.N. membership is the implicit threat of a veto at the U.N. Security Council by the United States, which would violate a solemn and binding pledge given by the United States not to veto states applying for U.N. membership.

"The votes are there already in the U.N. General Assembly to admit Palestine pursuant to the terms of its Uniting for Peace Resolution. It is the U.N. General Assembly that admits a member state, not the Security Council. Obama's blockage at the Security Council can be circumvented by the General Assembly acting under the Uniting for Peace Resolution to admit Palestine as a U.N. member state. By means of the Uniting for Peace Resolution, President Abbas could have full-fledged state membership for Palestine in the United Nations by the end of next week if that is what he wants to do."

UN Speech on Palestine: "Yes, Mr. Obama, Peace is Hard. . ."

September 21, 2011

The *New York Times* reports: "President Obama declared his opposition to the Palestinian Authority's bid for statehood through the Security Council on

Wednesday, throwing the weight of the United States directly in the path of the Arab democracy movement even as he hailed what he called the democratic aspirations that have taken hold throughout the Middle East and North Africa. 'Peace will not come through statements and resolutions at the UN,' Mr. Obama said, in an address before world leaders at the General Assembly. 'If it were that easy, it would have been accomplished by now.'"

Francis Boyle, fboyle at law.uiuc.edu

Today, Palestinian legislator Hanan Ashrawi raised the possibility of using the "Uniting for Peace" mechanism to get membership at the United Nations in a discussion webcast by the Institute for Middle East Understanding.

Professor of international law at the University of Illinois College of Law in Champaign and author of *Palestine, Palestinians, and International Law*, Boyle said today: "By means of the Uniting for Peace Resolution, the Palestinians could have full-fledged state membership for Palestine in the United Nations by the end of next week if that is what they want to do." See: "Palestinian UN Bid and Uniting for Peace."

Palestinian UN Bid and Uniting for Peace

September 19, 2011

The *Wall Street Journal* reports in "Palestinian UN Move Options at UN Lead to Legal Threat to Israel's Military," that: "If the Palestinian Authority succeeds in winning even an incremental upgrade of its status at the UN, it could subject Israel's military to international courts for actions in Palestinian territory—as well as allow Palestinian control of its Israeli-patrolled air space and national waters off Gaza.

"Palestinian Authority President Mahmoud Abbas said Friday he would seek full U.N. membership through the Security Council. If the U.S. vetoes that effort, as it has vowed to do, the Palestinians have a second option for membership: go to the General Assembly.

"Francis Boyle, a legal adviser to Mr. Abbas, told *The Wall Street Journal* that he has advised the Palestinian president to take this step, which is made possible through a resolution, known as Uniting for Peace, that was introduced by the U.S. in 1950 to circumvent repeated Soviet vetoes of Security Council measures to help South Korea battle the North."

Reports indicate President Obama will be meeting with Israeli Prime Minister Benjamin Netanyahu sometime before Wednesday when Obama is scheduled to speak at the UN. *Reuters* is reporting: "Abbas has said he will present the request for full UN membership during his speech to the General Assembly on Friday."

Francis Boyle, fboyle at law.uiuc.edu

Professor of international law at the University of Illinois College of Law in Champaign and author of *Palestine, Palestinians, and International Law*,

Boyle said today: "Many have claimed that if the U.S. does indeed veto the Palestinian UN bid, the only option would be for the Palestinians to pursue upgrading Palestine's current observer status at the UN. This is incorrect. As Palestinian diplomats have recently noted, they can get the UN General Assembly to admit Palestine as a UN member state pursuant to the terms of its Uniting for Peace Resolution 377 (1950). So Obama's veto at the Security Council can be circumvented by the General Assembly through the Uniting for Peace Resolution."

Boyle was also legal advisor to the Palestine Liberation Organization and Chairman Yasser Arafat on the Palestinian Declaration of Independence of Nov. 15, 1988, as well as to the Palestinian delegation to the Middle East peace negotiations and its chair, Dr. Haidar Abdul Shaffi, from 1991 to 1993.

See background on Uniting for Peace at the UN webpage

Boyle Appears in Wall Street Journal

September 18, 2011

Following his appearance on an IPA news release on Thursday, Francis Boyle was quoted in the *Wall Street Journal* Saturday discussing options for Palestinians seeking statehood if the U.S. vetoes the nation's efforts to gain recognition through the UN Security Council. Boyle, an adviser to Palestinian Authority President Mahmoud Abbas, believes the UN General Assembly could also be a potential route to membership. It would take a two thirds vote in the General Assembly to grant Palestine membership.

U.S. Vetoing Palestinian State It Claims to Support

September 15, 2011

Francis Boyle, fboyle at law.uiuc.edu

Professor of international law at the University of Illinois College of Law in Champaign and author of *Palestine, Palestinians, and International Law*, Boyle said today: "This week, President Obama has attacked the Palestinian UN membership bid as a 'distraction' and Secretary of State Clinton has claimed the U.S. 'strongly supports' the two-state solution but that the 'way of getting a lasting solution is through direct negotiations between the parties.'

"Negotiations with the Israelis were Plan A, but as I have advised the Palestinian leadership since 1987, Plan B would be to get UN full membership. The Israelis have refused to negotiate in good faith for all these years, so the Palestinians have now implemented Plan B. Far from being a distraction, a Palestinian UN bid would greatly enhance Palestinian rights. A UN member state of Palestine would be in a perfect position to bring Israeli officials before the International Criminal Court for their criminal attacks on Palestinians and illegal settlement activity. And every Palestinian living around the world would automatically become the citizen of a UN member state that is recognized by almost every state in the world. Palestinians would no longer be considered 'stateless.'

"Many have claimed that if the U.S. does indeed veto the Palestinian UN bid, the only option would be for the Palestinians to pursue upgrading Palestine's current observer status at the UN. This is incorrect. As Palestinian diplomats have recently noted, they can get the UN General Assembly to admit Palestine as a UN member state pursuant to the terms of its Uniting for Peace Resolution 377 (1950). So Obama's veto at the Security Council can be circumvented by the General Assembly through the Uniting for Peace Resolution, which was actually pioneered by the U.S. during the Korean War."

Boyle was legal advisor to the Palestine Liberation Organization and Chairman Yasser Arafat on the Palestinian Declaration of Independence of Nov. 15, 1988, as well as to the Palestinian delegation to the Middle East peace negotiations and its chair, Dr. Haidar Abdul Shaffi from 1991 to 1993.

Boyle is one of several contributors to the recent piece "Does the Palestinian UN Bid Threaten Refugee Rights?" in the Palestinian *Ma'an News Agency*, Aug. 29, 2011.

Al-Qaeda Wants U.S. to Stay? * Palestinian U.N. Membership
June 8, 2011
Francis Boyle, fboyle at law.uiuc.edu

Obama yesterday attacked the possibility of "Palestinians seeking a vote on statehood at the U.N. General Assembly" in September. Professor of international law at the University of Illinois College of Law in Champaign, Boyle served as legal advisor to the Palestine Liberation Organization and Yasser Arafat on the 1988 Palestinian Declaration of Independence, as well as to the Palestinian delegation to the Middle East peace negotiations from 1991 to 1993, where he drafted the Palestinian counter-offer to the now largely defunct Oslo Agreement. His books include *Palestine, Palestinians, and International Law* and the recently-released *The Palestinian Right of Return under International Law.*

Actually, the Ship Was Not Turkish-Flagged
June 7, 2010
Francis Boyle

Professor of international law at the University of Illinois College of Law in Champaign, Boyle said today: "The highest level officials of the Israeli government who ordered the attack upon the *Mavi Marmara* can be prosecuted by the International Criminal Court: Prime Minister Netanyahu, Defense Minister Barak, Foreign Minister Lieberman, General Ashkenazi and the rest of the Israeli council of seven ministers who ordered this criminal attack. Furthermore, under the ICC's Rome Statute any state party has the power to demand that these Israeli governmental officials be prosecuted."

Boyle's books include *Tackling America's Toughest Questions*. See: "Is the Israeli Blockade of Gaza Against the Law?," Explainer, June 1, 2010.

Background:

The Independent (UK): "The Hijacking of the Truth: Film Evidence 'Destroyed': Protesters say Israel had an assassination list. Israel says soldiers fired only in self-defence. So what really happened on 31 May?"

The Guardian (UK): "Gaza Flotilla Activists Were Shot in Head at Close Range: Nine Turkish men on board *Mavi Marmara* were shot a total of 30 times, autopsy results reveal."

Israel and Free Gaza Flotilla

June 2, 2010

Cindy and Craig Corrie are the parents of Rachel Corrie, who was killed by an Israeli army bulldozer in the Gaza Strip on March 16, 2003, while trying to prevent the demolition of the home of a Palestinian pharmacist, his wife and three young children.

A Free Gaza boat that is being readied to sail to Gaza is named for her. Among those on board are Irish Nobel Peace Laureate Mairead Corrigan-Maguire and former UN Assistant Secretary General Denis Halliday, who is also Irish.

The Corries, who have themselves been to Gaza twice and recently to Israel for a trial related to their daughter's killing, said today in a statement: "We call on the U.S. government and governments of the world to act now. First, the well-being of all the flotilla passengers still in Israel must be secured, and the identities of those killed and injured must be released immediately. Second, governments around the world must demand an independent investigation into the attack upon the flotilla and the killings that occurred. An Israeli-led investigation into an international incident of this magnitude is unacceptable. Our family's own experience has made it all too painfully clear that the Israeli military is unable or unwilling to adequately investigate itself. Third, the U.S. and other governments can and must insist that other boats from the flotilla, including the *MV Rachel Corrie*, named for our daughter, be permitted to sail through international waters to Gaza unobstructed. Finally, we demand that the governments of the world act as courageously as did the activists on the Free Gaza flotilla and, themselves, break the illegal and immoral siege of Gaza."

Francis Boyle

Professor of international law at the University of Illinois College of Law in Champaign, Boyle said today: "The Israeli attack on the Gaza flotilla violated the SUA Convention [Convention for the Suppression of Unlawful Acts Against the Safety of Maritime Navigation], to which Israel, Turkey, Ireland and the USA are all parties. This convention was pushed by the USA in reaction to the *Achille Lauro* hijacking and the murder of Leon Klinghoffer." See: "Is the Israeli Blockade of Gaza Against the Law?," Explainer, June 1, 2010.

Boyle's books include *Palestine, Palestinians, and International Law* and most recently *Tackling America's Toughest Questions.*

Carter: Netanyahu Adding Demands

June 16, 2009

The British newspaper the *Guardian* reports today that Jimmy Carter, who has been in Israel and just met with top Hamas officials in Gaza, said of Israeli Prime Minister Binyamin Netanyahu's recent speech: "My opinion is he raised many new obstacles to peace that had not existed under previous prime ministers . . . He still apparently insists on expansion of existing settlements, he demands that the Palestinians and the Arabs recognize Israel as a Jewish state, although 20 percent of its citizens here are not Jews. This is a new demand."

Carter also stated: "To me, the most grievous circumstance is the maltreatment of the people in Gaza, who are literally starving and have no hope at this time . . . They're being treated like savages. The alleviation of their plight to some means I think would be the most important [thing] the Israeli PM could do."

Francis Boyle

Boyle, a professor at the University of Illinois College of Law in Champaign, served as legal advisor to the Palestinian delegation to the Middle East peace negotiations from 1991 to 1993.

He said today: "Netanyahu has now shifted the goal-posts on the Palestinians by demanding that they recognize Israel as a 'Jewish State.' It would be as if the United States demanded that Iran recognize it as a 'White-Anglo-Saxon-Protestant State' as part of any peace settlement. Of course this demand is racist. It would likely lead to the denationalization of the 1.5 million Palestinians who are already second-class citizens of Israel and set the stage for their mass deportation to the Palestinian Bantustan envisioned by Netanyahu in this speech.

"Basically, Netanyahu [is trying] to stall and delay while Israel continues to develop and expand its illegal settlements in violation of the Fourth Geneva Convention of 1949, funded in substantial part by United States taxpayers." Boyle's books include *Palestine, Palestinians, and International Law* and most recently *Tackling America's Toughest Questions.*

Former Legal Adviser to Palestinians Blasts Bush

January 11, 2008

Francis Boyle

Professor of international law at the University of Illinois, Boyle is author of *Palestine, Palestinians, and International Law*. He said today: "Contrary to what many are saying—that Bush has not accomplished much in his trip to the Mideast—he has accomplished a great deal of harm.

"Bush called for 'new international mechanisms, including compensation, to resolve the [Palestinian] refugee issue.' This is an attempt to dismantle UN Resolution 194, which calls for the return of Palestinian refugees. When I was at the Middle East Peace Negotiations in 1991 as legal adviser to the Palestinian delegation, [then Secretary of State James] Baker instructed [his assistant Margaret] Tutwiler to publicly invoke Resolution 194, which she did. Bush's attempt to dismantle it is a major change in U.S. policy.

"Bush also said: 'The agreement must establish Palestine as a homeland for the Palestinian people, just as Israel is a homeland for the Jewish people.' Israel could use such an agreement to strip its Palestinian, non-Jewish citizens of Israeli citizenship, let them live in Israel, but say that now they can become citizens of Palestine. This is exactly what the South African Afrikaners did to Blacks with their bantustans during the apartheid era. Even worse, it could set the stage for the mass expulsion of Palestinians from Israel to a Palestinian bantustan.

"Bush's statements that the Palestinian state should be 'viable, contiguous, sovereign, and independent' and that 'Swiss cheese isn't going to work when it comes to the outline of a state,' sound substantial, but are rendered rather meaningless since he only said the U.S. is opposing 'settlement expansion'—meaning that current settlements, which effectively cut up the West Bank into apartheid-style bantustans, will remain and be annexed by Israel."

More Information

Israel's 40-Year Occupation · Palestinian Civil War? · USS Liberty

June 7, 2007

Francis Boyle

Professor of international law at the University of Illinois, Boyle is author of *Palestine, Palestinians, and International Law*. He writes in his most recent piece: "Palestinian President Mahmoud Abbas stated [Tuesday] that the Palestinians were on the verge of a civil war—as if he had nothing to do with it, in contrast to his predecessor . . . Israel and the United States are still doing everything humanly possible to promote a Palestinian civil war by means of arming, financing and encouraging comprador Palestinian surrogates toward that diabolical end." See "The 40th Anniversary of Occupation," *Palestine Chronicle*, June 6, 2007.

Will the UN Stop This War?

August 1, 2006

Francis Boyle

Professor of international law at the University of Illinois, Boyle suggests the establishment by the United Nations General Assembly of "an International Criminal Tribunal for Israel (ICTI) as a 'subsidiary organ' under UN Charter Article 22. The ICTI would be organized along the lines of the International Criminal Tribunal for Yugoslavia (ICTY), which was established by the Security Council . . . [T]he establishment of ICTI by the UN General Assembly would serve as a deterrent upon Israeli leaders such as Prime Minister Olmert, Defense Minister Peretz, Chief of Staff Halutz and Israel's other top generals because they will be prosecuted for their further infliction of international crimes upon the Lebanese and the Palestinians. Without such a deterrent, Israel might be emboldened to attack Syria . . . For the UN General Assembly to establish ICTI could stop the further development of this momentum towards a regional, if not global, catastrophe." Boyle is author of the books *Biowarfare and Terrorism* and *Destroying World Order*.

Interviews Available on Bush's Mideast Plan

June 25, 2002

Francis Boyle

Boyle is professor of international law at the University of Illinois College of Law. He was legal advisor to the Palestinian delegation to the Middle East peace negotiations from 1991 to 1993 and author of the forthcoming book *Palestine, Palestinians, and International Law*. He said today: "At least President Arafat was democratically elected by the vast majority of his people, unlike President Bush. The time frames seem deliberately designed by the Bush administration to punt on all critical issues beyond the 2004 presidential elections . . . As Israel repudiates Oslo and resumes its outright occupation of the West Bank, there is nothing for the Palestinians but vague promises of good intentions by the United States government that have never materialized during the past 35 years. Basically, Bush gave Sharon the proverbial green light to dump Arafat. Violence will continue and escalate."

U.S. and Israeli Policies: The Road Ahead

April 4, 2002

Francis Boyle

Professor of international law at the University of Illinois College of Law and legal adviser to the Palestinian delegation to the Middle East peace negotiations from 1991 to 1993, Boyle said today: "We must abandon the fiction that the U.S. government is an 'honest broker' in the Middle East . . . It has invariably sided with Israel against the Palestinians, as well as against the other Arab states. We need to establish some type of international framework to sponsor these negotiations where the Palestinian negotiators will not be subjected to the continual intimidation, bribery, and outright deceptions perpetrated by the U.S. and Israel." Boyle, who was General Agent for the Republic of Bosnia and Herzegovina before the International Court of Justice against the Milošević regime, added: "Milošević is on trial at The Hague for genocide, crimes against humanity and war crimes, whereas Sharon is on trial in Belgium for genocide, crimes against humanity and war crimes."

Interviews Available on Major Legal Issues
January 25, 2002
Francis Boyle
Professor of international law at the University of Illinois College of Law, Boyle sued Israeli Gen. Amos Yaron in a civil proceeding over the Sabra/Shatila massacre. He said today: "Yesterday a car bomb killed Elie Hobeika, a former militia chief whose forces carried out the 1982 massacre of Palestinian refugees in the Sabra and Shatila camps while surrounded by the Israeli army. Hobeika had recently indicated his willingness to testify against Israeli Prime Minister Ariel Sharon and other Israeli officials, including Yaron, at an ongoing criminal trial in Belgium for their role in the massacre. . ."
More Information

Interviews Available: Sharon vs. Hamas?
December 5, 2001
Francis Boyle
Professor of international law at the University of Illinois College of Law, Boyle said today: "Israel is acting in total violation of international law, including UN resolutions that allowed it into the UN in the first place. If something is not done quite soon to stop Israeli war crimes and crimes against humanity against the Palestinians, it could very well degenerate into genocide, literally fit that legal definition—if Israel is not there already. In this regard, Israeli Prime Minister Ariel Sharon is what international lawyers call a genocidaire—one who has already committed genocide in the past. There is currently a criminal case against Sharon in Belgium, using the Pinochet principle, for his role in the Sabra and Shatila massacres against Palestinian refugees. Sharon is ready, willing, and able to inflict genocide yet again upon the Palestinians."

Racism Conference
September 7, 2001
The UN conference on racism in Durban, South Africa is scheduled to end on Friday. The following analysts are available for interviews:
Francis Boyle

Professor of international law at the University of Illinois College of Law, Boyle said today: "The U.S. and Europe should not be allowed to use the Mideast to avoid seriously addressing the legacy of colonialism and slavery. Africans and their descendants are rightfully owed reparations. Rather than distracting from each other, it's important to see that Israeli practices are a continuation of colonialism—settler colonialism—and have a great deal in common with the European imperialism in the last half-millennium which we should at long last account for."

Major International Issues: * Racism Conference * Israel's Occupation
August 29, 2001
Francis Boyle
Professor of international law at the University of Illinois College of Law, Boyle said today: "UN Security Council Resolution 1322 [2000] 'calls upon Israel, the occupying Power, to abide scrupulously by its legal obligations and its responsibilities under the Fourth Geneva Convention. . .' There are 149 substantive articles of the Fourth Geneva Convention that protect the rights of every one of these Palestinians living in occupied Palestine. The Israeli government is currently violating, and has since 1967 been violating, almost each and every one of these. . ."

Camp David: Deadline?
July 19, 2000
Francis Boyle
Boyle, a professor at the University of Illinois College of Law in Champaign, served as legal advisor to the Palestinian delegation to the Middle East peace negotiations from 1991 to 1993. He said today: "The Palestinians have a very strong case they should take to the UN and the World Court. Everything that they are asking for—and then some—is contained in UN Resolution 181 and Resolution 194, both of which Israel accepted as a condition for its joining the UN. If Israel continues to refuse to let the refugees go home, or to share Jerusalem, Israel jeopardizes its position in the international community and its UN membership."

Director of the Middle East Children's Alliance, Lubin (who has just returned from the Mideast) said today: "If over 100,000 people from Russia could immigrate to Israel last year, then the time has come for the Palestinian children from the refugee camps to be allowed back to their rightful homes. Even if the Palestinians get 90 percent of the West Bank, we should bear in mind that that's just 22 percent of historic Palestine."

Human Rights, Trade and Foreign Policy
November 16, 1999

While President Clinton visits Turkey and tries to bring China into the World Trade Organization, the following analysts are available for comment:

Francis Boyle

Professor of International Law at the University of Illinois College of Law in Champaign, Boyle said: "Lost in the fuss about Mrs. Arafat's remarks is that Israel has used tear gas that caused a number of deaths, including many miscarriages, in violation of international law. And just recently Gen. Amos Yaron was appointed director-general of the Israeli Ministry of Defense. He bore command responsibility for the massacre of about 2,000 Palestinian and Lebanese civilians at the Sabra and Shatilla refugee camps in 1982 . . . Yaron should be behind bars."

PROSECUTING U.S. WAR CRIMINALS

Prosecuting Torture

December 11, 2014

AP reports: "UN Officials Demand Prosecutions for U.S. Torture."

Francis Boyle, fboyle at illinois.edu

Boyle is a professor at the University of Illinois College of Law and author of *Tackling America's Toughest Questions*. International Business Times reports: "Some human rights advocates have called for former President George W. Bush, Vice President Dick Cheney, Secretary of State Condoleeza Rice and others in Bush's administration to be tried for the abuses. Bush, Cheney, Rice and others were referred to the ICC [International Criminal Court] in 2010 by a team of prosecutors that later successfully levied war crimes charges against them in the independent and semi-symbolic Kuala Lumpur War Crimes Commission.

"Francis Boyle, a prosecutor in the Kuala Lumpur case and a professor at the University of Illinois College of Law, filed that complaint, but it remains pending. He said it's a good sign it wasn't immediately dismissed and that the Senate Intelligence Committee report could be what convinces an ICC prosecutor to open an investigation.

"'This is important because now we have an official branch of the U.S. government adopting and making these findings of fact,' he said. 'In addition to ICC prosecution, this now will help us pursue these individuals around the world [through the UN Convention Against Torture and Geneva Conventions]. All states signed to that convention, of which the U.S. is one of them, is required to have domestic legislation in place to prosecute torture. It does seem that if any of these individuals go outside of the U.S., we can go after them.'

"Boyle helped lobby the Swiss government to arrest Bush during a visit in 2011, which he, Human Rights Watch, and other rights groups said prompted

Bush to cancel that trip. Bush's spokesman said the group Bush was scheduled to speak but canceled because of security concerns.

"Donald Rumsfeld, former defense secretary under Bush, nearly cancelled a trip to Germany in 2005 after prosecutors there initially threatened him with war crimes case, but later backed down. In addition, the U.S. has pursued over 100 'Bilateral Immunity Agreements' with foreign states that essentially bar that state from referring U.S. officials—current or former—to the ICC.

"Boyle believes that bringing a case against Bush and his officials is crucial to rebuilding the ICC as a legitimate international court that doesn't just go after 'tin pot dictators' in Africa. He said he will submit follow-up appeals to the ICC after reading through the entirety of the [declassified sections of the] Senate report."

NATO and ICC: Power and Accountability

May 18, 2012

Francis Boyle, fboyle at law.uiuc.edu

Boyle is a professor at the University of Illinois College of Law and author of *Tackling America's Toughest Questions*. Yesterday, *AllAfrica.com* reported that Charles Taylor—in his first statements after being convicted by the UN Special Court on Sierra Leone: "President George W. Bush not too long ago ordered torture and admitted to doing so. Torture is a crime against humanity. The United States has refused to prosecute him. Is he above the law? Where is the fairness?" The report noted that "In January of 2010, one Professor Francis A. Boyle of the College of Law at the University of Illinois filed a Complaint with the International Criminal Court against President Bush and at least five of his senior officials for allegedly committing international crimes."

Just this week, Boyle returned to the U.S. from Malaysia and the Kuala Lumpur War Crimes Tribunal, which convicted Bush in absentia. He said today: "The International Criminal Court has become a joke and a fraud. I supported it originally. But no more. It has no credibility whatsoever. It just goes after tin-pot dictators in Africa while the real war criminals such as Bush, Blair and Netanyahu get off scot-free. Hence I went out to the Kuala Lumpur War Crimes Tribunal to convict Bush, Blair, Cheney, Rumsfeld and their consigliore lawyers."

Nobel Peace Prize Laureate Rebuffs U.S. State Department on Upcoming Summit

April 16, 2012

Mairead Maguire, who was awarded the Nobel Peace Prize for her work on Ireland and was scheduled to attend the Summit of Nobel Peace Laureates this month in Chicago, has canceled her appearance citing a statement by

U.S. Secretary of State Hillary Clinton that the State Department is an "active partner" in the event. Maguire notified associates, including other Nobel Prize Laureates, of her decision in a letter the Institute for Public Accuracy has obtained and is below.

The Nobel Summit leads up to the NATO Summit in Chicago. A video of Clinton's recent remarks is available here.

Critics of the State Department and NATO applauded Maguire's decision:

Francis Boyle, fboyle at law.uiuc.edu

Boyle is a professor at the University of Illinois College of Law and author of *Tackling America's Toughest Questions*. He said today: "It is well known that the so-called Nobel Peace Prize is awarded by Norwegian politicians and that Norway is a member of NATO. In other words the Nobel Peace Prize is awarded by NATO politicians in order to further their own political interests. And now we have the Nobel Prizers finally come out of the NATO closet." Boyle derided the notion of the U.S. State Department using the Nobel Peace Prize at the upcoming "NATO Warfest in Chicago. But of course the Nobel Peace Prize was awarded to Henry Kissinger. Nobel 'Peace Prize'? Tell that to millions in war after war—Vietnam, Yugoslavia, Iraq, Afghanistan, Libya, and now threatening Syria and Iran."

Boyle—who was a leading lawyer defending protesters during the fight against apartheid South Africa—noted that a video has also been released of former apartheid South African President Willem de Klerk touting his scheduled participation and interaction with Chicago students in conjunction with the upcoming events. Boyle noted that de Klerk "avoided testifying before the Truth and Reconciliation Commission—so from him there was no truth, no accountability, no prosecution."

Prosecuting Gadhafi, Prosecuting U.S. Leaders

June 29, 2011

The Washington Times editorialized Tuesday: "The Obama administration is backing the International Criminal Court's arrest warrants for Libyan leader Moammar Gadhafi. It is a dangerous precedent for the United States to rush to affirm the jurisdiction of this relatively new international body, particularly with a president whose counterterrorism strategy has made his name synonymous with 'targeted killing.' On Monday, ICC judges granted warrants for Col. Gadhafi, his son Seif al-Islam and regime intelligence chief Abdullah Sanussi. . .

'In 2010, American law professor Francis A. Boyle of the University of Illinois College of Law in Champaign, filed a complaint with the ICC prosecutor against Mr. Bush, Dick Cheney, Donald H. Rumsfeld, George Tenet, Condoleezza Rice and Alberto Gonzales for 'their criminal policy and practice of 'extraordinary rendition' perpetrated upon about 100 human beings.'

The dirty little secret is that renditions have continued—and some sources say increased—under the Obama administration. This, combined with the questionable legality of drone strikes under international law, could come back to haunt the White House if the ICC continues to expand its authority."

[Note: Obama, at his news conference today, made reference to the ICC case and repeated allegations of the Gadhafi regime using rape as a weapon. BBC reports: "Donatella Rovera from Amnesty International, who has spent three months in the country, said the organization did not have evidence of cases of rape so far."]

Francis Boyle, fboyle at law.uiuc.edu

Professor of international law at the University of Illinois College of Law in Champaign, Boyle said today: "In my 2010 ICC Complaint against Bush et al., which is still pending, I informed the ICC Prosecutor that the Obama administration publicly stated that it will continue the Bush et al. policy and practice of extraordinary renditions, which is really a euphemism for the enforced disappearances of human beings and their consequent torture by other States, and thus Crimes Against Humanity under the ICC Rome Statute. One of the charges against Colonel Gadhafi is the enforced disappearances of human beings as a Crime Against Humanity. Right now I do not have the documented facts necessary to file an ICC Complaint against President Obama and CIA Director Panetta, inter alia. But if and when such credible evidence emerges into the public record, I will file such an ICC Complaint against Obama, Panetta et al. if their 'extraordinary renditions' do not terminate immediately. In addition, the Obama administration's drone strikes in Afghanistan are subject to the jurisdiction of the ICC and should be terminated immediately because they are wreaking indiscriminate war crimes upon the civilian population of that benighted country and thus add up to Crimes Against Humanity under the ICC Rome Statute. The same general principles of international criminal law likewise apply to the CIA drone strikes in Pakistan."

Torture: * Prosecution * Protest

January 21, 2010

Francis Boyle

Boyle, a professor at the University of Illinois College of Law in Champaign, earlier this week submitted a complaint to the International Criminal Court charging Bush, Cheney, et. al with crimes relating to the "extraordinary rendition" and illegal detention of individuals. While the U.S. is not a signatory to the ICC, Boyle notes that many people detained by the Bush administration were detained in countries that were signatories of the ICC at the time of detention, and thus the Court has jurisdiction on those cases. See the complaint by Boyle to the prosecutor of the ICC, Luis Moreno-Ocampo.

Questions Not Asked: · Torturing People's Children · War Powers · Geneva Conventions

January 12, 2006

Francis Boyle

Boyle is professor of law at the University of Illinois. Alito stated Wednesday: "I think that the war powers are divided between the executive branch and the Congress."

Boyle said today: "Article I, Sec. 8 of the Constitution says: 'The Congress shall have power . . . to declare war. . .' The president has nothing to do with it. When Congress declares war, then that declaration triggers the Commander in Chief Clause of the Constitution. Alito is mistakenly attributing War Powers to the president in violation of the War Powers Clause of the U.S. Constitution and in violation of Congress's War Powers Resolution of 1973, which is 'the supreme Law of the Land' according to Article VI of the Constitution. Alito's argument is a fundamental alteration of one of the most basic principles for both separation of powers and checks and balances set up for our Republic by the Founders in the U.S. Constitution.

"But this unconstitutional argument for presidential war powers is part of the standard Federalist Society ideology propounded by its prominent members such as Alito, John Roberts, and John Yoo. It has led to the abuses of Guantanamo, Abu Ghraib, pervasive torture, 'extraordinary renditions,' criminal NSA spying on U.S. citizens, 'enemy combatants,' wholesale violations of the Geneva Conventions, assassinations, massive religious and racial profiling of Muslims/Arabs/Asians, an unconstitutional war against Iraq and the numerous other constitutional atrocities perpetrated by Bush's hyper-imperial presidency. The Democrats have not asked serious questions about most of these issues." Boyle is author of the book *Destroying World Order*.

Backers of International Court Challenge Nay-Sayers

July 17, 1998

WASHINGTON—As discussions on the International Criminal Court treaty were coming to a close in Rome today, backers of a strong Court criticized the U.S. delegation's end-game approach at the historic meeting. Some Court advocates took particular exception to the common argument that the Court would open a legal Pandora's box, saying that such allegations are a red herring. Among those available for comment are:

Francis Boyle

A professor of International Law at the University of Illinois College of Law, Boyle said: "The idea that U.S. soldiers on peacekeeping missions could be prosecuted under this is completely bogus. What they really want to do is still make it possible for U.S. soldiers—as well as civilians who conduct offensive, illegal operations—to escape jurisdiction. The Pentagon is concerned that future military operations such as its invasions of Grenada and Panama and its bombings of Tripoli and Benghazi would be found to be criminal. What came out of Nuremberg was that there should be one body of law, not only for the Nazi defendants but also for ourselves in the future. Now, here we are 50 years later trying to prevent it. They are also undoing years of U.S. jurisprudence, taking positions contradicting our own Army Field Manual."

ROMNEY

Romney's Bishophood and Mormonism

August 30, 2012

The Financial Times reports: "For months, Mitt Romney has been speaking about his Mormon faith only when pressed. On Thursday night, when he accepts the Republican party's nomination for president, his religion will be celebrated in prime time like never before."

Francis Boyle

Boyle is a professor at the University of Illinois College of Law and author of *Tackling America's Toughest Questions*. He said today: "The Mormon Bishop who succeeded Romney in Boston, Grant Bennett, will be speaking. Usually Bishops and Cardinals only lead prayers at Conventions. They don't give speeches. Romney's official positions in the hierarchy of the Mormon Church raise serious questions under the First Amendment to the U.S. Constitution. Romney must come clean and fully explain his official positions in the Mormon Church hierarchy and the extent to which he takes orders from their Prophet and Apostles. So far the mainstream news media have all given Romney a pass on this threat to the First Amendment."

"Romney is/was a Mormon Bishop and Archbishop. They take orders from the Mormon Prophet, roughly the Mormon equivalent of the Roman Catholic Pope. Constitutionally speaking under the First Amendment, Romney is not equivalent to either John Kennedy (a lay Catholic) or Joe Lieiberman (a lay orthodox Jew) or Jimmy Carter (a lay Baptist Sunday school teacher)."

"Critically, Kennedy said he would resign if there was a conflict and Romney conspicuously did not."

Boyle is a Magna Cum Laude graduate of Harvard Law School where he was section-mates with Willard Mitt Romney, now known as Mitt, as first year law students (1Ls) during the 1971-1972 academic year. They took all their first-year law courses together. He teaches courses on the Constitutional Law of U.S. Foreign Affairs, and Jurisprudence, among others.

See Kennedy's address from 1960.

Romney addressed the issue of religion and public office in 2007.

Mormonism: * Bigotry * President Romney's Bishophood a Threat to the First Amendment?

January 19, 2012

Francis Boyle, fboyle at law.uiuc.edu

Boyle is a professor at the University of Illinois College of Law and author of *Tackling America's Toughest Questions*. He said today: "Romney's official positions in the hierarchy of the Mormon Church raise serious questions under the First Amendment to the U.S. Constitution. Do the American people want the functional equivalent to the Mormon Pope and his College of Cardinals sitting in their Salt Lake Vatican City ordering the President of the United States what to do? Romney must come clean and fully explain his official positions in the Mormon Church hierarchy and the extent to which he takes orders from their Prophet and Apostles. So far the mainstream news media have all given Romney a pass on this threat to the First Amendment because big business supports Romney and the mainstream media is part of big business. But the mainstream media are protected by that same First Amendment that Romney threatens. The media have a First Amendment obligation to nail down Romney on these serious First Amendment issues."

"Romney is/was a Mormon Bishop and Archbishop. They take orders from the Mormon Prophet, roughly the Mormon equivalent of the Roman Catholic Pope. Constitutionally speaking under the First Amendment, Romney is not equivalent to either John Kennedy (a lay Catholic) or Joe Lieiberman (a lay orthodox Jew) or Jimmy Carter (a lay Baptist Sunday school teacher)."

"Critically, Kennedy said he would resign if there was a conflict and Romney conspicuously did not."

Boyle is a Magna Cum Laude graduate of Harvard Law School where he was section-mates with Willard Mitt Romney, now known as Mitt, as first year law students (1Ls) during the 1971-1972 academic year. They took all their first-year law courses together. He teaches courses on the Constitutional Law of U.S. Foreign Affairs, and Jurisprudence, among others.

Kennedy's address from 1960.

Romney addressed the issue of religion and public office in 2007.

From Mormon.org, see "Who is the Mormon Prophet Today?"

SYRIA

Syria Bombing "Illegal," Likely to "Prolong" Syrian War

April 14, 2018

The U.S., France and Britain bombed Syria Friday. This took place just before inspectors from the Organization for the Prohibition of Chemical Weapons were to begin their work in Syria.

Francis Boyle, fboyle at illinois.edu

Boyle is professor of international law at the University of Illinois College of Law. He was recently on an IPA news release: "Attacking Syria 'Impeachable.'" See his recent interview on WMNF, April 12, 2018. He also recently wrote the piece "America's 'Unlimited Imperialists'" for Consortium News, Oct. 25, 2018. Boyle's books include *Foundations of World Order* (1999) and *Destroying World Order* (2015).

Attacking Syria "Impeachable"

April 10, 2018

Francis Boyle, fboyle at illinois.edu

Boyle is professor of international law at the University of Illinois College of Law. He said today: "Any U.S. attack targeting the Syrian government or its forces would clearly violate both U.S. and international law. When Obama was in a similar position in 2013, his advisor Ben Rhodes [see below] has since commented that they turned back largely because they were afraid of impeachment. That fear is well founded. While the prospect of impeaching Trump is thrown around frequently for partisan purposes, on this issue, the Constitution is clear: Initiating a war or any such attack without authorization is clearly impeachable.

"Last year, at the National Press Club, Chairman of the Joint Chiefs of Staff, Gen. Joseph F. Dunford Jr., claimed the authority to target the Syrian government stemmed from the 2001 Authorization for the Use of Military Force. Gen. Dunford was totally incorrect. The AUMF passed after 9/11 has indeed been used to justify the bombing campaign purporting to target ISIS, but it cannot possibly be used to justify targeting the Syrian government.

"Excuses of 'humanitarian intervention' have no basis in international law and in these circumstances are transparently hollow. Israel apparently just attacked Syria (illegal) from Lebanese airspace (also illegal). Israel itself just openly admitted that it is killing Palestinian civilian protesters—part of a decades-long brazenly illegal policy. The U.S. representative to the UN, Nikki Haley, prevented even an inquiry by the UN into the matter. There's no evidence of any humanitarian concern here, simply a search for pretexts to pursue geopolitical goals which may well include carving up Syria."

Boyle's books include *Foundations of World Order* (Duke University Press).

In 2017, Ben Rhodes, Obama's Deputy National Security Advisor, and foreign policy speechwriter, told *Politico* that President Obama feared impeachment if he targeted the Syrian government:

Rhodes: "The only country in the world that was prepared to join us [in attacking the Assad government] was France. And we had no domestic legal basis. We actually had Congress warning us against taking action without congressional authorization, which we interpreted as the president could face impeachment."

Politico: "Really? Was the prospect of impeachment actually a factor in your conversations?"

Rhodes: "That was a factor. Go back and read the letters from Boehner, letters from the Republican members of Congress. They laid down markers that this would not be constitutional."

House Speaker John Boehner wrote to Obama in 2013: "It is essential you address on what basis any use of force would be legally justified and how the justification comports with the exclusive authority of Congressional authorization under Article I of the Constitution."

Are Claims About Syrian Sarin Attacks Propaganda Leading to More War?
June 27, 2017

BuzzFeed reports: "Syria appears to be preparing a new chemical weapons attack against its citizens, the White House said Monday, warning that if the weapons are again used, the U.S. will make the Syrian government 'pay a heavy price.' . . . Five U.S. defense officials reached by BuzzFeed News said they did not know where the potential chemical attack would come from, including one U.S. Central Command official who had 'no idea' about its origin."

From RT: "U.S. threats to Syria's legitimate government unacceptable—Kremlin."

See new interview with investigative journalist Seymour Hersh: "Trump Ignored Intel Before Bombing Syria" with The Real News. On Sunday, Hersh's piece "Trump's Red Line" was published in the German newspaper *Welt am Sonntag*. Hersh wrote: "On April 6, United States President Donald Trump authorized an early morning Tomahawk missile strike on Shayrat Air Base in central Syria in retaliation for what he said was a deadly nerve agent attack carried out by the Syrian government two days earlier in the rebel-held town of Khan Sheikhoun. Trump issued the order despite having been warned by the U.S. intelligence community that it had found no evidence that the Syrians had used a chemical weapon. . .

"'The Salafists and jihadists got everything they wanted out of their hyped-up Syrian nerve gas ploy,' the senior adviser to the U.S. intelligence community told me, referring to the flare up of tensions between Syria, Russia and America. 'The issue is, what if there's another false flag sarin attack credited to hated Syria? Trump has upped the ante and painted himself into a corner with his decision to bomb. And do not think these guys are not planning the next faked attack. Trump will have no choice but to bomb again, and harder. He's incapable of saying he made a mistake.'"

Francis Boyle, fboyle at illinois.edu

Boyle is professor of international law at the University of Illinois College of Law. See his recent interview with Dennis Bernstein at Consortium News: "A Baseless Justification for War in Syria," June 25, 2017. He said today: "The current posture of U.S., French and perhaps British policy in Syria is basically an invitation for some jihadist group to stage a chemical weapons attack in Syria. That would get blamed on Assad and the U.S. would bomb him. This is an intolerable, incredibly dangerous situation brought on by constant illegal U.S. meddling."

CNN recently reported: "Macron vows retaliation if chemical weapons used in Syria.

Bombing Syria: * Impeachable * Carve-Up Agenda

June 19, 2017

The *New York Times* reports: "Russia Warns U.S. After Downing of Syrian Warplane."

This afternoon at the National Press Club, Joint Chiefs Chairman and Marine Gen. Joseph Dunford was asked a question submitted by the Institute for Public Accuracy: "What's the legal justification for targeting Syrian government forces?" He claimed: "We are there and have legal justification under the Authorization for Use of Military Force, we are prosecuting a campaign against ISIS and Al-Qaeda in Syria." See video.

Francis Boyle, fboyle at illinois.edu

Boyle is professor of international law at the University of Illinois College of Law. He said today: "Gen. Dunford is totally incorrect. The AUMF passed after 9/11 has indeed been used to justify the bombing campaign purporting to target ISIS, but it cannot possibly be used to justify targeting the Syrian government. Those attacks are in fact clearly illegal and impeachable.

"Many have put forward dubious arguments for impeaching Trump—or arguments that they would never apply to a Democratic president. Similarly, some threatened Obama with impeachment and are not doing so now that Trump is engaging in exactly the activity they threatened Obama about. Hypocrisies and hypocrites abound.

"If we care about the rule of law, the most striking thing about Trump is his flagrant violation of the War Powers Clause of the Constitution in this targeting of the Syrian government. Now, the U.S. has been violating international law in terms of its drone assassination program and various bombing campaigns, like the one purporting to target ISIS in Syria. Many of these activities are justified by attempts to invoke the Authorization for the Use of Military

Force passed after the 9/11 attacks. A decade and a half after those attacks, that rationale is international legal nonsense, but it exists.

"In contrast, the targeting of forces of or allied with the Syrian government has no justification whatsoever. It is obviously impeachable—Obama's people say they were afraid of impeachment for exactly this [see below]. But pro-war Democrats don't raise it because it would put a constraint on the war-making capacities of the U.S. president—while they pretend to care about the rule of law.

"Many of the U.S. attacks on Syria have been around the so-called 'de-confliction zones.' These zones are de facto partitions of Syria in violation of its territorial sovereignty and political independence. This goes back at least to the Pentagon just after 9/11 telling retired General Wesley Clark that they wanted to target Iraq, and then Syria, Lebanon, Libya, Somalia, Sudan and, finishing off, Iran.

"Israeli strategic interests are obviously served by a breakup of Syria; as is the case for much of the U.S. establishment. The Saudis are clearly on board. The Russians, rhetoric aside, are likely simply looking for some scraps. The big losers are the Syrians and most of the other people of the region."

See recent report in the *Financial Times*: "Syria de-escalation deal stirs fears of carve-up by foreign powers." Also, see new report from the *Wall Street Journal*: "Israel Gives Secret Aid to Syrian Rebels."

Earlier this year, Ben Rhodes, Obama's Deputy National Security Advisor and foreign policy speechwriter, told *Politico* that President Obama feared impeachment if he targeted the Syrian government:

Rhodes: "The only country in the world that was prepared to join us [in attacking the Assad government] was France. And we had no domestic legal basis. We actually had Congress warning us against taking action without congressional authorization, which we interpreted as the president could face impeachment."

Politico: "Really? Was the prospect of impeachment actually a factor in your conversations?"

Rhodes: "That was a factor. Go back and read the letters from Boehner, letters from the Republican members of Congress. They laid down markers that this would not be constitutional."

House Speaker John Boehner wrote to Obama in 2013: "It is essential you address on what basis any use of force would be legally justified and how the justification comports with the exclusive authority of Congressional authorization under Article I of the Constitution."

Boyle was featured on an Institute for Public Accuracy news release in 2013 along with former Rep. Paul Findley: "* Key Author of War Powers Act: 'Obama has no Authority to Attack Syria' * Impeachment."

Trump's Syria Bombing Impeachable

May 19, 2017

CBS News reports: "U.S. aircraft conduct strike on Syrian army convoy."

Earlier this year, *The Hill* reported "Top aide: Obama worried about impeachment for Syria actions."

Rep. Ted Lieu (D-Calif.) tweeted Thursday after initial reports of the strike: "If true, this is FRICKIN ILLEGAL. Trump does not have Congressional authorization to attack Syria, a country that has not attacked US." He also tweeted: "Congress authorized President to use force in 2 cases: terrorists & Iraq. @realDonaldTrump has NO AUTHORIZATION to attack Syrian regime."

Francis Boyle, fboyle [at] illinois.edu

Boyle is professor of international law at the University of Illinois College of Law. He said today: "The U.S. strike clearly violates the War Powers Resolution, the War Powers Clause of the United States Constitution, and the United Nations Charter. It's impeachable.

"These so-called deconfliction zones are de facto partitions of Syria in violation of its territorial sovereignty and political independence."

The Hill report states: "President Obama's deputy national security adviser says in a new interview that the threat of impeachment 'was a factor' in Obama's decision not to pursue a tougher intervention policy in Syria.

"'We actually had Congress warning us against taking action without congressional authorization, which we interpreted as the president could face impeachment,' Ben Rhodes told *Politico Magazine*.

"When asked to elaborate, the president's adviser said that Republicans, including then-Speaker John Boehner (R-Ohio), made it clear that premature military action without congressional approval would be unconstitutional."

Trump Bombing "Illegal"

April 7, 2017

Francis Boyle, fboyle [at] illinois.edu

Reuters reports: "Russia calls for emergency U.N. meeting after U.S. strikes on Syria." Trump claimed on Thursday: "There can be no dispute that Syria used banned chemical weapons, violated its obligations under the Chemical Weapons Convention and ignored the urging of the U.N. Security Council."

Boyle is professor of international law at the University of Illinois College of Law. He said today: "The U.S. strikes are a clear violation of international law and the War Powers Clause of the U.S. Constitution. There is no evidence for any of Trump's claims."

Obama West Point Speech—Myths on Afghanistan, Syria, Honduras

May 28, 2014

Francis Boyle, fboyle at illinois.edu

Boyle is a professor at the University of Illinois College of Law and author of *Tackling America's Toughest Questions*. He said today: "The World Court ruled in the case *Nicaragua* brought against the U.S. in Nicaragua's favor, condemning the U.S.'s 'indirect form of support for subversive or terrorist armed activities within another State . . . These forms of action are therefore wrongful in the light of both the principle of non-use of force, and that of non-intervention' Thus, the U.S. and other states arming groups in Syria is illegal."

Key Author of War Powers Act: "Obama has no Authority to Attack Syria" * Impeachment

September 9, 2013

Paul Findley, findley1 at frontier.com

Available for a limited number of interviews, Findley served as a member of United States House of Representatives for 22 years. He was a key author of the War Powers Act and a leader in securing its enactment by overriding the veto of President Richard Nixon. He is also the author of six books. The Federal building in Springfield, Ill. is named for him.

He just wrote the piece "Obama has no Authority to Attack Syria," which states: "Despite his own recent statements to the contrary, President Barack Obama has no legal authority to assault the government of Syria even as 'a warning shot.' Neither the United States Constitution, nor the War Powers Act of 1973 gives him such authority in the absence of an emergency that allows Congress no time to react. Obama cannot cite the present situation as such an emergency, given his public statement that members of Congress need not act until the completion of their scheduled vacation. He has said that his proposal is 'not time sensitive.' If Congress fails to approve a resolution approving acts of war against Syria, he cannot order any military assault into Syria."

"On several recent occasions the President and administration officials have mentioned a 'sixty day' period during which he has authority to act without approval of Congress. Such authority does not exist. It is a misreading of a provision of the War Powers Act that provides only Congress with oversight constraints on executive actions . . ." Findley also recently wrote the piece "Syria—a War We Should Reject."

Francis Boyle, fboyle at illinois.edu

Boyle is a professor at the University of Illinois College of Law and author of *Tackling America's Toughest Questions*. Boyle drafted articles of impeachment that were introduced by the late Rep. Henry Gonzalez against President George H. W. Bush in 1991. Boyle said today: "Impeachment is the remedy for a president taking extra-constitutional action. Obama claims he has the authority to attack Syria when—under the Constitution—he does not."

See: "Cornel West: It's 'Grounds For Impeachment' If Obama Bombs Syria Without Congressional Approval."

A "Dodgy Dossier" Instead of a Congressional Debate?

August 30, 2013

UN weapons inspectors are reportedly leaving Syria on Saturday.

Francis Boyle, fboyle at illinois.edu

Boyle is a professor at the University of Illinois College of Law and author of *Tackling America's Toughest Questions*. He said today: "The test the Dossier [PDF] uses is 'high confidence'—but the appropriate standard by the International Court of Justice (in the *Corfu Channel* case) is 'beyond a reasonable doubt.' The Dossier notes that it does not 'confirm' the allegations against Syria. So the U.S. intelligence community refuses to 'confirm' that the Syrian government did it."

"Kerry claimed in his remarks: 'We assess that the opposition has not used chemical weapons.' But Carla Del Ponte of the UN commission said they did. See: BBC: 'UN's Del Ponte says evidence Syria rebels "used sarin" Similarly, Kerry claimed 'We intercepted communications involving a senior official. . .' But the *Wall Street Journal* already reported that came from Israeli intelligence."

"Concrete Suspicions" Syrian REBELS—Not Government—Used Sarin Gas Says UN Investigator

May 6, 2013

The BBC reports in "UN's Del Ponte Says Evidence Syria Rebels 'Used Sarin'" that Carla Del Ponte, a member of the Independent International Commission of Inquiry on Syria, stated that the investigation has so far found that nerve gas appeared to be "used by the opponents, by the rebels. And we have no indication at all that the government, the authority of the Syrian government, had used chemical weapons." See full BBC report, including video of Del Ponte.

Francis Boyle, fboyle at illinois.edu

Boyle is a professor at the University of Illinois College of Law and most recently author of *Destroying Libya and World Order*. He said today: "I have worked personally with Carla Del Ponte. She has an enormous amount of credibility. By the logic of Obama's 'red line' should he now enter the U.S. on the side of the Syria government?"

"In fact, as is true for almost every previous invocation of the doctrine of so-called 'humanitarian intervention' in modern history going all the way back to the mid-19th century, the application of the Responsibility to Protect Doctrine to Syria is based upon outright lies, propaganda and half-truths—as with all the baseless accusations over the last several weeks regarding the Syrian government using nerve gas and calls for U.S. military intervention. The Israeli strikes on Syria are obvious violations of international law. None of this of course excuses any violation of international human rights law that might have been committed by the Assad government."

TRUMP

International Court Caving to Trump Pressure

April 15, 2019

The *New York Times* reports: "Hague Court Abandons Afghanistan War Crimes Inquiry."

. . .

Also see Institute for Public Accuracy news release from last week: "Trump ICC and Iran Moves: Latest Attacks on International Law" with Prof. Francis Boyle, who filed the original complaint against Bush administration officials to the ICC and his interviews with The Real News: "Sec. of State Pompeo Protecting Bush Jr. from War Crimes Prosecution."

Trump ICC and Iran Moves: Latest Attacks on International Law

April 9, 2019

Francis Boyle, (217) 333-7954, fboyle@illinois.edu

Boyle is professor of international law at the University of Illinois College of Law. His books include *Foundations of World Order* (Duke University Press).

In "Trump Designates Iran's Revolutionary Guards a Foreign Terrorist Group" the *New York Times* reports: "The timing of Mr. Trump's announcement appeared aimed at giving Prime Minister Benjamin Netanyahu of Israel a final boost in a tight re-election campaign before a vote on Tuesday."

Boyle said today that the administration's move is "a complete negation and violation of the Third Geneva Convention of 1949 and thus a war crime. It opens us up to reprisals against our own military forces. Under the laws of war, reprisals against military personnel are permissible. This is continuing down the path of Bush Junior determining that Taliban and Al Qaeda are not protected by the Geneva Conventions, which was rejected by the U.S. Supreme Court in the *Hamdan* decision. . . . . Iran could now determine that U.S. Special Forces, Seals, Green Berets, Rangers, etc. are terrorists and thus do not benefit from the Third Geneva Convention. Apparently, for that reason, the Pentagon was against it."

Iran's Supreme National Security Council has responded to the U.S. government move by designating the U.S. Central Command (CENTCOM) and all the "forces connected to it" as a "terrorist group."

Secretary of State Mike Pompeo recently announced "a policy of U.S. visa restrictions on those individuals directly responsible for any I.C.C. [International Criminal Court] investigation of U.S. personnel. This includes persons who take or have taken action to request or further such an investigation. These visa restrictions may also be used to deter I.C.C. efforts to pursue allied personnel, including Israelis, without allies' consent."

Boyle referred cases against top U.S. government officials to the International Criminal Court. He also advised Mahmoud Abbas to accept the jurisdiction of the International Criminal Court.

In an interview published Monday with The Real News, Boyle said the "I.C.C. investigation, despite what Pompeo said, is not really against U.S. soldiers in Afghanistan. The I.C.C. does not have jurisdiction as it were to go after low-level soldiers. Basically, the I.C.C. in the case of the United States, would be going after the President, the Secretary of Defense, the Secretary of State, the head of the C.I.A." See: "Sec. of State Pompeo Protecting Bush Jr. from War Crimes Prosecution."

. . .

Emergency Powers "Impeachable": "All You Need is One Brave Member"

February 14, 2019

The *New York Times* reports: "Trump Plans National Emergency to Build Border Wall as Senate Passes Spending Bill."

Francis Boyle, fboyle@illinois.edu

Boyle is professor of international law at the University of Illinois College of Law. He was legal adviser to Rep. Henry B. González when he released classified material on the House floor in 1992 in an attempt to impeach George H. W. Bush following the start of the the Gulf War and wrote the first draft of the Gonzalez Impeachment Resolution. Bush would later write in his memoirs that if the Gulf War "drags out, not only will I take the blame, but I will probably have impeachment proceedings filed against me."

Boyle said today: "While establishment Democrats are eyeing various legal challenges to the possibility that Trump will declare a national emergency to get around Congress not agreeing on as much funding for a border wall as he would like, the most direct remedy is impeachment. A Bill of Impeachment could consist of articles including for (1) violating Article 1, Section 7 of the United States Constitution: 'All Bills for raising Revenue shall originate in the House of Representatives. . .' (2) Article 1, Section 8 of the Constitution: 'No Money shall be drawn from the Treasury, but in Consequence of Appropriations made by Law. . .' (3) It also violates the Federal Anti-Deficiency Statute.

"This should be initiated immediately. All you need is one brave member of the U.S. House of Representatives to meaningfully assert that body's Power of the Purse. Trump's indications that he will override that legislative power and the seeming acquiescence by some Democrats is illegitimate and dangerous and subverts a fundamental premise of the Constitution."

. . .

Is Threat of Emergency Powers to Override Power of the Purse Impeachable?

January 11, 2019

The *Washington Post* reports: "Trump administration lays groundwork to declare national emergency to build wall."

Francis Boyle, fboyle at illinois.edu

Boyle is professor of international law at the University of Illinois College of Law. He was legal adviser to Rep. Henry B. González when he released classified material on the House floor in 1992 in an attempt to impeach George H. W. Bush following the start of the Gulf War and wrote the first draft of the Gonzalez Impeachment Resolution. Bush would later write in his memoirs that if the Gulf War "drags out, not only will I take the blame, but I will probably have impeachment proceedings filed against me."

Boyle said today: "While establishment Democrats are eyeing various legal challenges to the possibility that Trump will declare a national emergency to get around Congress not agreeing on as much funding for a border wall as he would like, the most direct remedy is impeachment. A Bill of Impeachment could consist of articles including for (1) violating Article 1, Section 7 of the United States Constitution: 'All Bills for raising Revenue shall originate in the House of Representatives. . .' (2) Article 1, Section 8 of the Constitution: 'No Money shall be drawn from the Treasury, but in Consequence of Appropriations made by Law. . .' (3) It also violates the Federal Anti-Deficiency Statute. This could be initiated on Tuesday when the House reconvenes. All you need is one brave member of the House of Representatives to meaningfully assert that body's Power of the Purse. Trump's indications that he will override that legislative power and the seeming acquiescence by some Democrats is illegitimate and dangerous."

. . .

UKRAINE

Ukraine Agreement: 'Propaganda' and Low Expectations?

April 17, 2014

BBC reports: "Russia, the U.S. and the European Union have said that all sides have agreed to steps to 'de-escalate' the crisis in Ukraine. . .

"Following the Geneva talks, Russian Foreign Minister Sergei Lavrov, U.S. Secretary of State John Kerry and EU foreign policy chief Catherine Ashton said there was agreement that all illegal military formations in Ukraine must be dissolved, and that everyone occupying buildings must be disarmed and leave them."

Francis Boyle, fboyle at illinois.edu

Boyle is a professor at the University of Illinois College of Law. His books include *Foundations of World Order* (Duke University Press: 1999) and *Tackling America's Toughest Questions* (2009). He said today, "Ukraine did not commit itself to constitutional reform and it was very cleverly and deviously drafted language. So no agreement upon this issue. It says nothing about Ukraine staying out of NATO; and it is not a good sign that this was not a joint [media] conference by Lavrov and Kerry.

"Kerry's allegations [about East Ukraine anti-Semitism] sound like propaganda to me given . . . all the anti-Semitic statements coming out of Kiev and the warning by the [Ukrainian Chabad Chief] Rabbi Reuven Azman of Kiev [for Jews to leave Ukraine].

"So it does not sound to me as if Kerry is proceeding in good faith here, which is a bad sign.

"Even if they have agreed upon what Lavrov said they agreed upon, how are they going to get the people on the ground on either side to comply?"

* Is Annexation of Crimea Legal? * Contrast with Iraq War

March 19, 2014

Francis Boyle, fboyle at illinois.edu

Boyle is a professor at the University of Illinois College of Law. His books include *Foundations of World Order* (Duke University Press: 1999). He said today: "U.S. officials are condemning Russia for annexing Crimea after a referendum. I personally thought Russia should not annex Crimea, but it's ludicrous for U.S. officials to be attacking Russia's actions. Consider their record in backing bombings in Libya, assassination by drones in Yemen, Pakistan and elsewhere and, perhaps most notably, aggressive war in Iraq—which began 11 years ago this week."

Ukraine: Exploding the Myths, Outlining Solutions

March 3, 2014

Francis Boyle, fboyle at illinois.edu

Boyle is a professor at the University of Illinois College of Law. His books include *Foundations of World Order* (Duke University Press: 1999). He said today: "John Kerry is claiming to stand for international law and invokes the 1994 Budapest Agreement. Of course the U.S. has repeatedly violated international law, with the Iraq invasion (which Kerry voted for) and numerous other instances. But even in this case, if you examine the Victoria Nuland [assistant secretary of state] tape, it's clear that the U.S. was plotting a coup in the Ukraine and a coup is what happened. So Russia is only the second country guilty of violating Ukrainian sovereignty and the Budapest Agreement in response to the previous violations by the Obama administration."

[Audio on *YouTube* of Nuland with Geoffrey R. Pyatt, U.S. ambassador to Ukraine, determining which Ukrainian politicians should and should not be in government. At one point, Nuland talks about using UN Secretary General Ban Ki Moon for her purposes rather than the EU, saying "fuck the EU." *Transcript.*]

Ukraine Crisis: How Cooler Heads Can Prevail
February 27, 2014
Francis Boyle, fboyle at illinois.edu

Boyle is a professor at the University of Illinois College of Law. His books include *Foundations of World Order* (Duke University Press: 1999). He said today: "While talking about storming the parliament in Simferopol and Russian war maneuvers, [Christiane] Amanpour on CNN this morning invoked the Budapest Agreement saying that Russia must stay out, they have a legal obligation. This is noteworthy because the Budapest Agreement also states that the U.S., Russia, Ukraine, and UK need to immediately jointly 'consult'—meaning meet at least at the foreign minister level. [Text below; see *Financial Times* "Ukraine's new premier invokes treaty in bid to resist Russia."]"

"These mechanisms of international law are critical because the First World War started this way in 1914—exactly a century ago. The Serbian terrorist [Gavrilo] Princip assassinated Archduke Franz Ferdinand in Sarajevo, the heir to the throne of the Austrian-Hungarian Empire. The Austrian-Hungarian emperor got the backing of the German Kaiser for an ultimatum to Serbia over it. Serbia offered to submit the dispute to the Permanent Court of Arbitration at The Hague, which was rejected by Austria-Hungary. Serbia's ally the Russian Tsar mobilized the Russian army. Then the Kaiser gave the order to execute their Schleifen Plan, attacking both to their east and west. Ten million people died for nothing."

The Budapest Agreement (Signed in 1994 upon Ukraine getting rid of its nuclear weapons and entering the Nuclear Nonproliferation Treaty as a non-nuclear power):

. . .

1. The Russian Federation, the United Kingdom of Great Britain and Northern Ireland and the United States of America reaffirm their commitment

to Ukraine, in accordance with the principles of the Final Act of the Conference on Security and Cooperation in Europe, to refrain from economic coercion designed to subordinate to their own interest the exercise by Ukraine of the rights inherent in its sovereignty and thus to secure advantages of any kind;

2. The Russian Federation, the United Kingdom of Great Britain and Northern Ireland and the United States of America reaffirm their commitment to seek immediate United Nations Security Council action to provide assistance to Ukraine, as a non-nuclear-weapon State party to the Treaty on the Non-Proliferation of Nuclear Weapons, if Ukraine should become a victim of an act of aggression or an object of a threat of aggression in which nuclear weapons are used;
3. The Russian Federation, the United Kingdom of Great Britain and Northern Ireland and the United States of America reaffirm, in the case of Ukraine, their commitment not to use nuclear weapons against any non-nuclear weapon State party to the Treaty on the Non-Proliferation of Nuclear Weapons, except in the case of an attack on themselves, their territories or dependent territories, their armed forces, or their allies, by such a State in association or alliance with a nuclear-weapon State;
4. Ukraine, the Russian Federation, the United Kingdom of Great Britain and Northern Ireland and the United States of America will consult in the event a situation arises that raises a question concerning these commitments.

Partitioning Ukraine? Threats to Jews and Others; Does Brzezinski Want to Partition Russia?

February 25, 2014

BBC reports: "Ukraine's interim President Olexander Turchynov has warned of the dangers of separatism following the ousting of President Viktor Yanukovych. His comments came amid continuing opposition in Ukraine's Russian-speaking regions to the new administration in Kiev. The formation of a unity government has been delayed until Thursday."

Francis Boyle, fboyle at illinois.edu

Boyle is a professor at the University of Illinois College of Law and author of *Tackling America's Toughest Questions*. Boyle said today: "The Ukrainian Parliament terminated Russian as an alternative official language, thus illegally stripping about 30 percent of Ukraine's population of their basic human rights. And there is no effective government to speak of." Boyle argues that "under these circumstances international law would permit Russian-speaking sections of Ukraine to move toward secession if they so desire."

He also notes: "In Kiev there are public demands for murdering Russians, Jews, and Communists by neo-Nazi, fascist and rightist groupings. The situation is so dire that the Ukrainian Chabad Chief Rabbi Reuven Azman has recommended that Jews leave the city and perhaps the country." See in the *Jewish Press*: "Ukrainian Jews Urged to Leave Kiev."

Boyle also criticized Zbigniew Brzezinski (who has advised President Obama on foreign policy and appeared on Fareed Zakaria's CNN program on Sunday) as well as much of the U.S. foreign policy establishment as having "a long-term anti-Russian bias." Boyle noted that Brzezinski "started the Afghan Mujahidin war against the Soviet Union in Afghanistan and bragged about it. Brzezinski wants to do to the Russian Federation what was done to the Soviet Union—crack it up into pieces." Boyle graduated from the same Harvard PhD Program that produced Brzezinski before him.

Zbigniew Brzezinski wrote in "A Geostrategy for Eurasia" in the journal *Foreign Affairs* (1997): "Russia's first priority should be to modernize itself rather than to engage in a futile effort to regain its status as a global power. Given the country's size and diversity, a decentralized political system and free-market economics would be most likely to unleash the creative potential of the Russian people and Russia's vast natural resources. A loosely confederated Russia—composed of a European Russia, a Siberian Republic, and a Far Eastern Republic—would also find it easier to cultivate closer economic relations with its neighbors. Each of the confederated entities would be able to tap its local creative potential, stifled for centuries by Moscow's heavy bureaucratic hand. In turn, a decentralized Russia would be less susceptible to imperial mobilization."

VENEZUELA

Venezuela Intervention: Pretexts and Solutions

January 25, 2019

Francis Boyle, (217) 333-7954, fboyle@illinois.edu

Secretary of State Pompeo has announced he is going to New York for a UN Security Council meeting Saturday regarding Venezuela. Boyle is professor of international law at the University of Illinois College of Law. He said today: "The U.S. government refusing to withdraw its officials from Venezuela may well set up a pretext for further intervention or blockade." Boyle's books include *Foundations of World Order* (Duke University Press).

. . .

WAR POWERS

Does Trump Decide on War?

February 9, 2018

NBC News reports today: "Democratic Sen. Tim Kaine is demanding the release of a secret memo outlining President Trump's interpretation of his legal authority to wage war.

"Kaine, a member of the Armed Services and Foreign Relations Committees, sent a letter Thursday night to Secretary of State Rex Tillerson seeking a 7-page memo the administration has kept under wraps for months . . .

"There is a new urgency to obtain the memo given increasing U.S. involvement in Syria and recent Trump administration rhetoric on North Korea. Shortly after the 2017 bombing raid [on Syria], several members of Congress called on Trump to justify it under U.S. and international law. Article I of the U.S. Constitution gives Congress the power to declare war . . .

"'The fact that there is a lengthy memo with a more detailed legal justification that has not been shared with Congress, or the American public, is unacceptable,' Kaine said in the letter to Tillerson, obtained by NBC News."

The *Washington Post* reports in "U.S. troops may be at risk of 'mission creep' after a deadly battle in the Syrian desert": "The Syrian government accused the United States of 'aggression' in launching the strikes, which it said killed 'scores' of people. Russia denounced the U.S. presence in Syria as 'illegal' and accused the United States of seeking to seize Syria's oil."

Francis Boyle, fboyle at illinois.edu

Boyle is professor of international law at the University of Illinois College of Law. He said today: "There's no 'mission creep,' it's clear the U.S. government has been using ISIS as a pretext to illegally intervene in Syria. None of the stated rationales for U.S. military involvement—including the 2001 Authorization for the Use of Military Force or alleged 'self-defense' or buttressing the 2002 authorization regarding Iraq—are remotely legally valid. Syria has a sovereign government, the U.S. government should get out. The AUMFs should be rescinded.

"This memo that Kaine refers to was likely written by these Federalist Society lawyers that Trump has surrounded himself with, just like George W. Bush did."

On September 13, 2001, Boyle warned on an Institute for Public Accuracy news release that the 2001 AUMF would be like the "Tonkin Gulf Resolution, which the Johnson administration used to provide dubious legal cover for massive escalation of the Vietnam War."

Last year, after Chairman of the Joint Chiefs of Staff Gen. Joseph F. Dunford Jr. claimed that the authority to attack Syria stemmed from the 2001 AUMF, Boyle stated: "What the U.S. government is getting away with here is incredible. Gen. Dunford is citing the 2001 AUMF to go after Al Qaeda as justification to go after a secular government—Syria—that is actually fighting Al Qaeda, as well as ISIS." See "Need to 'Repeal the Perpetual Illegal Wars.'"

Boyle's books include *Foundations of World Order: The Legalist Approach to International Relations* (Duke University Press).

Need to "Repeal the Perpetual Illegal Wars"

June 21, 2017

Charlie Savage of the *New York Times* reports in "Senators Wrestle With Updating Law Authorizing War on Terrorist Groups" that: "Asked at a luncheon on Monday at the National Press Club in Washington what legal basis the United States had to attack Syrian government forces, the Chairman of the Joint Chiefs of Staff, Gen. Joseph F. Dunford Jr., claimed the authority stemmed from the 2001 law because the American military presence in Syria was predicated on fighting Al Qaeda and the Islamic State there.

"But on Tuesday, the ranking Democrat on the Senate committee, Senator Benjamin L. Cardin of Maryland, said, 'The most recent use of this, in regards to activities in Syria, certainly had nothing to do with the attack on our country on September the 11th.'"

The question at the National Press Club to Dunford was submitted by Sam Husseini of the Institute for Public Accuracy and was featured on an IPA news release on Monday: "Bombing Syria: * Impeachable * Carve-Up Agenda."

Boyle is professor of international law at the University of Illinois College of Law. He said today: "What the U.S. government is getting away with here is incredible. Gen. Dunford is citing the 2001 AUMF to go after Al Qaeda as justification to go after a secular government—Syria—that is actually fighting Al Qaeda, as well as ISIS.

"Congress should not be in the business of 'updating' any authorization of continuing these wars, which are clearly illegal under international law. Congress should be in the business of repealing these bogus domestic authorizations. No one in 1970 was working to 'update' the Gulf of Tonkin Resolution. At least no one who was not a laughing stock. Congress was working to repeal the Gulf of Tonkin resolution, to defund the war—not to perpetuate illegal war for another generation. Congress now needs to repeal the perpetual illegal wars. The War Powers Clause of the Constitution, as well as the War Powers Resolution are being flagrantly violated."

KEY AUTHOR OF WAR POWERS: ISIL AUMF COULD BE WORSE THAN VIETNAM AUTHORIZATION

February 12, 2015

Paul Findley, findley1 at frontier.com

Available for a limited number of interviews, Findley was a member of Congress from Illinois for 22 years and was a principal author of the War Powers Resolution of 1973. He resides in Jacksonville, Ill. The Federal building in Springfield, Ill. is named for him. He said today: "If I were still in Congress I would oppose any resolution that authorizes further involvement there. Our forces have been killing Muslims by the tens of thousands for the past decade in the misleading label of anti-terrorism. Bombing kills innocent people whose friends are furious over these killings.

"It has greater potential for trouble than the Tonkin Gulf Resolution in 1964 that I voted for, only after getting Republican Leader Gerald Ford's assurance that it was not the equivalent of a declaration of war [on Vietnam].

"Congress should have used its responsibility to call a halt long ago to war measures. Instead of such measures, I believe in enforcing world law through international institutions. The current war over religion in the Middle East could make the Vietnam War look like a Sunday School picnic." Findley was recently profiled in the *Jacksonville Journal-Courier*. His books include *They Dare to Speak Out.*

Francis Boyle, fboyle at illinois.edu

Boyle, who has worked with Findley for years, is a professor at the University of Illinois College of Law and author of *Tackling America's Toughest Questions*. He said today: "Of course Obama is wrong to state that existing statutes give him any authority he needs to wage war against ISIL.

"In the cover letter, Obama would use special forces, which is how the Vietnam War started. Once you have ground troops over there in combat, there is really no way to prevent escalation or to call it off and he knows it. What happens when one of our soldiers is captured and killed by ISIL? What kind of jingoism will that unleash and what escalations will that facilitate?

"He only talks about 'tailoring' the 2001 AUMF. It should be repealed, not 'tailored.'

"This Resolution sets a dangerous precedent. Up until the 2001 AUMF, all War Powers Resolutions had been adopted with respect to a State, not alleged terrorist organizations that can operate anywhere in the world as defined by the President. This Resolution continues in that dangerous path, basically substituting ISIS for al-Qaeda and continuing to wage a global war on terrorism. So if Obama cannot plausibly invoke the 2001 Resolution because there is no connection to 9/11 as required therein, he will simply invoke this Resolution. Between the two resolutions you can have the U.S. government waging war all over the world.

"The Resolution states: 'The authority granted in subsection (a) does not authorize the use of the USAF in enduring offensive ground combat operations.' In other words, it does indeed authorize the use of USAF in offensive ground combat operations. 'Enduring' is in the eye of the beholder. Three years from now could have another 100,000 troops back in Iraq and maybe Syria too.

"Congress cannot lawfully give him authorization to use military force against Syria. That requires the permission of the Syrian government, which they do not have, or else the authorization of the Security Council, which they do not have. As for Iraq, [Iraqi Prime Minister Haider] al-Abadi is a puppet government that Obama installed and therefore has no authority under international law to consent to U.S. military operations in Iraq. It is like in Vietnam when we had our puppets there asking us to conduct military operations there."

ISIS and UN; Peace Arrests at White House

September 24, 2014

Professor at the University of Illinois College of Law, Boyle is author of *Tackling America's Toughest Questions* and *Biowarfare and Terrorism.* He said today: "The Obama administration wants a Security Council Resolution today, not simply as ex post facto justification for the illegal and unconstitutional bombing it is already conducting in Syria and Iraq. The Pentagon has said this 'war' against terrorism will go on for years. So, this Resolution may well be the legal fig leaf for bombing countries all over the world under the pretext that he is trying to stop the movements of terrorist groups between them. Acting under U.N. Charter Chapter 7 enforcement powers, the draft Resolution can arguably be interpreted to create a bogus right of 'hot pursuit' against alleged transnational terrorists anywhere in the world . . . The President—as well as Congress—are in total violation of their responsibilities under the War Powers Clause of the United States Constitution and Congress's own War Powers Resolution of 1973."

Key Author of War Powers Resolution: "Attack on Iraq Would Violate Constitution"

July 7, 2014

The Nation writes: "Left-Right Coalition of 80 House Members Wants Congress to Check and Balance Iraq Intervention."

Paul Findley, findley2 at frontier.com

Available for a limited number of interviews, Findley served as a member of United States House of Representatives for 22 years. He was a key author of the War Powers Resolution and a leader in securing its enactment by overriding the veto of President Richard Nixon. He is also the author of six books. The Federal building in Springfield, Ill. is named for him. He said today: "Just as with threats to attack Syria last year, an attack on Iraq and/or Syria today would violate the Constitution and the War Powers Resolution. As with any president, he [President Obama] commits an impeachable offense if he does not follow the Constitution. Some observers misread a section of the War Powers Resolution as giving the president 60 days to make war without a declaration from Congress. The section cited actually sets limits over war making in the event of an attack upon the United States, its territories, or armed forces, which is not the case in either Iraq or Syria. In my view, a tight rein on presidential war making is more important today than ever before." Last year Findley wrote the piece "Obama has no Authority to Attack Syria."

Francis Boyle, fboyle at illinois.edu

Boyle, who has worked with Findley for many years, is a professor at the University of Illinois College of Law and author of *Tackling America's Toughest Questions*. He said today: "President Obama has now incrementally introduced about 800 U.S. troops armed for combat into Iraq in three stages, each without Congressional authorization, which clearly violates the terms of the War Powers Resolution. This is precisely what the War Powers Resolution was intended to prevent—another incremental military escalation along the lines of the Vietnam War. The Obama administration has also threatened to bomb Syria as well as Iraq, either one of which would violate the War Powers Clause of the Constitution as well as the War Powers Resolution. It is not legitimate for the president—or members of Congress—to make de facto arrangements that violate the Constitution and the War Powers Resolution."

Key Author of War Powers Resolution: "Attack on Iraq Would Violate Constitution"

June 19, 2014

Paul Findley, findley1 at frontier.com

Available for a limited number of interviews, Findley served as a member of United States House of Representatives for 22 years. He was a key author of the War Powers Resolution and a leader in securing its enactment by overriding the veto of President Richard Nixon. He is also the author of six books. The Federal building in Springfield, Ill. is named for him. He said today: "Just as with threats to attack Syria last year, an attack on Iraq would violate the Constitution and the War Powers Resolution. As with any president, he [President Obama] commits an impeachable offense if he does not follow the Constitution." Last year Findley wrote the piece "Obama has no Authority to Attack Syria."

Francis Boyle, fboyle at illinois.edu

Boyle, who has worked with Findley for years, is a professor at the University of Illinois College of Law and author of *Tackling America's Toughest Questions*. He said today: "This could escalate in any number of ways—exactly what the War Powers Resolution was supposed to stop. It's not legitimate for the president—or members of Congress—to make arrangements that violate the Constitution and the War Powers Resolution. Obama just stated that the 300 U.S. troops would be doing training, but CNN reports his spokesperson Jay Carney stated they would also 'provide airfield management security and logistic support.' Does this mean that they will become the required forward air controllers for the targeted and precise military action that Obama says he is preparing? If the U.S. is going to target ISIS, will it be limited to Iraq or will it eventually go into Syria?"

War Powers

July 8, 2008

Former Secretaries of State James Baker III and Warren Christopher have formed a commission on war powers and have published a piece in today's *New York Times*. They are advocating replacing the 1973 War Powers Resolution.

Francis Boyle

Professor of international law at the University of Illinois, Boyle said today: "The President is already required to 'consult' with Congress, which repeated Presidents have either refused to do, or else have done grudgingly. In fact they have done more consultation with foreign governments than they have with our own Congress when it comes to launching foreign wars of aggression around the world.

"The President and the Congress do not 'share' the war powers. Under Article 1, Section 8 of the U.S. Constitution, the war powers are textually vested in both Houses of the U.S. Congress, not the President. The President only has constitutional authority to repel a 'sudden attack' upon the United States and its armed forces.

"The War Powers Resolution was intended to redress the unconstitutional imbalance created by a series of imperial Presidents going back to Truman's unconstitutional Korean War and culminating in Johnson's unconstitutional Vietnam War, with 36,000 dead Americans and 58,000 dead Americans, respectively. In 2002 President George W. Bush lied to the American people and Congress to procure a fraudulent War Powers Resolution authorization to use military force against Iraq . . . There is nothing wrong with the War Powers Resolution except for imperial Presidents who believe they are above the Constitution and the laws of the United States."

Boyle's most recent book is *Protesting Power: War, Resistance and Law* (Rowman and Littlefield Inc.).

War Powers

January 9, 2007

UPI is reporting: "If Congressional Democrats want to block any proposed escalation in U.S. troop levels in Iraq, as new House Speaker Nancy Pelosi,

D-Calif., hinted at the weekend, they have the constitutional authority and the legal power to do so, according to some scholars."

The following legal analysts are available for media interviews:

Francis Boyle

Professor of international law at the University of Illinois, Boyle said today: "Concerning the proposed 'surge' by the Bush administration of 20,000-plus U.S. troops into Iraq, this requires further authorization by the U.S. Congress under the terms of the War Powers Resolution. Section 4(a)(3) makes it quite clear that the War Powers Resolution is triggered . . . 'In the absence of a declaration of war [which we do not have for Iraq], in any case in which United States Armed Forces are introduced . . . (3) in numbers which substantially enlarge United States Armed Forces equipped for combat already located in a foreign nation. . .'

"We currently have about 140,000 troops in Iraq. Sending in an additional 20,000-plus would 'substantially enlarge' those forces. Therefore, the Bush administration would require further authorization from Congress for this euphemistic 'surge,' which is really a substantial escalation. Failure to obtain additional authorization from Congress for this substantial enlargement of U.S. Armed Forces in Iraq would constitute an impeachable offense under the terms of the United States Constitution for violating the Constitution's War Powers Clause and Congress's own War Powers Resolution."

Impeachment in Perspective

September 17, 1998

WASHINGTON—As the nation considers the future of the Clinton presidency, some legal scholars and policy analysts are putting the Starr report in a broader context of governmental wrongdoing. Among those available for comment:

Francis Boyle

Professor of Law at the University of Illinois College of Law, Boyle said: "The impeachment clause is meant to deal with crimes against the state, subverting the Republic. Starr has not yet presented evidence of such a threat to the Republic. This is not to say that there is no reason to impeach Clinton. There are grounds for impeachment—for example, the illegal bombings of Sudan and Afghanistan, which violated both domestic and international law, including the U.S. Constitution." Boyle added: "Our system of government was in jeopardy in the Reagan Iran-Contra scandal." The White House had "basically set up an underground government. But no one really made an effort to impeach Reagan over that—though documents show that Reagan and his people were concerned about impeachment."

Analysts Available on U.S. Missile Attacks

August 21, 1998

Interviews are available with these specialists on international law and the Middle East:

Francis Boyle

A professor of International Law at the University of Illinois College of Law, Boyle said: "The U.S. attacks were clearly illegal. Particularly the attack on Sudan was without reason. The Sudanese government can probably sue the U.S. in the World Court over this."

YEMEN

Myths on * Yemen * Armenian Genocide

April 24, 2015

Francis Boyle, fboyle at illinois.edu

Boyle is a professor at the University of Illinois College of Law and author of *Tackling America's Toughest Questions*. He said today: "The U.S. blockade of Yemen is illegal. A naval blockade is an act of war and the administration has no authorization from the U.S. Congress or the Security Council for this."

Bibliography

Abunimah, Ali. *One Country: A Bold Proposal to End the Israeli-Palestinian Impasse*. New York, NY: Metropolitan Books, 2006.

Adler, David G., and Larry N. George, Editors. *The Constitution and the Conduct of American Foreign Policy*. With a foreword by Arthur Schlesinger, Jr. Lawrence, KS: University Press of Kansas, 1996.

Al-Ani, Abdul-Haq, and Tarik Al-Ani. *Genocide in Iraq: The Case Against the UN Security Council and Member States*. With a foreword by Joshua Castellino. Atlanta, GA: Clarity Press, 2012.

Allison, Graham. *Destined for War: Can America and China Escape Thucydides's Trap?* Boston, MA: Houghton Mifflin Harcourt, 2017.

Anderson, Tim. *Axis of Resistance: Towards an Independent Middle East*. Atlanta, GA: Clarity Press, 2019.

Anghie, Antony. *Imperialism, Sovereignty and the Making of International Law*. Cambridge: Cambridge University Press, 2005.

Anonymous. *A Warning*. London: Little, Brown, 2019.

Archer, Jules. *The Plot to Seize the White House*. New York, NY: Skyhorse, 2007. First Published 1973 by Hawthorn Books (New York, NY).

Arend, Anthony C., and Robert J. Beck. *International Law and the Use of Force*. London: Routledge, 1993.

Aruri, Naseer H. *Dishonest Broker: The U.S. Role in Israel and Palestine*. Cambridge, MA: South End Press, 2003.

Avery, Michael, and Danielle McLaughlin. *The Federalist Society: How Conservatives Took the Law Back from Liberals*. Nashville, TN: Vanderbilt University Press, 2013.

Bader, Jeffrey A. *Obama and China's Rise: An Insider's Account of America's Asia Strategy*. Washington, DC: Brookings Institution Press, 2012.

Balakrishnan, Gopal. *The Enemy: An Intellectual Portrait of Carl Schmitt*. London: Verso, 2000.

Barry, John M. *The Great Influenza: The Epic Story of the Deadliest Plague in History*. New York, NY: Penguin, 2018. First Published 2004 by Viking (New York, NY).

Beard, Charles A. *An Economic Interpretation of the Constitution of the United States*. New York, NY: Free Press, 1913.

———. *President Roosevelt and the Coming of the War, 1941: A Study in Appearances and Realities*. New Haven, CT: Yale University Press, 1948.

Benjamin, Medea. *Inside Iran: The Real History and Politics of the Islamic Republic of Iran*. New York, NY: OR Books, 2018.

Benner, Erica. *Be Like the Fox: Machiavelli's Lifelong Quest for Freedom*. New York, NY: Penguin, 2017.

Bernays, Edward. *Propaganda*. With an Introduction by Mark C. Miller. Brooklyn, NY: Ig Publishing, 2005. First published 1928 by H. Liveright (New York, NY).

Bernstein, Dennis J. *Follow the Money: Radio Voices for Peace and Justice, Pacifica Radio Network KPFA's Flashpoints Interviews 2009–2016. With a Foreword by Mumia Abu-Jamal*. Edited by Riva Enteen. South Lake Tahoe, CA: Left Coast Press, 2018.

Black, Charles L. *Impeachment: A Handbook*. With a Foreword by Akhil R. Amar. New Haven, CT: Yale University Press, 1974.

Blum, William. *America's Deadliest Export Democracy: The Truth about US Foreign Policy and Everything Else*. New York, NY: Zed Books, 2013.

———. *Killing Hope: US Military and CIA Interventions Since World War II*. Monroe, ME: Common Courage, 1995.

Boal, Iain, T. J. A. Clark, Joseph Matthews, and Michael Watts. *Afflicted Powers: Capital and Spectacle in a New Age of War*. London: Verso, 2005.

Bonifaz, John C. *Warrior-King: George W. Bush and the Looming Irrelevancy of Our Courts, Congress, and Constitution*. With a Foreword by John Conyers, Jr. New York, NY: Nation Books, 2003.

Boucheron, Patrick. *Machiavelli: The Art of Teaching People What to Fear*. Translated by Willard Wood. New York, NY: Other Press, 2020. First published 2017 by Édition des Équaters (Paris).

Boyle, Francis A. *Biowarfare and Terrorism. With a Foreword by Jonathan King*. Atlanta, GA: Clarity Press, 2005.

———. *The Bosnian People Charge Genocide: Proceedings at the International Court of Justice Concerning Bosnia v. Serbia on the Prevention and Punishment of the Crime of Genocide. With an Introduction by Marshall Harris, a Preface by Chandra Muzaffar and a Foreword by Frank McCloskey*. Amherst, MA: Aletheia, 1996.

———. *Breaking All the Rules: Palestine, Iraq, Iran, and the Case for Impeachment*. Atlanta, GA: Clarity Press, 2008.

———. *The Criminality of Nuclear Deterrence. With a Foreword by Philip Berrigan*. Atlanta, GA: Clarity Press, 2002.

———. *Defending Civil Resistance Under International Law*. Greenburgh, NY: Transnational, 1987.

———. *Defending Civil Resistance Under International Law*. Salem, OR: Center for Energy Research, 1988. First Published 1987 by Transnational (Greenburgh, NY). Microfiche.

———. *Destroying Libya and World Order: The Three-Decade US Campaign to Terminate the Qaddafi Revolution*. Atlanta, GA: Clarity Press, 2013.

———. *Destroying World Order: U.S. Imperialism in the Middle East Before and After September 11*. Atlanta, GA: Clarity Press, 2004.

———. *Foundations of World Order: The Legalist Approach to International Relations (1898–1922)*. Durham, NC: Duke University Press, 1999.

———. *Free Puerto Rico!: Puerto Rico and the Puerto Ricans Under International Law*. Edited by Ramón Nenadich. Cayey, PR: Editorial Borikén, 2016.

———. *The Future of International Law and American Foreign Policy*. Greenburgh, NY: Transnational, 1989.

———. *Palestine, Palestinians, and International Law*. Atlanta, GA: Clarity Press, 2003.

———. *Protesting Power: War, Resistance, and Law*. Lanham, MD: Rowman and Littlefield, 2008.

———. *Restoring the Kingdom of Hawaii: The Kanaka Maoli Route to Independence*. Atlanta, GA: Clarity Press, 2015.

———. *The Palestinian Right of Return Under International Law*. Atlanta, GA: Clarity Press, 2011.

———. *Tackling America's Toughest Questions: Alternative Media Interviews*. Atlanta, GA: Clarity Press, 2009.

———. *The Tamil Genocide by Sri Lanka: The Global Failure to Protect Tamil Rights Under International Law*. Atlanta, GA: Clarity Press, 2010.

———. *The Tamil Genocide by Sri Lanka: The Global Failure to Protect Tamil Rights Under International Law*, 2nd edition. Atlanta, GA: Clarity Press, 2016.

———. *United Ireland, Human Rights and International Law*. Atlanta, GA: Clarity Press, 2012.

———. *World Politics and International Law*. Durham, NC: Duke University Press, 1985.

Bracken, Paul. *The Second Nuclear Age: Strategy, Danger, and the New Power Politics*. New York, NY: Times Books, 2012.

Brisard, Jean-Charles, and Guillaume Dasquié. *Forbidden Truth: U.S.-Taliban Secret Oil Diplomacy and the Failed Hunt for Bin Laden*. Translated by Lucy Rounds, with Peter Fifield and Nicholas Greenslade. With Introductions by Joseph Trento and Wayne Madsen. New York, NY: Nation Books, 2002.

Brownlie, Ian. *Principles of Public International Law*, 7th edition. New York, NY: Oxford University Press, 2008.

Brzezinski, Zbigniew. *The Grand Chessboard: American Primacy and Its Geostrategic Imperatives*. New York, NY: Basic Books, 1997.

Buchanan, Patrick J. *Churchill, Hitler, and "The Unnecessary War": How Britain Lost Its Empire and the West Lost the World*. New York, NY: Crown, 2008.

———. *Suicide of a Superpower: Will America Survive to 2025?* London: Thomas Dunne Books, 2011.

Bugliosi, Vincent. *The Betrayal of America: How the Supreme Court Undermined the Constitution and Chose Our President*. With a Foreword by Molly Ivins and Gerry Spence. New York, NY: Nation Books, 2001.

Bugliosi, Vincent. *The Prosecution of George W. Bush for Murder*. Cambridge, MA: Vanguard, 2008.

Burgo, Joseph. *The Narcissist You Know: Defending Yourself Against Extreme Narcissists in an All-About-Me Age*. New York, NY: Touchstone, 2015.

Burroughs, John, Jacqueline Cabasso, Felicity Hill, Andrew Lichterman, Jennifer Nordstrom, Michael Spies, and Peter Weiss. *Nuclear Disorder Or Cooperative Security?: U.S. Weapons of Terror, the Global Proliferation Crisis, and Paths to Peace: An Assessment of the Final Report of the Weapons of Mass Destruction Commission and Its Implications for U.S. Policy*. Edited by Michael Spies and John Burroughs. With a Foreword by Zia Mian. New York, NY: Lawyers' Committee on Nuclear Policy, 2007.

Campbell, David. *National Deconstruction: Violence, Identity, and Justice in Bosnia*. Minneapolis, MN: University of Minnesota Press, 1998.

Carter, Jimmy. *Palestine: Peace Not Apartheid*. New York, NY: Simon and Schuster, 2006.

Center for Constitutional Rights. *Articles of Impeachment Against George W. Bush*, 2nd edition. Hoboken, NJ: Melville House, 2006.

Chabris, Christopher, and Daniel Simons. *The Invisible Gorilla: And Other Ways Our Intuitions Deceive Us*. New York, NY: Crown, 2010.

Chomsky, Noam. *Failed States: The Abuse of Power and the Assault on Democracy*. New York, NY: Metropolitan Books, 2006.

———. *Global Discontents: Conversations on the Rising Threats to Democracy. Interviews with David Barsamian.* New York, NY: Metropolitan Books, 2017.

———. *Hegemony or Survival: America's Quest for Global Dominance*. New York, NY: Metropolitan Books, 2003.

———. *Hopes and Prospects*. Chicago, IL: Haymarket Books, 2010.

———. *Imperial Ambitions: Conversations on the Post-9/11 World. Interviews with David Barsamian.* New York, NY: Metropolitan Books, 2005.

———. *Interventions*. San Francisco, CA: City Lights Books, 2007.

———. *Making the Future: Occupations, Interventions, Empire and Resistance*. San Francisco, CA: City Lights Books, 2012.

———. *Occupy*. Brooklyn, NY: Zuccotti Park Press, 2012.

———. *Power Systems: Conversations on Global Democratic Uprisings and the New Challenges to U.S. Empire*. Interviews with David Barsamian. New York, NY: Metropolitan Books, 2013.

———. *Requiem for the American Dream: The 10 Principles of Concentration of Wealth and Power*. Edited by Peter Hutchison, Kelly Hyks, and Jared P. Scott. New York, NY: Seven Stories, 2017.

———. *What We Say Goes: Conversations on U.S. Power in a Changing World*. Interviews with David Barsamian. New York, NY: Metropolitan Books, 2007.

———. *Who Rules the World?* New York, NY: Metropolitan Books, 2016.

Chomsky, Noam, and C. J. Polychroniou. *Optimism over Despair: On Capitalism, Empire, and Social Change*. Chicago, IL: Haymarket Books, 2017.

Chossudovsky, Michel. *America's "War on Terrorism,"* 2nd edition. Pincourt, QC: Global Research, 2005.

———. *The Globalization of War: America's "Long War" Against Humanity*. Montréal: Global Research, 2015.

Clarke, Richard A. *Against All Enemies: Inside America's War on Terror*. New York, NY: Free Press, 2004.

Coates, Benjamin A. *Legalist Empire: International Law and American Foreign Relations in the Early Twentieth Century*. New York, NY: Oxford University Press, 2016.

Cockburn, Alexander, and Jeffrey S. Clair, Editors. *Dime's Worth of Difference: Beyond the Lesser of Two Evils*. Petrolia, CA: CounterPunch, 2004.

———. *The Politics of Anti-Semitism*. Petrolia, CA: CounterPunch, 2003.

Cockburn, Alexander, and Jeffrey S. Clair. *Imperial Crusades: Iraq, Afghanistan and Yugoslavia: A Diary of Three Wars*. London: Verso, 2004.

Cockburn, Patrick. *The Occupation: War and Resistance in Iraq*. London: Verso, 2006.

———. *War in the Age of Trump: The Defeat of ISIS, the Fall of the Kurds, the Conflict with Iran*. London: Verso, 2020.

Cohen, Stephen F. *War with Russia? From Putin and Ukraine to Trump and Russiagate*. New York, NY: Hot Books, 2019.

Cohn, Marjorie. *Cowboy Republic: Six Ways the Bush Gang Has Defied the Law*. Sausalito, CA: PolipointPress, 2007.

Cole, David. *Enemy Aliens: Double Standards and Constitutional Freedoms in the War on Terrorism*. New York, NY: New Press, 2003.

Cole, David, and James X. Dempsey. *Terrorism and the Constitution: Sacrificing Civil Liberties in the Name of National Security*. With a Foreword by Nancy Talanian and Kit Gage. New York, NY: New Press, 2006. First published 1999 by First Amendment Foundation (St. Petersburg, FL).

Coll, Steve. *Ghost Wars: The Secret History of the CIA, Afghanistan and Bin Laden, from the Soviet Invasion to September 10, 2001*. London: Penguin, 2005.

Cox, Harvey. *The Market as God*. Cambridge, MA: Harvard University Press, 2016.

Crabb, Cecil V., and Pat M. Holt. *Invitation to Struggle: Congress, the President, and Foreign Policy*, 2nd edition. Washington, DC: CQ Press, 1984.

Dahl, Robert A. *How Democratic is the American Constitution?*, 2nd edition. New Haven, CT: Yale University Press, 2003.

Damrosch, Lori F., Louis Henkin, Sean D. Murphy, and Hans Smit. *International Law: Cases and Materials*, 5th edition. St. Paul, MN: West Academic, 2009.

Dean, John W. *Worse Than Watergate: The Secret Presidency of George W. Bush*. New York, NY: Little, Brown, 2004.

Dennett, Charlotte. *The People V. Bush: One Lawyer's Campaign to Bring the President to Justice and the National Grassroots Movement She Encounters along the Way*. Hartford, VT: Chelsea Green Publishing, 2010.

Dower, John W. *The Violent American Century: War and Terror Since World War II*. Chicago, IL: Haymarket Books, 2017.

Dunbar, David, and Brad Reagan, Editors. *Debunking 9/11 Myths: Why Conspiracy Theories Can't Stand Up to the Facts*. Edited by David Dunbar and Brad Reagan. With a Foreword by John McCain. New York, NY: Hearst Books, 2006.

Ebenstein, William, and Alan Ebenstein. *Great Political Thinkers: Plato to the Present*, 6th edition. Belmont, CA: Wadsworth Group, 2000.

Elden, Stuart. *Foucault: The Birth of Power*. Cambridge, UK: Polity, 2017.

Ellsberg, Daniel. *The Doomsday Machine: Confessions of a Nuclear War Planner*. New York, NY: Bloomsbury, 2017.

Ellwood, Wayne. *The No-Nonsense Guide to Globalization*. Oxford: New Internationalist, 2001.

Engdahl, F. W. *Full Spectrum Dominance: Totalitarian Democracy in the New World Order*. London: Third Millennium Press, 2009.

———. *Manifest Destiny: Democracy as Cognitive Dissonance*. Wiesbaden, DE: mine.Books, 2018.

Engelhardt, Tom. *The End of Victory Culture: Cold War America and the Disillusioning of a Generation*. New York, NY: BasicBooks, 1995.

Farer, Tom. *Confronting Global Terrorism and American Neo-Conservatism: The Framework of a Liberal Grand Strategy*. New York, NY: Oxford University Press, 2008.

Fein, Bruce. *American Empire Before the Fall. With a Foreword by Walter Jones*. Edited by Daniel McCarthy. Scotts Valley, CA: CreateSpace, 2010.

———. *Constitutional Peril: The Life and Death Struggle for Our Constitution and Democracy*. New York, NY: Palgrave Macmillan, 2008.

Fields, A. B. *Rethinking Human Rights for the New Millennium*. New York, NY: Palgrave Macmillan, 2003.

Finkelstein, Norman G. *Beyond Chutzpah: On the Misuse of Anti-Semitism and the Abuse of History*. Oakland, CA: University of California Press, 2005.

Fisher, Louis. *The Constitution and 9/11: Recurring Threats to America's Freedoms*. Lawrence, KS: University Press of Kansas, 2008.

———. *Constitutional Conflicts Between Congress and the President*, 4th edition. Lawrence, KS: University Press of Kansas, 1997. First published 1978 by St. Martin's Press (New York, NY).

Fisher, Roger. *Improving Compliance with International Law*. Charlottesville, VA: University of Virginia Press, 1981.

Fisher, Roger, Elizabeth Kopelman, and Andrea K. Schneider. *Beyond Machiavelli: Tools for Coping with Conflict*. Cambridge, MA: Harvard University Press, 1994.

Fisk, Robert. *The Great War for Civilisation: The Conquest of the Middle East*. New York, NY: Alfred A. Knopf, 2005.

Forsythe, David P. *The Politics of International Law: U.S. Foreign Policy Reconsidered*. With an Afterword by Francis A. Boyle. Boulder, CO: Lynne Rienner, 1990.

Frank, Justin A. *Bush on the Couch: Inside the Mind of the President*, Rev. edition. New York, NY: HarperCollins, 2007. First published 2004 by ReganBooks (New York, NY).

Funk, Kevin, and Steven Fake. *Scramble for Africa: Darfur-Intervention and the USA*. Montréal: Black Rose Books, 2009.

Gellman, Barton. *Angler: The Cheney Vice Presidency*. New York, NY: Penguin, 2008.

Glennon, Michael J. *National Security and Double Government*. New York, NY: Oxford University Press, 2015.

Goldsmith, Jack. *The Terror Presidency: Law and Judgment Inside the Bush Administration*. New York, NY: W. W. Norton, 2007.

Gordon, Rebecca. *American Nuremberg: The U.S. Officials Who Should Stand Trial for Post-9/11 War Crimes*. New York, NY: Hot Books, 2016.

Greenberg, Karen J. *Rogue Justice: The Making of the Security State*. New York, NY: Crown, 2016.

Greenburg, Jan C. *Supreme Conflict: The Inside Story of the Struggle for Control of the United States Supreme Court*. New York, NY: Penguin, 2007.

Griffin, David R. *The 9/11 Commission Report: Omissions and Distortions*. Northampton, MA: Olive Branch, 2005.

———. *The New Pearl Harbor Revisited: 9/11, the Cover-up, and the Exposé*. With a Foreword by Richard Falk. Northampton, MA: Olive Branch, 2004.

Guzman, Andrew T. *How International Law Works: A Rational Choice Theory*. New York, NY: Oxford University Press, 2008.

Haas, Michael. *George W. Bush, War Criminal? The Bush Administration's Liability for 269 War Crimes*. With a Foreword by Benjamin B. Ferencz. Westport, CT: Praeger, 2009.

Helderman, Rosalind S., and Matt Zapotosky. *The Mueller Report Presented with Related Materials by The Washington Post*. New York, NY: Scribner, 2019.

Henkin, Louis. *Foreign Affairs and the United States Constitution*, 2nd edition. New York, NY: Oxford University Press, 1996.

Henkin, Louis, Sarah H. Cleveland, Laurence R. Helfer, Gerald L. Neuman, and Diane F. Orentlicher. *Human Rights*, 2nd edition. New York, NY: Foundation Press, 2009.

Henkin, Louis, Stanley Hoffmann, Jeane J. Kirkpatrick, Allan Gerson, William D. Rogers, and David J. Scheffer. *Right V. Might: International Law and the Use of Force*. With a Foreword by John T. Swing. New York, NY: Council on Foreign Relations, 1989.

Herman, Edward S., and David Peterson. *The Politics of Genocide*. With a Foreword by Noam Chomsky. New York, NY: Monthly Review Press, 2010.

Herring, George C. *From Colony to Superpower: U.S. Foreign Relations since 1776*. New York, NY: Oxford University Press, 2008.

Hersh, Seymour M. *Chain of Command: The Road from 9/11 to Abu Ghraib*. New York, NY: HarperCollins, 2004.

Hiro, Dilip. *After Empire: The Birth of a Multipolar World*. New York, NY: Nation Books, 2010.

———. *Iraq: In the Eye of the Storm*. New York, NY: Nation Books, 2002.

Hirst, David. *The Gun and the Olive Branch: The Roots of Violence in the Middle East*. New York, NY: Nation Books, 2003. First published 1977 by Faber and Faber (England).

Hoffmann, Stanley, and Frédéric Bozo. *Gulliver Unbound: America's Imperial Temptation and the War in Iraq*. Lanham, MD: Rowman and Littlefield, 2004. First published 2003 by Editions Louis Audibert (Roubaix, FR).

Holbrooke, Richard C. *To End a War*. New York, NY: Random House, 1998.

Holtzman, Elizabeth, and Cynthia L. Cooper. *Cheating Justice: How Bush and Cheney Attacked the Rule of Law and Plotted to Avoid Prosecution – And What We Can Do about It*. Boston, MA: Beacon Press, 2012.

———. *The Impeachment of George W. Bush: A Practical Guide for Concerned Citizens*. New York, NY: Nation Books, 2006.

Honig, Jan W., and Norbert Both. *Srebrenica: Record of a War Crime*. New York, NY: Penguin, 1997. First published 1996 by Penguin (London).

Horwitz, Morton J. *The Warren Court and the Pursuit of Justice*. New York, NY: Hill and Wang, 1998.

Hulse, Carl. *Confirmation Bias: Inside Washington's War Over the Supreme Court, from Scalia's Death to Justice Kavanaugh*. New York, NY: HarperCollins, 2020.

Ikenberry, G. J. *Liberal Leviathan: The Origins, Crisis, and Transformation of the American World Order*. Princeton, NJ: Princeton University Press, 2011.

Immerwahr, Daniel. *How to Hide an Empire: A History of the Greater United States*. New York, NY: Farrar, Straus and Giroux, 2019.

Johnson, Rebecca, and Angie Zelter, Editors. *Trident and International Law: Scotland's Obligations*. Edinburgh: Luath, 2011.

Johnson, Chalmers. *Blowback: The Costs and Consequences of American Empire*. New York, NY: Metropolitan Books, 2000.

———. *Dismantling the Empire: America's Last Best Hope*. New York, NY: Metropolitan Books, 2010.

———. *Nemesis: The Last Days of the American Republic*. New York, NY: Metropolitan Books, 2006.

———. *The Sorrows of Empire: Militarism, Secrecy, and the End of the Republic*. New York, NY: Metropolitan Books, 2004.

Johnstone, Diana. *Queen of Chaos: The Misadventures of Hillary Clinton*. Petrolia, CA: CounterPunch, 2015.

Johnstone, Paul H. *From MAD to Madness: Inside Pentagon Nuclear War Planning*. With Commentary by Diana Johnstone. Atlanta, GA: Clarity Press, 2017.

Kaplan, David A. *The Most Dangerous Branch: Inside the Supreme Court's Assault on the Constitution*. New York, NY: Crown, 2018.

Kaplan, Fred. *The Bomb: Presidents, Generals, and the Secret History of Nuclear War*. New York, NY: Simon and Schuster, 2020.

Kattan, Victor, Editor. *The Palestine Question in International Law*. With a Foreword by John Dugard. Surrey, UK: British Institute of International and Comparative Law, 2008.

Keenan, Jeremy. *The Dark Sahara: America's War on Terror in Africa*. New York, NY: Pluto, 2009.

Khalidi, Rashid. *Resurrecting Empire: Western Footprints and America's Perilous Path in the Middle East*. Boston, MA: Beacon Press, 2004.

———. *The Iron Cage: The Story of the Palestinian Struggle for Statehood*. Boston, MA: Beacon Press, 2006.

Klein, Naomi. *The Shock Doctrine: The Rise of Disaster Capitalism*. New York, NY: Picador, 2007.

Kolko, Gabriel. *The Age of War: The United States Confronts the World*. Boulder, CO: Lynne Rienner, 2006.

Kovalik, Dan. *The Plot to Attack Iran: How the CIA and the Deep State Have Conspired to Vilify Iran*. New York, NY: Skyhorse, 2018.

Kovel, Joel. *Overcoming Zionism: Creating a Single Democratic State in Israel/Palestine*. London: Pluto, 2007.

Laderman, Charlie, and Brendan Simms. *Donald Trump: The Making of a World View*, Rev. edition. London: I. B. Tauris, 2017. First published 2017 by Endeavour Press (London).

Laffin, Arthur J., and Anne Montgomery, Editors. *Swords into Plowshares, Vol. 1: Nonviolent Direct Action for Disarmament, Peace, Social Justice, Rev. edition*. Marion, SD: Rose Hill Books, 1996.

Laffin, Arthur J., Editor. *Swords into Plowshares, Vol. 2: A Chronology of Plowshares Disarmament Actions, 1980–2003. With a Foreword by Daniel Berrigan, S.J.* Marion, SD: Rose Hill Books, 2010.

Lammers, Nancy, Editor. *Powers of Congress*, 2nd edition. Washington, DC: Congressional Quarterly, 1982.

Lauria, Joe. How I Lost by Hillary Clinton. With a Foreword by Julian Assange. Introduced and Annotated by Joe Lauria. New York, NY: OR Books, 2017.

LeBlanc, Lawrence J. *The United States and the Genocide Convention*. Durham, NC: Duke University Press, 1991.

Leverett, Flynt, and Hillary M. Leverett. *Going to Tehran: Why the United States Must Come to Terms with the Islamic Republic of Iran*. New York: Metropolitan Books, 2013.

Lindorff, Dave, and Barbara Olshansky. *The Case for Impeachment: The Legal Argument for Removing President George W. Bush from Office*. London: Thomas Dunne Books, 2006.

Liu, Mingfu. *The China Dream: Great Power Thinking and Strategic Posture in the Post-American Era*. With a Foreword by Liu Yazhou. New York, NY: CN Times Books, 2015.

Lofgren, Mike. *The Deep State: The Fall of the Constitution and the Rise of a Shadow Government*. New York, NY: Viking, 2016.

Loo, Dennis, and Peter Phillips, Editors. *Impeach the President: The Case Against Bush and Cheney*. New York, NY: Seven Stories, 2006.

Madsen, Wayne. *The Manufacturing of a President: the CIA's Insertion of Barack H. Obama, Jr. into the White House*. Scotts Valley, CA: CreateSpace, 2012.

Mandel, Michael. *How America Gets Away With Murder: Illegal Wars, Collateral Damage and Crimes Against Humanity*. London: Pluto Press, 2004.

Martyanov, Andrei. *Losing Military Supremacy: The Myopia of American Strategic Planning*. Atlanta, GA: Clarity Press, 2018.

Massad, Joseph A. *The Persistence of the Palestinian Question: Essays on Zionism and the Palestinians*. London: Routledge, 2006.

Mayer, Arno J. *Plowshares into Swords: From Zionism to Israel*. London: Verso, 2008.

Mayer, Jane. *The Dark Side: The Inside Story of how the War on Terror Turned into a War on American Ideals*. New York, NY: Doubleday, 2008.

Mazower, Mark. *Governing the World: The History of an Idea, 1815 to the Present.* New York, NY: Penguin, 2012.

McCormack, Gavan. *Target North Korea: Pushing North Korea to the Brink of Nuclear Catastrophe.* New York, NY: Nation Books, 2004.

Mearsheimer, John J., and Stephen M. Walt. *The Israel Lobby and U.S. Foreign Policy.* New York, NY: Farrar, Straus and Giroux, 2007.

Mikovits, Judy, and Kent Heckenlively. *Plague of Corruption: Restoring Faith in the Promise of Science.* With a Foreword by Robert F. Kennedy, Jr. New York, NY: Skyhorse, 2020.

Müllerson, Rein. *Dawn of a New Order: Geopolitics and the Clash of Ideologies.* London: I.B. Tauris, 2017.

National Commission on Terrorist Attacks. *The 9/11 Commission Report: Final Report of the National Commission on Terrorist Attacks Upon the United States.* New York, NY: W. W. Norton, 2004.

Nazemroaya, Mahdi D. *The Globalization of NATO.* With a Foreword by Denis J. Halliday. Atlanta, GA: Clarity Press, 2012.

Nepstad, Sharon E. *Religion and War Resistance in the Plowshares Movement.* Cambridge: Cambridge University Press, 2008.

Neustadt, Richard E., and Ernest R. May. *Thinking in Time: The Uses of History for Decision Makers.* New York, NY: Free Press, 1986.

Nichols, John. *The Genius of Impeachment: The Founders' Cure for Royalism.* New York, NY: New Press, 2006.

Niebuhr, Reinhold. *Reinhold Niebuhr: Major Works on Religion and Politics.* Edited by Elisabeth Sifton. New York, NY: Library of America, 2015.

Ohlin, Jens D. *The Assault on International Law.* New York, NY: Oxford University Press, 2015.

O'Keefe, Thomas A. *Bush II, Obama, and the Decline of U.S. Hegemony in the Western Hemisphere.* New York, NY: Routledge, 2018.

Ostrovsky, Victor, and Claire Hoy. *By Way of Deception: The Making and Unmaking of a Mossad Officer.* New York, NY: St. Martin's Press, 1990.

Parenti, Michael. *The Culture Struggle.* New York, NY: Seven Stories, 2006.

———. *Face of Imperialism.* Boulder, CO: Paradigm Publishers, 2011.

———. *Superpatriotism.* San Francisco, CA: City Lights Books, 2004.

Parsi, Trita. *A Single Roll of the Dice: Obama's Diplomacy with Iran.* New Haven, CT: Yale University Press, 2012.

———. *Treacherous Alliance: The Secret Dealings of Israel, Iran, and the United States.* New Haven, CT: Yale University Press, 2007.

Paul, Ron. *Swords into Plowshares: A Life in Wartime and a Future of Peace and Prosperity.* Clute, TX: Ron Paul Institute, 2015.

Paust, Jordan J. *Beyond the Law: The Bush Administration's Unlawful Responses in the "War" on Terror.* Cambridge: Cambridge University Press, 2007.

———. *International Law as Law of the United States*, 2nd edition. Durham, NC: Carolina Academic Press, 2003.

Perkins, John. *Confessions of an Economic Hit Man.* San Francisco, CA: Berrett-Koehler, 2004.

Perloff, James. *COVID-19 and the Agendas to Come Red-Pilled*. Burlington, MA: Refuge Books, 2020.

Petras, James. *The Arab Revolt and the Imperialist Counterattack*. Atlanta, GA: Clarity Press, 2011.

———. *The End of the Republic and the Delusion of Empire*. Atlanta, GA: Clarity Press, 2016.

———. *Rulers and Ruled in the US Empire: Bankers, Zionists, Militants*. Atlanta, GA: Clarity Press, 2007.

———. *Zionism, Militarism and the Decline of US Power*. Atlanta, GA: Clarity Press, 2008.

Phillips, Peter. *Giants: The Global Power Elite*. New York, NY: Seven Stories, 2018.

Pilger, John. *The New Rulers of the World*. London: Verso, 2003.

Polk, William R. *Crusade and Jihad: The Thousand-Year War Between the Muslim World and the Global North*. New Haven, CT: Yale University Press, 2018.

Posner, Gerald. *Pharma: Greed, Lies, and the Poisoning of America*. New York, NY: Avid Reader Press, 2020.

Prideaux, Sue. *I Am Dynamite!: A Life of Nietzsche*. New York, NY: Tim Duggan Books, 2018.

Quigley, Carroll. *The Anglo-American Establishment*. San Pedro, CA: GSG and Associates, 1981.

Quigley, John. *The Case for Palestine: An International Law Perspective*, Rev. edition. Durham, NC: Duke University Press, 2005.

———. *The Statehood of Palestine: International Law in the Middle East Conflict*. Cambridge: Cambridge University Press, 2010.

Rashid, Ahmed. *Descent Into Chaos: The US and the Failure of Nation Building in Pakistan, Afghanistan, and Central Asia*. London: Penguin, 2009.

———. *Taliban: Militant Islam, Oil, and Fundamentalism in Central Asia*. New Haven, CT: Yale University Press, 2001.

Reinhart, Tanya. *Israel/Palestine: How to End the War of 1948*. New York, NY: Seven Stories, 2002.

———. *The Road Map to Nowhere: Israel/Palestine Since 2003*. London: Verso, 2006.

Richardson, Louise. *What Terrorists Want: Understanding the Enemy, Containing the Threat*. New York, NY: Random House, 2007.

Riemen, Rob. *To Fight Against This Age: On Fascism and Humanism*. New York, NY: W. W. Norton, 2018.

Risen, James. *Pay Any Price: Greed, Power, and Endless War*. Boston, MA: Houghton Mifflin Harcourt, 2014.

Ritter, Scott. *Scorpion King: Americas Suicidal Embrace of Nuclear Weapons from FDR to Trump*. With a Foreword by William R. Polk. Atlanta, GA: Clarity Press, 2020.

Rohde, David. *Endgame: The Betrayal and Fall of Srebrenica, Europe's Worst Massacre Since World War II*. Boulder, CO: Westview Press, 1998.

Roy, Olivier. *The Politics of Chaos in the Middle East*. Translated by Ros Schwartz. New York, NY: Columbia University Press, 2008.

Rubenberg, Cheryl A. *The Palestinians: In Search of a Just Peace*. Boulder, CO: Lynne Rienner, 2003.

Rucker, Philip, and Carol Leonnig. *A Very Stable Genius: Donald J. Trump's Testing of America*. New York, NY: Penguin, 2020.

Ruppert, Michael C. *Crossing the Rubicon: The Decline of the American Empire at the End of the Age of Oil*. With a Foreword by Catherine A. Fitts. Gabriola Island, BC, Canada: New Society Publishers, 2004.

Salaita, Steven. *Israel's Dead Soul*. Philadelphia, PA: Temple University Press, 2011.

Sand, Shlomo. *The Invention of the Jewish People*. Translated by Yael Lotan. London: Verso, 2009.

Sandel, Michael J. *Justice: What's the Right Thing to Do?*. New York, NY: Farrar, Straus and Giroux, 2009.

Savage, Charlie. *Power Wars: The Relentless Rise of Presidential Authority and Secrecy*. New York, NY: Little, Brown, 2015.

———. *Takeover: The Return of the Imperial Presidency and the Subversion of American Democracy*. New York, NY: Little, Brown, 2007.

Scahill, Jeremy. *Dirty Wars: The World is a Battlefield*. Enhanced Edition for Nook. New York, NY: Nation Books, 2013.

Schlesinger, Arthur M. *The Imperial Presidency*. Boston, MA: Houghton Mifflin, 1986. First Published 1973 by Atlantic (Boston, MA).

Schmitt, Carl. *The Nomos of the Earth in the International Law of the Jus Publicum Europaeum*. Translated and Annotated by G. L. Ulmen. New York, NY: Telos, 2006.

Scruton, Roger. *Conservatism: An Invitation to the Great Tradition*. New York, NY: All Points Books, 2018. First Published 2017 by Profile Books (London).

Sensini, Paolo. *Sowing Chaos: Libya in the Wake of Humanitarian Intervention*. Translated by Alexander M. Synge. With a Foreword by Cynthia McKinney. Atlanta, GA: Clarity Press, 2016.

Simms, Brendan. *Unfinest Hour: Britain and the Destruction of Bosnia*. London: Penguin, 2001.

Smith, Grant F. *Foreign Agents: The American Israel Public Affairs Committee from the 1963 Fulbright Hearings to the 2005 Espionage Scandal*. Washington, DC: Institute for Research: Middle Eastern Policy, 2007.

Smith, Grant F., and Michael Scheuer. *Spy Trade: How Israel's Lobby Undermines America's Economy*. Washing, DC: Institution for Research: Middle Eastern Policy, 2008.

Springmann, J. M. *Goodbye, Europe? Hello, Chaos?: Merkel's Migrant Bomb*. Washing, DC: Daena, 2014.

———. *Visas for Al Qaeda: CIA Handouts That Rocked the World*. Washing, DC: Daena, 2014.

Stent, Angela. *Putin's World: Russia Against the West and with the Rest*. Cornwall: Twelve, 2019.

Stiglitz, Joseph E. *Globalization and Its Discontents*. New York, NY: W. W. Norton, 2003.

Stone, Oliver, and Peter Kuznick. *The Untold History of the United States*. New York, NY: Gallery Books, 2012.

Swanson, David. *War Is a Lie*. Charlottesville, VA: Printed by the Author, 2010.

Swisher, Clayton E. *The Truth About Camp David: The Untold Story About the Collapse of the Middle East Peace Process*. New York, NY: Nation Books, 2004.

Talhami, Ghada H. *Palestinian Refugees: Pawns to Political Actors*. New York, NY: Nova Science, 2003.

Tarpley, Webster G. *Barack H. Obama: The Unauthorized Biography*. Joshua Tree, CA: Progressive, 2008.

Tedeschi, Robert F. *The U.S. Constitution and Fascinating Facts about It*. Greens Farms, CT: Tiger, 1993.

Teles, Steven M. *The Rise of the Conservative Legal Movement: The Battle for Control of the Law*. Princeton, NJ: Princeton University Press, 2008.

Tigar, Michael E. *Law and the Rise of Capitalism*. With the Assistance of Madeleine R. Levy. New York, NY: Monthly Review Press, 2000.

———. *Thinking about Terrorism: The Threat to Civil Liberties in Times of National Emergency*. Chicago, IL: American Bar Association, 2007.

Trump, Donald J., and Tony Schwartz. *Trump: The Art of the Deal*. New York, NY: Ballantine Books, 1987.

Turse, Nick. *Tomorrow's Battlefield: U. S. Proxy Wars and Secret Ops in Africa*. Chicago, IL: Haymarket Books, 2015.

Vega, Elizabeth D. *United States V. George W. Bush Et Al*. New York, NY: Seven Stories, 2006.

Wallace, Rebecca M. *International Law: A Student Introduction*. London: Sweet and Maxwell, 1986.

Wendt, Alexander. *Social Theory of International Politics*. Cambridge: Cambridge University Press, 1999.

Wilcox, Francis O., and Richard A. Frank, Editors. *The Constitution and the Conduct of Foreign Policy: An Inquiry by a Panel of the American Society of International Law*. New York, NY: Praeger, 1976.

Williamson, Myra. *Terrorism, War and International Law: The Legality of the Use of Force Against Afghanistan in 2001*. Surrey, UK: Ashgate, 2009.

Witt, John F. *Lincoln's Code: The Laws of War in American History*. New York, NY: Free Press, 2012.

Wittes, Benjamin. *Law and the Long War: The Future of Justice in the Age of Terror*. London: Penguin, 2009.

Wolff, Michael. *Fire and Fury: Inside the Trump White House*. New York, NY: Henry Holt, 2018.

———. *Siege: Trump Under Fire*. New York, NY: Henry Holt, 2019.

Wolin, Sheldon S. *Democracy Incorporated: Managed Democracy and the Specter of Inverted Totalitarianism – New Edition*. Princeton, NY: Princeton University Press, 2008.

Woodward, Bob. *Bush At War*. New York, NY: Simon and Schuster, 2003.

———. *Fear: Trump in the White House*. New York, NY: Simon and Schuster, 2018.

———. *Obama's Wars*. New York, NY: Simon and Schuster, 2010.
———. *Plan of Attack*. New York, NY: Simon and Schuster, 2004.
———. *State of Denial: Bush at War, Part III*. New York, NY: Simon and Schuster, 2006.
———. *The War Within: A Secret White House History 2006–2008*. New York, NY: Simon and Schuster, 2008.

Index

About the Author

Francis A. Boyle is professor of law at the University of Illinois College of Law and also professor in the Unit for Criticism and Interpretive Theory in the College of Liberal Arts and Sciences at the University of Illinois in Urbana-Champaign. He was the Parhad Lecturer at the Faculty of Medicine for the University of Calgary in Canada in 2001. He was the Bertrand Russell Peace Lecturer at McMaster University in Canada in 2007. He drafted the U.S. domestic implementing legislation for the Biological Weapons Convention of 1972, known as the Biological Weapons Anti-Terrorism Act of 1989, which was passed unanimously by both Houses of the U.S. Congress and signed into law by President George Bush Senior. He served on the Board of Directors of Amnesty International USA from 1988 to 1992. He served as legal adviser to Chairman Yasser Arafat and the Palestine Liberation Organization on the Palestinian Declaration of Independence of November 15, 1988, and its creation of the State of Palestine that is now a United Nations Observer State. From 1991 to 1993 he served as legal adviser to the Palestinian Delegation to the Middle East Peace Negotiations and its Chair Dr. Haidar Abdul Shaffi, who instructed him to draft the Palestinian counteroffer to the now-defunct Oslo Agreement.

In 1993 he represented the Republic of Bosnia and Herzegovina before the International Court of Justice, where he won two World Court Orders overwhelmingly in favor of Bosnia against Yugoslavia to cease and desist from committing all acts of genocide in violation of the 1948 Genocide Convention. He also represented the Republic of Bosnia and Herzegovina at the Owen-Stoltenberg Negotiations in Geneva in 1993, where he prevented Bosnia's destruction as a State, saved Bosnia's membership in the United Nations Organization, and stopped the ethnic cleansing of 1.5 to 2 million *more* Bosnians. He was Attorney of Record for the Mothers of Srebrenica and

Podrina before the International Criminal Tribunal for the Former Yugoslavia and secured the indictment of Yugoslav president Slobodan Milošević for almost every crime in the ICTY Statute, including two counts of genocide: one for Srebrenica and the second for Bosnia in general. He started the Divestment/Disinvestment Campaign against Israel in 2000 and at the request of Palestinian Civil Society joined with them in 2005 to form the Palestinian Boycott, *Divestment*, and Sanctions (BDS) Campaign.